AWAKENING
FROM THE DREAM

A KUNDALINI MEMOIR

LOTUS LINDLEY

BALBOA.
PRESS

A DIVISION OF HAY HOUSE

Author Photo Credit: Zachary Tristen Copyright 2012

Balboa Press books may be ordered through booksellers or by contacting:

Balboa Press
A Division of Hay House
1663 Liberty Drive
Bloomington, IN 47403
www.balboapress.com
1 (877) 407-4847

Because of the dynamic nature of the Internet, any web addresses or links contained in this book may have changed since publication and may no longer be valid. The views expressed in this work are solely those of the author and do not necessarily reflect the views of the publisher, and the publisher hereby disclaims any responsibility for them.

The author of this book does not dispense medical advice or prescribe the use of any technique as a form of treatment for physical, emotional, or medical problems without the advice of a physician, either directly or indirectly. The intent of the author is only to offer information of a general nature to help you in your quest for emotional and spiritual well-being. In the event you use any of the information in this book for yourself, which is your constitutional right, the author and the publisher assume no responsibility for your actions.

Any people depicted in stock imagery provided by Getty Images are models, and such images are being used for illustrative purposes only. Certain stock imagery © Getty Images.

Print information available on the last page.

ISBN: 978-1-9822-2642-8 (sc)
ISBN: 978-1-9822-2641-1 (hc)
ISBN: 978-1-9822-2643-5 (e)

Library of Congress Control Number: 2019904567

Balboa Press rev. date: 06/17/2019

CONTENTS

PART I

PART II

PART III

INTRODUCTION

Though this story is a personal account of the first decade of my spiritual awakening journey, it's really a story for those who traverse their own inner adventure. I trust you'll find relatedness. This is my hope, my prayer, my intention.

I love to write but have never thought of myself as a writer. Journals upon journals hold the processing of my spiritual awakening journey. *Awakening from the Dream: A Kundalini Memoir* began as a personal integration process of this first decade of a reborn life, so to speak.

From there it sat on a shelf for almost another decade, until it became clear to me, when working with clients, that my story had value to others in the midst of their spiritual unfolding.

Kundalini awakenings are becoming more common yet are still misunderstood and confusing, even for those going through this mysterious process. It is most often talked about intellectually, conceptually, or in rudimentary terms. All of these ways are appropriate, but they are very incomplete because there isn't a logical way to communicate the mystery within the confines of the intellect.

This is why the mystics, saints, poets, and wise men and women spoke or speak in metaphor, parable, symbolism and rhyme. Sometimes their words register to the intellect as nonsense, but the heart and soul perk up the inner ears so that they may hear.

The experiential reality of awakening is highly personal, based on present life experiences and the past lives of a soul. All karma will be called to the surface, programming will be dissolved, identity will be dismantled, ego will be purified, and devotion will be an anchor. The rousing of this divine energy of Source that resides within all human beings is the psycho-spiritual evolutionary transformational force that forever alters our perception of God, reality, life, and the self.

This process can be daunting, expansive, mind-blowing, heart-opening, physically challenging, and blissfully freeing. It isn't uncommon for individuals, whether consciously seeking the rousing of the mysterious divine Kundalini energy or stumbling upon it as I did, to end up on an uncontrollable roller-coaster ride of confusion, bliss, fear, ecstasy, loss, divine unification, and dark nights of the soul.

For me, I found great solace during the initial phase in the very few and far between personal experiential accounts of the awakening journeys of other people. Given the transformation of consciousness that takes place, unless someone else has undergone these same radical shifts, one can feel very alone, misunderstood, isolated, and fearful. I hope my story brings the same kindred connection that I found. May these pages be a balm to soothe anxiety and loneliness, and may they serve as a lighthouse of hope that there is a shore to be reached amid internal storms.

The publication of my story is now two decades past the original dramatic unfolding. Much has changed in the perceptions written of in these pages. The change isn't a discounting of what was understood at that time, but more of the continuous expansion of perception that happens naturally over time. Our awakening doesn't end. Transformation continues always. Therefore, our humanness simply continues to deepen the learning as consciousness expands into higher wisdom.

Awakening from the Dream: A Kundalini Memoir takes you with me into the unknown corridors of a Kundalini awakening. From a green, innocent, naive, and unexpected entrance into a whole new life, I asked questions, deciphered soul communication, touched higher realms, and recognized my own divine embodied reality. My sense is that if you are here with me, you will find that kindred connection of soul-to-soul companionship.

Regardless of where you are in your spiritual journey, I invite you to explore this as a reflection of your own experiences, even as the specifics differ. Seek the subtle energetic messages to help guide, inform, and offer inspiration for deeper reflection. The higher teachings passed on here are for all of us. The truth is, we are all transforming and are all being called to listen more closely within our own hearts and awaken from the dream.

A FEW WORDS ABOUT THE LENS OF THE MEMOIR

The relevance of *Awakening from the Dream: Kundalini Memoir* is now better timed than I could have imagined. Collectively, we are seeing the rise of awareness of the divine feminine. When my journey first began, this was barely a concept. Kundalini yoga, taught by Yogi Bhajan, wasn't yet mainstream. And perspectives such as Ascension, which I now equate with Kundalini awakening, were for many still in the New Age fringe.

My story is one that is seen through the lens of the yogic tradition, a Shakti-Kundalini path, which differs from the Kundalini yoga mentioned above. The Shakti path isn't as easily found. However, the awakening experience of this divine feminine force is activating in more and more people. Many are actively seeking this soul call of deeper spiritual connection without understanding there is direct route, which is Divine Mother, Shakti Kundalini.

Twenty years ago, there were fewer people whose divine essence was sparked. Today, this inner fire is igniting abundantly, and I'm certain *Awakening from the Dream: A Kundalini Memoir* will find its way into the perfect hands. I'm very excited for the spiritual trajectory of humanity. As you read my story, I invite you to allow boxes and labels to fall away. You will see the gift of grace is extended through the expansion of consciousness. We are then asked to step up and hone our will to develop that deeper knowing through disciplined practice. Please see that the divine guidance in the pages that follow may be directed to me personally, yet it carries a vibration and wisdom meant for all of us. Though the characters, situations, and lessons that unfold are mine, please *feel* the underlying reflections that you can take into your own personal awakening journey.

More than anything, I hope you find enjoyment and deeper connection of faith and trust, an expanded awareness of the world within us, and the unseen divine guidance all around us, assisting us with an unconditional Love. You are now invited to a journey of the living mystery, traveling side by side with me into the unknown territory of Spirit and Soul in these early green years as I awaken.

PREFACE

I found myself distant from the familiar and felt a strange lurking melancholy within as I finally escaped my dark little apartment after the strange bout of sickness. The sickness had struck almost immediately on my way home from work on the bus from downtown Portland. Sitting, sipping a green juice, and chatting with Evan, my bus buddy, I had warmed up slightly during the thirty-minute ride. It was December, which meant it was pouring rain and dark. The temperature was bearable even though I wasn't partial to cold. Since I'd been working at the outdoor flower stand for the past three years, I'd developed a thicker skin. Through rain and shine I often preferred to walk home most days, but after working the closing shift, I felt appreciation for the ride and the company.

Once home, stripping off the wet clothes and hanging them on the heater, I couldn't wait to be submerged in a hot bath. My sweet kitty Urisk would take this opportunity to jump up onto the side of the tub and offer his greeting. We had just met one another a few weeks earlier. Just recently I had moved out on my own, away from Carl—again—but this time it was for good, I decided. And it was time for a fuzzy little friend. I got him on a whim, as was the tendency with most things, and trusted that parenting would be good for me while moving forward from the past. Urisk, still a bit shy, had been kept isolated in a box, in which I'd found him when I picked him up on that night of whimsy. The ad was brief and to the point: "Available immediately." The kittens were ready for the taking. I wasn't keen on the guy who had kept these little beings in the garage, and I was even less impressed with him when he led me to the box with this new companion, isolated from the others. There was no way I could leave the kitten there. I fell instantly in love.

Upon Urisk's arrival to his new home, I tried to make him feel safe, but the only place he wanted to be was under the bed. Keeping his food and water close to the bed for him at first, I slowly, after a few days, moved it three feet or so away into the kitchen, after he'd acclimated to his new home. Fortunately the apartment was a studio, sparse in belongings, so he couldn't get lost. The bed, the only piece of furniture in the place other than the small kitchen table and chairs, enabled him to stay in close proximity. His time of courage was after lights out, once I'd fallen asleep. It was then that his little form with its sharp claws would scale the covers of the bed and pounce. I playfully moved my feet around and let him attack them, then ran my hands along each side of my body to feel him chasing them in the darkness of night. By morning he'd have returned to his safe haven under the bed.

The name Urisk was a suitable name for him after I'd witnessed his struggles in the world. I'd found this name in a book I had on fairies years ago. In the book, Urisk was a big creature who found shelter under a bridge, frightened by the presence of passers-by. Breaking the name down as U-risk, I felt this would be a suitable characteristic as the kitten grew more secure and learned to trust. It was also appropriate for me. I felt Urisk and I had some wonderful healing energy to share with one another. Eventually he showed himself more and more. Tub time lured him out from below the bed upon my arrival home at the end of the day, and it became a favorite time for us both.

That particular night, after the bus ride, tub time was pleasant. I made a small dinner for myself, and then Urisk joined me for a short time on the bed, in the light, while I journaled and sipped tea. When he'd had his fill of company, under the bed he went, until the wee hours of the morning.

The conclusion to the night was an evening grieving ritual. This evening ritual prevented the fearful buildup of grief or doubts about the inevitable decision I'd made to end my relationship. It was comforting to me to honor whatever expressions needed to come forth with this practice. Lighting one candle that sat on the TV across the room, with tea, cigarette, and ashtray poised, I pushed play on the stereo to listen to some Mazzy Star.

Trying to climb out of the thick darkness of this relationship felt like tearing a strap off of Velcro. Me and my former lover's wounds of fear, power, control, sex addiction, and abandonment fit like a hand in a glove. Five years of doing our best to make the relationship work had met its end. His path was his art. Mine was simply to reclaim any and all of myself that I'd lost. In my last journal entry before I'd left, sitting on the couch and staring off into the city from our loft, I wrote that somehow I felt like this ending was final. I asked myself what it all had been for and about, and though I didn't understand then the deep karmic tie Carl and I had to each other, I had a sense there was a spiritual significance to our relationship's ending.

I'd been offering myself up to this grief for a couple of weeks now and found there was less intensity, fewer tears, and more peace. Each night, after I felt complete, off went the light as I slipped into bed. This ritual taught me that the *fear of pain* is often more painful than the actual experience of the emotions. Momentary closure would envelop me in a pillow of peace as I drifted off to sleep. The morning would come fast enough, along with the rain and perhaps wind that was forecasted.

Having slept for only a couple of hours, I looked at the clock. I felt like a flu had overtaken me in an instant. With stomach cramping and head spinning, I made my way to the bathroom and vomited violently, thankfully into the toilet. Confused, my only deduction was that the juice must have been bad and I had food poisoning. This wouldn't be the first time I'd experienced food poisoning, so I hoped to just ride it out. The night wore on as a tremendous headache began to pound my head open, coupled with vomiting and diarrhea. Sleep wasn't to be had. I got a cold cloth for my head, lying as still as possible and waiting until I could call Fiona, my boss, to let her know I was super sick.

At 5:00 a.m., dialing the phone, barely able to open my eyes, I made the call. My eyes felt bludgeoned, or at least what bludgeoning must feel like, and swollen. Everything hurt, and I knew that this wasn't food poisoning. Fiona answered the phone, groggy but awake, as she had to be up for the flower market pickup.

"It's me. I can't come in. I'm so sick. Thought it might be food poisoning, but don't really know. Sorry."

"Oh, sweetie. I'm so sorry." Fiona was always so generous in her sentiments. "No worries. Just take care of yourself, and feel better. Can I bring you anything?"

I could hardly talk. "No thanks. I'll keep you posted. So sorry." Hanging up, I could feel guilt from long ago creep in. Whenever I had to call in sick, which hardly ever happened anymore, it always lingered in the back of my mind, *Does she believe me? Does she think I'm lying?* Back in the days of drinking, I lied often and feigned being sick without a thought of how it affected anyone else. Man, how things had changed in just six years.

After getting some fluid into my body, I crawled back into bed and attempted to find comfort. Once I was in bed, there seemed to be no tracking of days or time. I knew my mother had called and left a couple of messages, as had Fiona, but I just couldn't bring myself to speak. Although I was in a lot of pain and agony, including not being able to walk to the bathroom, I had to crawl in order to expel what was ready to leave my body. It seemed like forever since I'd opened my eyes. Was I asleep or awake? Neither or both?

There were points when it felt as though I had split into various levels of awareness. There was a part of me that didn't even seem to be affected by any degree of the suffering taking place. It felt as if I, or my mind, was being restrained from any normal internal antics of my hypochondriac tendencies, such as, *Am I going to die? Oh my God, is this some horrible disease flaring up that I need to see a doctor for?* Or, *Oh no, what if I'm really sick and no one finds me?!* Instead, my thoughts were very detached, such as, *This is odd,* from a removed place within myself. *I'm not worried at all. I'm going to be fine. I must be cleansing.*

For the first couple of days, from that deep space within, I saw that my physical body was feeling the turmoil, and yet not. I wasn't experiencing the body as mine. It was as if there was a screen inside my mind and I was watching a movie of past experiences and memories, particularly those of the most recent couple of years with Carl. There was a sensation of a tar-like gook peeling off me—or out of me. There were feelings of sadness, fear, and rage that seemed to rise up from nowhere, only to be dissolved in some strange undertow.

Urisk continued to arise in the blackness, but he and I had little interaction. At times I felt his little form resting by my feet, and at one point I realized he was nestled up under my arm, purring. I experienced a silent elation as this was the first buzz of purr that I'd experienced coming from him. That alone brought a moment of joy. It was as if he knew, even at his very young age, that just the stillness and quietude was necessary.

I didn't sleep, at least not normal sleep. There were times when I thought I was dreaming, except that I was simultaneously aware that I thought I was dreaming. It was like a circus house full of mirrors inside my head. There were conversations taking place that were snippets of memories, and other conversations that were completely foreign with voices just as unknown. Even the things that were said that made sense to me were forgotten as quickly as they appeared.

Days later, who knew how many, I finally answered my mother's call. She was getting worried, as we rarely went more than a day or two without contact. When I answered the phone, barely able to talk, needless to say there was great concern on my mom's end.

"Honey! What's wrong? You sound horrible. What's happening?"

"I've been so sick. Still feeling horrible, but I can open my eyes better now."

"Well, I'm coming over after work. You should go to a doctor. It's been days since this has been happening, obviously. Otherwise you would have been able to call. I'll take you to the doctor."

"No. Please. I'm getting better. I just need to sleep." I didn't want to explain anything and knew on a deep level that this wasn't a regular illness with a doctor's cure.

"I want to come by and see that you're okay. I'll bring you some juice and some food. Is there anything else you need?"

"No. That's fine. I can't promise I'm going to eat anything. Actually, I may need food for Urisk. It was low, if I recall, the last time I filled his bowl." I'd filled his bowl as much as it would hold the day or so before and changed his water. I didn't want to neglect him if getting out of bed came to be impossible.

"Okay. I'll see you in a couple of hours." My mother ended on the note, "I love you."

"Thanks. You too." We had a wonderfully close relationship in many ways; however, like most mother–daughter, parent–child relationships, ours wasn't without its trials and tribulations.

When my mother arrived, her concern was not abated. "I really think you need a doctor. When did you eat last? Have you been drinking anything? I brought you some soup. Let me heat it up."

I really just wanted quiet, but I was able to be somewhat present and was not feeling as debilitated.

"What would feel really good, if you don't mind, is if you'd run me a bath. I haven't had one at all. And honestly, I don't need a doctor. Thanks, though."

"Okay. If you think you're really on the mend. And, of course, a bath it is. I'll do that first and then get the soup heating for you. Maybe I should change the sheets?" she called out to me as the tub began to fill. "They're pulled and twisted all over the place, and I'm sure fresh ones will feel good after the bath."

"That would be sooo good. The first day or so, I was dripping with sweat. That's when I still thought it was food poisoning." It felt so good to be climbing into the tub. It didn't matter that it had barely started to fill. "Yes. Water," I murmured as I lowered myself down.

My mom came in to inquire about what was wrong.

"I think I've just had a bad flu. I'm feeling better. Thanks for the soup. I'll eat just a bit when I get out though. I'm ready to get back into bed. I'm appreciative, but it's all a bit exhausting." I closed my eyes in order to be present with the nourishment of the water. I didn't want to talk anymore. I was tired.

The bed was changed, nibbles of food had been eaten, liquids had been sipped, and Urisk had been fed. And, oh yeah: "Honey, I cleaned Urisk's kitty litter. I guess he really does exist! Rest, and I'll call you tomorrow." With me feeling like a five-year-old again, all tucked in, she kissed me goodbye and departed.

It was only a matter of moments before I drifted back off into this odd limbo-land inside. It seemed this time that much of the previous darkness had been washed away. Instead, I began to witness wisps of color dancing through my mind, through my brain, through my thoughts. It was quite difficult to discern or describe. And there seemed to be sound to the colored wisps, which weren't audible in the normal way of hearing but were still very present. Instances of lightness, maybe even joy, arose from some internal hiding place.

Just in the last few weeks I'd bought a couple of new books, one on Rastafarianism and another on herbalism. I had also observed an interest in Buddhism sparking. These last years had been filled with so much darkness and heaviness, I was feeling the need to shift perspectives and consciousness. While I slept, I felt like a sponge, soaking in things I'd been reading and other things I had no idea from whence they came. Energy was prevalent in a variety of forms within the inner landscape, yet it was absent of any clear meaning.

Even as I'd intuited that there was a cleansing taking place—and now I felt certain of it—the awareness seemed to come from out of nowhere. Cleansing was an unknown concept to me. However, the part of me that wanted to question, to understand intellectually, or to know, was held in a place of suspension, and the job was simply to allow, feel, witness, sleep, dream, and listen.

Two and a half weeks later I resurfaced, as if rising from the dead. I was weak, but my appetite came on with a vengeance. But something was different. Actually, a few things were *very* different as I resumed my life.

One of the first things I noticed was that my body didn't want any meat. Though I'd been finding meat less and less desirable over the years, I still ate fish and turkey—until now, that is. It took a few days for me to notice it, but even when I was in a hungered state, meat held absolutely no appeal. Without too much more thought, I adjusted accordingly.

The second relinquishment that the body was making was coffee. I entirely lacked any desire for it. Granted, nights were designated as teatime, but my love for coffee might as well have been an aspect of my identity. I considered myself a coffee snob, and in Portland, Oregon, I wasn't alone. The darker, the stronger, the better. No milk or cream to ruin its thrust, only a touch or two of sugar. I loved coffee, and being sober, good coffee was how one partied! But alas, something else was amiss. I wasn't going to give it up so easily, but my enjoyment of it would never be the same again.

The oddest part was the ways in which I was thinking about these changes. Somehow, in certain moments, I still felt detached from myself. This was most obvious when it felt as if something else was making decisions, or someone else, other than me. For instance, the body was making choices and making changes that were coming from a source of knowing that I didn't know of, if that makes any sense. I pondered this curiosity, and then the train of thought would vanish as if it had never begun.

My little studio apartment was in Northwest Portland. This was a cute neighborhood of shops, restaurants, coffee shops, and great old homes, including the Alano club where twelve-step meetings were held. These rooms held the AA meetings where I'd finally gotten sober after four years of relapses. My whole community was made up of AA members. I'd worked at the club for a period of time and attended meetings daily for years until the last year or so. And I felt as though my spiritual birth had been through AA. Here, I had grown from feeling a visceral repulsion toward the word *God* to settling first on the reference to a higher power, and then graduating to find a sprout of trust in God.

I loved the Northwest neighborhood, and it held many memories for me, some beautiful, some dramatic, some frightening. As I felt better, in order to gain my strength back after being sick, I made it a point to walk back and forth to work regardless of the weather. Particularly on my walks home in the evening, I noticed a sense of floatiness overtaking me. It was coupled with a sense of distance or detachment, similar to what I'd felt during the illness. *Am I dissociating?* I wondered, feeling like I used to when I smoked pot.

The Christmas season was just passing, and walking down Northwest Twenty-Third Avenue, with all the trees lit, I had a sense of joyful freedom; shops were open, and people were bustling here and there. On one specific day, I felt the affinity I had for this neighborhood, and at the same time I was aware that I didn't belong anymore. There was a numbness accompanying this realization. And like with many things, I knew it was time to leave.

There were few things that I did slowly or even with too much forethought. Spontaneity was both a weakness and a strength. While I had realized years ago that I was sometimes like a snowball rolling down a mountain, out of control, growing larger and larger, it rarely made me pause for long.

Walking by Coffee People a few times on the way home, I saw friends who were hanging out before or after meetings. When I stopped to visit, it became ever the more apparent that I no longer had anything to say. While on one hand it troubled me, because it felt that overnight I'd lost some kind of stable footing in my world, on the other hand, it felt like what I needed next couldn't be found in these old stomping grounds or with familiar comrades.

Within a month, I was setting up house across town in Southeast Portland.

Energy. What's up with energy? This was a topic I'd been pondering more and more often. My whole realm of relating had shifted to this abstract description for everything. Everything seemed to be understood as energetic vibrations, frequencies, feelings, sensations. But what did any of that even mean?

"Can I just say that I love you, but I really am hating 'energy this, energy that' lately." Fiona was obviously feeling irritated one day at work, but she never failed to speak as pointedly as needed, with sprinkles of love.

I didn't feel defensive about Fiona's remark. It hadn't been the first as of late, and I understood where she was coming from. Giggling somewhat self-consciously, I tried again to explain what I was realizing more clearly on a sensory level, without having an intellectual understanding.

"This and that." I tapped the flower stand, indicating the false belief in its solidity. "That's what I'm saying. Everything is energy. This is hard and solid, but it's just energy. Everything has some kind of energetic quality behind it. Everything is energy. And I know I'm talking about it a lot, but that's because it's what I'm realizing. Everything we feed ourselves is energy, and that isn't limited to only the food we eat. It's like this." I continued, "For years I fed myself dark, dysfunctional movies and heavy depressing music and lived in an overly stimulated, darkly sexualized relationship and environment with Carl. I read books that were disturbing. All of this is energy food for the mind, the emotions, and the senses. And now, I'm realizing that I need to feed myself energy that has more lightness, joy, peace, and love."

"Well, can you find a different word to use? I understand somewhat what you're saying, but the whole energy thing sounds kind of hippyish / New Agey." Fiona continued, "I get that Southeast Portland feels different from Northwest Portland. So you're saying that this feeling is a different energy or vibe."

"Vibe." I snorted. "Would you rather I use *vibe*?"

We both laughed just before Fiona could say under her breath, "See. You're up in Southeast not even a month with all the hippies, and you're using the lingo."

As we went back to doing our work, changing the water in the flower buckets, I now felt I needed to come to my own defense. I said, "This started before I moved into Southeast. It's why I moved to Hawthorne to begin with. The energy called, and it's not about the predominant Hawthorne hippy population."

Really, I didn't understand much of this yet either. I simply knew that it was time to break away from all the energy of the past and start anew. Southeast Portland spoke to me. Right around the time of the move, the distance and detachment feelings became a deep ache in the pit of my stomach. The loss of an old life was no doubt a piece of it.

Maybe I'm lonely? I thought, *After all, I've cut myself off from community, my neighborhood, and familiar support.* But what I knew was that this ache, this loneliness, was a feeling that I never wanted to be without. *Hmm. How strange is that?*

A new road was outstretched before me. Not that I knew this then, as Urisk and I were settling into our new abode, taking risks together to evolve. This ache, the lonely longing, came and went, ebbed and flowed like all things in life. In its absence I longed for its return. In its presence, I felt whole and at home, in need of nothing from the outside. Contrary to what might be assumed, the only words I could find to describe this feeling were "quietly joyful and peaceful." Although I'd mistaken the ache for depression, loss, and sadness in the beginning, I now recognized it to be a deeper presence and a deeper call of … soul? But a call to what, exactly, was still a mystery.

Over the next few years, from 1996 to 2000, I followed an internal compass and allowed myself to be propelled through personal intentional trials. I chose a path and a community of intense personal growth that intertwined with my spiritual evolution. An intuition that from a young age I had learned to question at best and squelch at worst was now speaking more strongly as I honored its guidance. I began studying herbalism and enrolled in a yearlong class about energy work. After my breakup with Carl, I'd spent a year of being single for the first time since I was a teenager. Carl was the final wake-up call that my love radar wasn't working particularly well, and I needed to find out who I was without being in a relationship. After that year, I'd been blessed with two wonderful partnerships, Jace and Caleb, in the space of five years. Both were tremendously healing and loving.

My heart was burst open in a way I'd never experienced before through the love of my two dogs, Ochoco and Lotus, whom Jace and I parented together. Not desiring to be a parent, I found that animals were my children. They served as my primary vehicle for learning about sacrifice, putting other beings before myself, and experiencing the growth that comes from being responsible for another life. Though nothing to the extent of raising human children and the maturing process that doing such a thing invokes, this was the miniature version of unconditional love and parenthood that introduced these lessons into my life. In time, caregiving for the elderly became a secondary lesson of self-sacrifice. Urisk, however, always remained my little guy, although he carried different lessons for me than the larger furry four-legged creatures did.

From Southeast Portland to Oregon City with Jace, and back to Portland, in the years 1998 through 2000, my primary struggle that continued to bring about much grief and confusion was "What am I going to be when I grow up?" Except I was grown up, supposedly.

I was in my thirties yet still grasping for the elusive expression of gifts, talents, passions, and purpose. I felt driven to create a career. Purpose and passions became exhausting, revealing some of my thickest stories and beliefs of what I lacked, along with feelings of unworthiness; and required the deepest digging.

My baggage, like the baggage all of us have, is both unique and shared. Just when I believed I'd reached the goal I'd been working toward, in 2000, with a feeling that I'd finally arrived and with excitement that the greatest challenges and greatest blessings were ready to come to fruition, something unknown began to quietly wave from other realms.

> Your path was laid out before you, traveling the ruts then through.
> You wore the suit mended and tailored, beyond the holes and tears.
> Alive in your quest to be, to show, to be seen in the emergence.
> And now, to die to the lostness, stripping away the armor that you sewed.

PART I

PART I

1

"Happy birthday to me," I spoke out loud to myself. I looked out the window of my favorite room in our small, 1920-something bungalow. The Love Room was what Caleb and I called the sunroom. It was all glass windows with French doors connecting the living room. Staring out the window at the summer gray sky of June, I thought, "Yep. Gray. Just how I feel."

I couldn't tell if the gray was comforting or depressing me further. I didn't quite know what to do with myself. My energy level was almost nil. No students. No workshop. Only two twelve-hour caregiving shifts, and that alone was enough to drag me deeper into the depths of despair. How long would I have to do this work that triggers so much frustration and disdain, regardless of my love for the patients?

An identity crisis was at hand. I'd been so focused, so active, working so hard toward this goal to teach Nia for the last couple of years. All that passion and direction felt like it had been ripped out from under my feet. Though I knew my passion and excitement weren't gone forever, only resting, it created a sense of isolation and confusion. I felt completely lost.

With my head in my hands, I processed the feelings out loud. "I mean, it's no wonder, really, that I don't want to be around anyone. I feel like I've failed. And after pushing myself for these last three years, trying to get *there*, I'm just so tired. Cocooning is all I feel like doing. I'm just so fucking tired. I'm so tired." And off to sleep I'd go, once again, escaping from the pressing reality.

Since my mysterious illness in the winter of 1996, I'd been on a crash course toward raising consciousness. Not that I would've known to call it that, but anyway, unbeknownst to me, that's precisely what was taking place. In 2001, after a period of time substitute teaching classes for others, I felt ready to commit to teaching my own Nia classes. The studio had been leased, flyers had been distributed, the first few routines were down solid, and I felt ready to overcome my issue of stage fright. My stress levels were naturally running high after these years of hard work both within myself and in the outer world, and my confidence felt truly on the rise. I'd been striving to build a career based on what I felt passionate about, as well as what I was gifted in. I was feeling excited, strong, and ready to emerge into who I wanted to be.

On the morning that was to be the first class, I awoke with intense dizziness. Rising out of bed, managing to stumble a few feet, I then collapsed on the hardwood floor outside the bathroom. Lying there spinning, with nausea and a headache growing, all I could think of, with desperateness, was, *I have to make it to the class!* It quickly became obvious I wasn't going anywhere but back into bed.

My partner at the time, Caleb, did his best to support, encourage, and console me. "Sweetie, it'll be okay. It's just the first day. Can I call the studio for you to let them know, so that they can tell people to check in next week?"

"There's no other choice, is there?!" I growled at him, then instantly felt bad. I dismissed him indirectly by pulling the covers over my head. I hated being seen like this. I felt pathetic. Tears wanted to come, but crying seemed to make the dizziness worse. Frustration and an internal crowd with a barrage of stories rushed at me the entire rest of the day, pointing out all the failure I'd be facing if I didn't get it together soon.

The next day at my naturopathic doctor's office, I was informed I had vertigo and adrenal fatigue. Suzy, my doctor, sent me home with three homeopathic remedies for prolonged emotional discomfort from grief and shock, mental strain, and chronic stress.

"These sound pretty extreme, don't you think?" I commented to Suzy, through mild dizziness.

She and I had been through things like this before. "I feel it's appropriate. I've been telling you that you need to slow down for a while. Now, it looks like you have no choice. You need to rest. You need downtime. Your adrenals are in serious need of rest and nourishment. You need to stop."

"But what am I supposed to do with these new classes?!" I was starting to feel emotional, which meant first and foremost that the expression was anger. "I've worked so hard for this. I can't just say, 'Sorry, can't make it!'"

"Listen. Get some rest. Give yourself a couple of weeks. Take the remedies, and then come back and we'll see how everything is looking. Nothing is forever." Suzy felt compassion, but she wasn't surprised by the situation. It'd been just a matter of time.

My resistance to Suzy's instruction was vehement. I was determined not to miss any more than the first two classes that initial week. I knew that if I just took control of the situation with some rest, took the remedies, and did a little practice of the routines, I'd be good to go the next week.

Well, in spite of my plans, the fact was that the couch became my worst enemy and best friend for weeks. I fretted about two other important projects in the works, and it soon became apparent that those, too, would not be coming to fruition in the near future. During my third week on the couch, the class schedule was canceled and the lease broken. Even the caregiving job was put on the back burner, which brought me financial stress. The body saw to it that the only activities that would be taking place were sleeping, lying, or sitting.

For three weeks the dizziness kept me immobile, while the rage and fear within kept me suffering. Slowly, little by little, a crumbling started taking place as I felt the failure of all I'd worked for. Whether or not I could reassess and move forward when the vertigo was relieved didn't even have space to enter my mind. The stories about failure, the fears of how I'd never be able to create what I wanted in life, and the insecurities that I felt would never be overcome all surfaced. Being practically a prisoner of the couch (or bed), I couldn't get away from myself, my mind, and the ongoing persistent thoughts. I cried, raged, swore, and grieved, and slowly, when there was no more fight left, parts of me began to die.

The day the vertigo hit, Caleb set off on a three-week kayak trip, which he'd been planning on for quite some time, on my insistence. I was so grateful to be able to go through this alone. I did much better on my own. Pulling myself up by my own bootstraps was my comfort zone. Vulnerability was not one of my strengths. I would have just felt pathetic with him around. Once again, I sat humbled and humiliated and depressed, witnessing a burgeoning pattern.

Another roar had captured me and become a meow. I had a way of creating waves and managing their razor-sharp edges. Whether those edges were internal or external, I pushed them to a fine point. I always seemed oblivious to the whittling down of the edge to its point, often failing to see the point getting finer and finer. For years I felt in control, my inner voice screaming. My ego had me believing the screams were out of passion and joy, of course. However, there were other shadows interwoven. In the shadow hid a need to prove my worth, which disguised itself in a number of different expressions.

Right after receiving my Nia White Belt certification in 2000, I became obsessed with learning every routine I could. I did love what I was doing, but that passion was out of proportion to all other aspects of my life.

"Sweetie, let's go out and play this afternoon!" Caleb had suggested one day.

"I can't. I need to practice," I replied while dancing, counting the beats.

"But you've been in here for hours already. You can take a break, don't you think?"

I didn't like to be pulled away from dancing until I felt ready. "Babe, I need to practice. This is what I love. This is my passion. I need to work. This is how I have fun. Maybe tomorrow afternoon, okay?" My voice had an edge, ready to attack if I wasn't left alone.

Caleb never failed in honesty. "I think your passion is more like an addiction."

He left the room knowing I wouldn't get what he was seeing, and he was right. I assumed *he didn't get it* and went about my "fun" for a few more hours.

Reflecting back on this, it is clear to me that I had a knack for expressing my passion and love all over the place. We'd had been living in a community with eight other friends during all this focused practice time, and Caleb wasn't the only one to request my companionship. Others also wanted to spend time with me. However, other than being focused on this goal, another burden I carried was that I wasn't able to *receive*. I wasn't able to understand that others valued my company. When questioned by friends about spending time together, I expressed the love for my passion with anxiety, adrenaline, expectation, and ego. My presence in those moments was enough to zap those closest to me like a plug socket short-circuiting. I saw, in the forced quietude, that I wasn't having the fun I'd thought. I was disconnected from the people closest to me and blind to the fact that I was beginning to tread on thin air, the point whittling away.

And now, trapped on the couch, in the interim of tantrums, imprisoned by my own misery, I began to notice a subtle surrendering taking place within my being. Beyond my doing, I was beginning to feel an allowance for everything just as it was. Every now and then, I started to feel better, only to find that if I had the slightest inkling of a thought about moving forward with some plan, be it a new agenda or an old plan (for there was always a plan), the vertigo would come right back. For most of that first month, reading or journaling wasn't even an option. Literally, I was left with just being. The message from the Universe, from my body, and from my soul was that *everything* had to stop for whatever was to come next. When I really received the message, when my true surrender occurred at the tail end of that month, something deep within me changed. And in that place of surrender, I found, once again, that familiar ache in the pit of my stomach that had been covered with striving and proving. I found myself once again sensing a sacred emptiness within.

> I'm longing for You, moving toward You,
> The ache of surrender etching the way.
> Losing myself to be with You, going deeper to be You,
> The ache of surrender etching the way.

These words played as a song over and over as I sat on the couch, my perch in the Love Room. The room looked out over our large backyard with the oldest apple tree in the neighborhood, secluded by a high fence. The house, the smallest in the area, had at one time sat on an apple orchard and had the largest lot prior to becoming a real suburban neighborhood. The perch on which I found my solace was perfect for watching the skies to the south and west. I began to see clearly that the last few years had been out of control with my obsession for accomplishment. Nothing had been allowed to flow in an organic process. I attacked and pushed at every turn. I believed it was passion. With the grace that came with emptying out, it became clear to me that my ego had been in full swing for quite some time.

While my creative impulse was genuine, my ego carried stories of my fear of failure, of not becoming something, which fueled my aggressive doing-ness.

This was the paramount drive that overshadowed the inspired gifts I held. It was evident that the homeopathic remedies were, in fact, sadly accurate. As my insides quieted, I began to connect to a peace, calm, and wholeness that was already present within, as well as to the beauty of nature outside.

I sat for hours dreamily watching the rain and the clouds, watching the sky shift from its darkness to light, shadow to sun. My body began to soften, then melt. Days upon days of this stillness and silence brought to the surface old hidden wounds and sorrow.

"I'm longing for You, moving toward You"

As old emotions rose in this spaciousness, they gently moved through my being, untethered. Yes, there was pain, tears, feelings of loss. But it was as if they moved through and out of me on a gentle current. There was no story or resistance or judgement to what arose and was released. There was peace, love, and tenderness expressed by something deep within and around me, but completely intangible. And I had to be in a state of spaciousness to feel its subtle presence.

"The ache of surrender etching the way"

There was a beauty and bliss in the ebbing and flowing. I saw all I'd worked for in a new light. None of it mattered anymore, at least not in the way I had thought. All the ideas and answers I believed about who or what I thought I was faded into a mist of what had been. Wants and needs became less and less. Resting in this contentment and wholeness, and just being in the stillness that had been imposed upon my life, I saw that all was perfect. Who would have thought that just being in stillness could be so powerful?

"I'm longing for You, moving toward You"

With my edges softened, the stories quieted and the vertigo lifted. I was more open and fluid when Caleb arrived home from his trip. These softer qualities, which he appreciated, allowed the space for us to connect more deeply. However, the fluid in my right ear that had emerged as the vertigo retreated remained. This fluid was to become an important teacher for me. There was a new understanding forming, an understanding that body and soul will use whatever means possible to help us along our journey, but we must be willing students.

A sensation of a kind of billowing, an expansive spaciousness, emerged throughout these days of just being. As the weather warmed, I entered my thirty-seventh year and witnessed how my whole life had just turned completely around in a short span of time. This wasn't how I anticipated going into a new year, but for now, I'd given up the fight to control it, the ache of surrender etching the way.

2

This period of time had been confusing and emotionally painful albeit beautiful. I couldn't tell if I was depressed and lost or just emptied out. Finally able to return to work with the elder gentleman I cared for, I seemed to be able to hold it with acceptance rather than with the previous, energy-draining resistance. There were no clues left as to what I wanted or needed anymore. The only thing for certain was that I was experiencing an identity crisis, yet I didn't have the deeper understanding that it was a death process in continuation. The death had begun in 1996, with the mystery flu that set my life on a new course. I was once again being invited, compelled, dragged by my ankles, by some unknown force that was demanding I die to all I had believed relevant. And this force made itself known through the physical body.

Paradoxically, I was feeling both weaker and stronger in my sense of self. I was welcoming a new vulnerability and fragility, though in the past it would have been quite frightening. The phrase I used to express this experience was "raw pink skin." So fragile and tender. There was an intrinsic soft, gentle, humbling power in the vulnerability. I longed to be that raw pink skin.

As I continued to find balance, I was content to do the caregiving, spend time with Caleb, read, meditate, sit on my perch in the Love Room, and spend time in as little clothing as possible stretched on the grass in the backyard, or out in the garden, feeling the breeze, sun, earth, and cool grass against my skin. There was an absence of my obsession to prove I was someone by doing or achieving or becoming something. I felt a sense of wholeness just as I was. I embraced that ache in my gut, which in the emptiness of too many distractions seemed to expand and bring me closer to God. God had been calling me through that longing ache in the gut.

But what was this song?

> I'm longing for You, moving toward You,
> The ache of surrender etching the way.
> Losing myself to find you, going deeper to be You,
> The ache of surrender etching the way.

The song had been singing itself in my mind. It seemed like it was lingering in the background, twirling around other thoughts. Then when all was quiet, it would move to the forefront. I found it both comforting and curious.

With the remaining issue of fluid in the ear, my doctor Suzy suggested I remove all dairy, sugar, caffeine, pastas, and meat from my diet. Since I only ate fish on rare occasions, the meat wasn't an issue. I limited the coffee intake and drank it only in spurts. Without the dairy, the fluid began to drain, but not without imparting a few precious lessons before it did so.

When the body is understood as a way in which the soul communicates with us, illness, disease, and even "clumsy" accidents become a sacred language. Each of my maladies became an opportunity to listen to deeper communication and guidance for healing, which came from within. The path of the body was the journey I'd embarked upon.

I'd become acutely aware that I had very subtle levels of stress that weren't experienced consciously, that is, not until "the ear" became a teacher. Again, detachment was the overarching experience, as if parts of me had identities of their own and each had its own agenda. During this time it was the ear teaching me. The ear began to alert me to feelings of emotional discomfort or self-consciousness, which triggered fluid rising in the ear, the result of extremely subtle constriction. I had no idea before the ear that it was stressful for me to meet new people. And even more surprising to see, I became stressed by some of those I considered close friends, when under certain circumstances the fluid would be triggered to rise. While consciously "I" felt fine and comfortable, and while my personality engaged in its natural way, subconsciously, somewhere, there lurked unease. The ear made this evident as deep stress created a subtle constriction, making me conscious of the subtle stress by the fluid rising. The ear was acting as a biofeedback system.

One day as I was lying on the couch and watching the sky, I felt the urge to talk to the ear. I wasn't particularly focused on the communication that began to take place; it felt more akin to daydreaming and talking to myself. Then at one point, I moved my hand up to rest over my right ear and massaged my neck gently.

"I'm not angry at you, you know," I softly spoke. "I'm just so tired of all these body sensations, all the body stuff. I'm tired of not hearing very well. I'm tired of the echo inside my head. I'm just so tired, I guess." I drifted off for a moment, closing my eyes in order to really feel what I was saying.

I continued, "I think I'm super sad somewhere too."

"You don't have to try so hard," replied the ear.

"I see that clearer now, I guess," I confirmed.

"Just relax and breathe," guided the ear.

Obliging, I did just that.

"Feel everything. Slow down. Stay slow." The ear paused for a few moments. "It's okay to feel little, to feel afraid or vulnerable."

Tears began to stream down my face. "Grr." I growled at the tears. "I hate those feelings." And then I sobbed and sobbed. And as I sobbed, I felt fluid draining away.

"It's good to cry. You need to cry." The ear continued to guide. "You're draining out all the lies. This is a time of nurturing yourself. Be soft."

The words that were spoken within me melted away the false protection of anger and resistance, and I felt waves of peace mingling with eons of grief, peeling off in layers.

"I so want to be soft," I sobbed, wiping my nose on the only thing available, my sleeve.

"I want to be gentle. I feel so out of control of everything right now. And yet sometimes this feels so right that I want to keep melting away. Other times, I get freaked out."

The ear informed me, "It's natural to feel what you're feeling. The truth is, you aren't in control. It's just the way it is. Control is an illusion. You're in a time of deepening and opening. For now, you are the student, and this body is your teacher."

Startled, I thought suddenly, *Why does this actually sound like a conversation?* I felt a moment of confusion regarding who was talking to whom. I thought I was talking to myself. "I mean, who else could I be talking to?" I asked myself.

There was silence. I thought for a few seconds about the right side, the masculine side, of the body. Then I heard, "Too much masculine. Too little feminine." Had I said that to myself? And then when my thoughts moved to the quality of congestion, I heard, "You're congesting your truth and receptivity of self."

I was on hyperalert now. These answers couldn't possibly have come from me. Could they? I understood the answers and how they applied, but it didn't feel like it was me, my mind, responding.

Silence again. I closed my eyes, felt my breath, and allowed myself to relax. No more thinking. No more questions. I just wanted to rest.

As I drifted off, I thought I heard the song again:

> I'm longing for You, moving toward You,
> The ache of surrender etching the way ...

There was a vague wondering that floated through my awareness, asking, "Who is that singing?"

> Losing myself to find You, going deeper to be You,
> The ache of surrender etching the way.

And in the final fall into dreamland, I heard before dropping into the deeper sleep, "It's all okay. You're being stripped of your misunderstood strengths."

3

After a few months of solid rest, I felt in balance and harmony. My state of mind was clear, and emotionally I felt more open than perhaps I ever had before. On deeper levels there was healing taking place, and wounds that had been bullied over were revealing themselves with some hope of being received.

Even Urisk was basking in this harmony. On a sunny afternoon as I was listening to some music and reading, Urisk made his way to my little couch perch to visit. He hadn't been the cuddliest little guy, but then again, in his four years he'd faced some challenges with a mother who wasn't the most present. He was already timid when we came together, and my ways weren't always the most soothing or stabilizing. We'd moved a few times. For a time, with my previous partner Jace, Urisk lived primarily outdoors and had to share attention with two larger dogs. And I'd been quite involved for a couple of years in my own career preparation, without much energy or attention for much else other than work.

But on this day, Urisk wandered in, and not just to pass through. He joined me on the couch. He climbed up by my feet. Leaning forward, he allowed me to pet him for a stroke or two on his head and face. He didn't have a very high tolerance for affection, and I stopped when it seemed he'd had enough.

I greeted him, "Hi, buddy. So nice to have you join me. Are you gonna hang out with me for a while?"

I wasn't counting on him staying for long, but before I could carry on much more with this presumption, he curled up by my feet. I was thrilled. I sat and watched him, for how long I didn't know. His relaxation was visible. His body softened, and at some point his breath released with a deeper exhale. I recognized this had been my process as well, the releasing of the body when true letting go occurs.

But the cherry on top followed next. Urisk stretched himself out and slowly rolled onto his back, exposing his belly. He finally felt safe. I was finally safe for him. I cried and cried quietly, joyfully, for each of us. "I'm so sorry, buddy, that I haven't been able to offer you safety before this, but I'm happy we're here together now," I whispered through tears of guilt and gratitude. "What a teacher you've been, and I didn't even see it. We're mirrors for each other. Thank you." *When we heal ourselves, we allow healing for others.*

4

Years back, when I'd first moved over to the Southeast Hawthorne area in 1997, I was intrigued with a Kundalini yoga class. Although it was just a couple of blocks away, the time just didn't seem right. It was as if some voice buried in my mind said, "Not yet." Without too much regard, I never really thought about it again.

I hadn't been active at all since the vertigo. No dancing with Nia or Sweat Your Prayers, no nothing. My body was feeling achy, and movement was calling. It was while pondering my options that I heard from within, this time not buried in the mind but front and center, "Yoga now." In the same instant I felt an internal *Yes!* ring out, and the secondary thought rushed through my mind: *Whose voice is this?*

I hadn't heard much from it, or heard the song, since the day I had the conversation with the ear. That was a curious experience, but I couldn't come up with any answers about its origin, and all the information that I'd received was a true fit for me. Caleb seemed to think it was my higher self talking. That made as much sense as anything I could think of. After that, it had fallen out of my awareness. And now, here it was, having returned, saying I should start yoga.

There was a Bikram studio not far up the road. We were living in Northeast Portland, and this studio was up on Freemont. The next day I enrolled in the thirty-day special. I loved everything about it: the heat, the structure, the athleticism. I was hooked. The first couple of weeks, I felt so energized, completely in the flow of whatever life brought my way, and joyful.

During my first visit to the studio, I saw a picture hanging on the wall in the hallway. The image was not of Bikram Choudhury. It was another Indian gentleman, very handsome, older, whom I felt intrigued by. After class, I saw a book by him on one of the end tables in the reception area. There didn't need to be any voice present to let me know I needed to buy the book and meet him. I read through the book with a thirst I hadn't recognized in myself before. Though much of the content of this teacher's book was foreign to me, it was also resonant with my inner longing, the ache within. This was a spiritual teacher, a guru who'd been in the United States since the 1960s. The book talked about discipleship, Kundalini, ego, and states of addiction or, one could say, attachments. His website was easily found, and it said he would be offering a weeklong yoga retreat in Colorado next spring. I decided, in the same quickened intuitive way I decided most things, that I would attend.

In the meantime, I was appreciating the Bikram practice. By the end of the month, however, I was experiencing some kind of burning sensation at the base of my spine. I decided to ask one of the instructors about it. After class one day, I saw the teacher who had just taught at the reception desk.

"Hi. Thanks for the class. It felt great," I complimented.

"Wonderful! I'm happy you enjoyed it," Paul responded.

"I have a question for you."

"Shoot," said Paul.

"Well, a few days ago I started getting a crazy burning and itching sensation at the sacrum. The burning and itching is almost constant. I'm rubbing it all the time, trying not to use my nails. And then every so often, I get this feeling like the sacrum is … stretching. Is that possible?"

"You're probably just having a cleansing response. Just keep doing yoga. It'll change," he said with a reassuring squeeze to my shoulder. Then he walked away.

I felt like the explanation sounded accurate. So, I kept doing Bikram, kept sweating, and kept hoping that the itching would fade away. A month later, it was still there, only to a much less degree. Feeling satisfied that cleansing was taking place and soon it would not be an issue, I no longer felt preoccupied with the sensations.

Yet as the itching seemed to subside, my practice was becoming very unpleasant. Oddly, there was a growing tightness in some areas of my body. My body had always been really flexible and balanced, but things were definitely changing in my physical structure. I was also experiencing more acute anger and agitation, to the extent that I'd decided to skip the classes and practice at home for a while. It was in the privacy of home where it became clear to me that there were some big emotions trying to break free.

The first time tears streamed down my cheeks while in child's pose didn't surprise me. However, the rage that blew forth from the hamstrings took me quite off guard. It was during these home practices that I could release emotions that disguised themselves as stress and tightness in the body. When the emotions released, I found deeper relaxation and had the sense of more space in my body.

Repressed emotions, thought forms, and negative beliefs are stress patterns in the body, mimicking tensions and chronic pain. In their release, it felt like a whole new world was opening up to me.

One day after an especially intense practice, I heard what seemed like a poem being recited—from the inside. I wanted to say it was coming from my mind, yet I couldn't be sure. I grabbed a pen and paper and wrote it out:

> She circled her fear, aware of the voices calling caution.
> She questioned to whom they truly belonged.
> Disregarding them, she looked at her fear head-on.
> With shaking limbs, she felt their bindings.

Moving into her fear, a rush, a jolt, passed through her,
leaving her boundless and free, standing stronger than ever.

There was no mistaking the pertinence to what had just been written, in conjunction with what my practice had entailed, but I had not formed this writing. At least not my conscious mind. And yet there it was. I couldn't help but wonder if all of this had to do with the vertigo. It seemed like that was when the song began. And now this. Was it related to all the rest and relaxation, all the openness after letting go? Granted, I did love those states where the mind felt empty or when it seemed as though my whole being was floating like the clouds. I was most grateful for the softness that had been introduced to me and how that affected all my relationships. I felt more open, accepting, and loving in general. But I wasn't sure how much I understood exactly what the song, and now this poem, was communicating. Furthermore, how was it even conceivable that I could be writing or singing inside myself sentiments that I, myself, didn't even understand? I was beginning to feel like a mystery to myself.

5

The summer months flew by. I still needed to monitor my stress and energy levels, wondering if I would ever recover from the adrenal fatigue. Most of the time I felt quite strong, but every now and again I encountered waves of sleepiness. My contentment in life and my energy ups and downs prevented me from getting too caught up in what was to come next, especially in the way of a career or what my heart's work was anymore. For now, I accepted that I'd continue caregiving. And as long as I stayed in acceptance, I suffered less. Inspiration seemed to be mysteriously kept at bay, which helped me to remain on an even keel.

My practice continued mostly at home and occasionally in a class at the Bikram studio. My relationship with the yoga practice was up and down. Intuitively, I just seemed to understand the emotional release experienced through the body. At first it was startling, but after these last few months, it was like second nature. There were phases of agitation, and there were phases of much joy and peace.

One dream in particular brought a smile to my face every time I remembered it. In the dream I was arching backward in camel pose, and I *felt* giggles and laughing coming from my chest, illuminated in swirls of color, which represented the heart energy. My thought upon waking was, *Wow! Things must really be changing!*

For Thanksgiving, Caleb and I invited both sides of our family over for the holiday dinner. I was feeling so grateful for life and those I loved, and I wanted to share what I could with them. Many of my attachments and perceived unmet needs from family felt like they were fading away. *Maybe I'm finally maturing!* I thought to myself.

There is no escaping family dynamics that are painful, confusing, and inhibiting. Since I'd gotten sober, I'd been steadily working to heal the perceived wounds and hurts from my growing up. However, what was becoming clearer was the perception that I had chosen my family. Or I could say that the soul chooses the family to be born into, so that it may learn specific lessons or impart lessons. In the early days of my sobriety, I focused on acknowledging the places of my pain and suffering. I allowed myself to get angry, to blame this or that person or event for my suffering. This was helpful psychologically and emotionally for my ego's development. As I moved into this new realm, there was no more blame. I felt it was all perfect. It didn't mean I was free from projecting, or accusing, or reliving the patterns that had been established, but it did mean that now I was free to perceive these things differently. I was gaining more and more evidence through this new way of practicing that, indeed, the soul, this personality expression, had led me to exactly whom and what I needed, and had determined how I needed them or it, for my life's journey. This higher awareness enabled less attachment to the egoic pain and a greater connection to unconditional love when I was "awake" enough to perceive from that higher place.

Thanks to my yoga and meditation practice, I felt fluid, calm, generous, and unattached throughout the holiday. In the past, even though I enjoyed hostessing, my previous modus operandi was to be bogged down with stress, perfectionism, control, and rushing. No one wanted to be around me in those preparty hours, but yoga had transformed all of that. It felt fulfilling to have an opportunity to give to those we loved, to create a sacred space to hold our families in. At each moment throughout the day, I chose love and acceptance, trusting that energy to remedy any stumbles through the day. I drifted through the festivities with an open heart and in love with everyone there, especially with Caleb for going along with the idea. What wasn't perfect was released with no worries or clinging. It had been our first holiday hosting, and I felt wonderful about how it had gone that night as I sat reflecting on the evening in my second-favorite relaxation spot, the hot bath.

6

Finally in May, 2002, the date was nearing for my travels to Colorado to see this teacher who had captured my heart and imagination. I knew intuitively that this trip was a life changer. There weren't a lot of words for the feeling that fit accurately. Doom? Loss? Mystery? Excitement? None of them were quite right, and each emotion was contrary to the next. I did feel the need, however, to make a tea date with my mother before I departed.

With two days left before I was to depart for the retreat, my mom and I were sitting one evening after work in Common Grounds Coffee Shop on Hawthorne. Small talk and catching up a bit was the preliminary focus, then I started feeling restless and emotional. I interrupted the present topic of conversation.

"So I'm leaving for Colorado in a couple of days, and for some reason I really wanted to see you before that," I began rather seriously.

I had my mom's attention. "Okay. Why do you seem so tense?"

"Well, I'm not sure. I'm really looking forward to this, but ya know, I don't know anything about the retreat. It just feels really big and maybe a little scary."

"Scary? If you're feeling scared or nervous, I don't understand why you still want to go. Do you think it's unsafe or that something bad is going to happen?" she inquired.

"No. Not quite like that, not as if bad things await. It's more of a feeling that everything is going to be different." I paused for a minute. "Do you remember when I first went to Naka Ima?"

"Yeah."

"As you know, that was one of those spur-of-the-moment, intuitive impulses I followed. I saw the flyer, and I was completely in the dark as to what that workshop really was, or what the weekend would entail, but I just knew I had to go! I registered the next day, and three weeks later I was off."

"Right. I remember. The beginning of the end of your relationship with Jace and losing the dogs," recalled my mom.

"Exactly!" I almost shouted. "The day I packed the car to head down there, I placed a picture of Jace, Ochoco, and Lotus on the dashboard. I wanted them with me, yes. But I knew I needed to remember them as they were, and how much I loved them, because I had this … feeling, this desperation … like now, doom or something. I knew that everything would forever be changed. And it was. I was completely different, and my life as it was no longer worked. This is the same thing." I was almost in tears.

"So what do you think is going to change? Are you afraid of losing Caleb?" my mom asked. "Things, life always changes, and we adjust. You went through those changes, but then everything has worked out for the best, right? It was hard, and there were some hard lessons, but you're happy now."

I was feeling self-conscious. I always felt like my mother thought I was too serious, too intense, too emotional. And here I was proving those beliefs right again. But I forged onward.

"I'm feeling that this will affect *our* relationship. I know it sounds weird, but I'm afraid that whatever this is has to do with you and me. I know, it sounds weird and dramatic. I feel that we've overcome many of our differences in the past, but there is this sense that a new gap is forming ... or will form. I don't know. I just wanted to see you and tell you I loved you and that I don't want to lose our relationship."

"Honey." My mother moved to hug me, but I withdrew slightly. I was feeling little and silly. I didn't really know how to receive consoling from my mother in that moment. "It's all going to be okay. I think you're overreacting a little. You're going to go and have a great time doing yoga. There isn't anything to worry about!"

The conversation switched topics, we sipped the last of our tea, and then we went our separate ways.

7

There I sat in the meeting space at the abbey in Colorado with forty or so other students awaiting the teacher, or guru. The first yoga class of the retreat, and those that followed over the subsequent five days, was in no way like Bikram yoga. Led by one of the lead yoga teachers, it was not only relaxing and gentle but also extremely meditative at the same time. As I became more relaxed, I started to lose track of the initial disappointment that had run through my mind during the first class. At first I'd felt frustrated when the class first began, grumbling to myself, "I'm not going to break a sweat or get any kind of workout doing this." In the end, I felt grand, similar to how I felt when I lay on my perch in the Love Room, just being and watching the sky. Open. Spacious. Whole.

At the beginning of the session with the teacher, whom everyone refers to as Gurudev, everyone rose to their feet and bowed respectfully when he entered the room. I clumsily followed their lead. Just before he sat, he bowed to us students as well. He said nothing as one of the students brought him an accordion-looking instrument, which I later learned was a harmonium. He opened with a prayer and an invocation of his gurus before him. Their pictures were on the table next to him, along with a glass, a pitcher of water, and a small lovely vase of flowers.

The chanting began, and I did my best to pronounce what was being said. Finally I caught on just as it was ending. Gurudev then guided us all in a meditation. My mind wasn't quieting easily. There were thoughts about the beautiful gold coverings on the tables, and the flowers sitting along the bottom of the small stage that elevated Gurudev just slightly above the students. I loved his long flowing white robe and how easily he took his seat and remained silent. There was no need to speak immediately or at all. *What is a guru?* I thought to myself. I'd read about the term in his book, but I wasn't sure I truly understood it. I saw the term often in *Yoga Journal*, as the word was making its way into pop culture. There were gurus for everything. That irritated me. Even though I may not have understood what *guru* meant, I knew that the term had been cheapened and misused. *More shall be revealed*, I thought, as he was ending the meditation.

"What the majority of people call yoga is not yoga. You think in your classes that you put your body in positions, the positions learned as in hatha yoga, and you are doing yoga. Instead what you are practicing is conflict, stress, and competition." Gurudev had begun most directly, I thought. I panned the room, wondering if anyone was going to be offended.

"Then you leave, you get in your cars, you go home and watch TV, and you don't realize true yoga is something you practice in all of life. The purpose of yoga is to bring the darkness of unconscious patterns into the light. The purpose of yoga is to return to the Source that the soul is." He finished his introduction. I was even more intrigued. What did I know about yoga? Nothing. Nothing I'd read in magazines spoke like this.

All of sessions with Gurudev, whom everyone seemed to regard with great affection and reverence, were compelling and resonated with me deeply. When he spoke about our attachments, of energy, and of the internal conflicting voices and drive of ego, I recognized my most recent past clearly. As he described that we must have a healthy ego before we can choose to let go of it, to purify its hold on our identity, I instantly saw in a flash these last years since I'd separated from Carl. I'd been working so hard to find myself, to prove myself to others, to recognize my own worth, and to create a life I could be proud of. Isn't that what we all want?

Ego building had been taking place. For most of my life I'd felt my ego was upside down, or inverted somehow, and my mission, without consciously knowing it, was to get it turned right side up. And if I was understanding how Gurudev's talk applied to me, this ego building had been strengthening before this fall from which I'd been recovering for almost a year now. *A healthy ego has to be established in order to be at choice, to let go and surrender.* How interesting. A healthy ego had been stabilizing with teaching, responsibility, overcoming many self-destructive belief patterns, and believing in my worth from within, not depending on what others thought of me.

And when Gurudev talked about the doer and allowing the doing to be done *through* us rather than *by* us, this sparked a "Wow!" through my entire being, which was odd because I wasn't even sure of its meaning. But there was an internal response from something, somewhere inside of me, that *knew*. I could see how the doer, this ego force, had been in full power, until I experienced a different force, the vertigo, stopping me, moving me into this new way of just being. I knew I was onto something. It was almost making sense yet was not quite within reach.

The days of the retreat were filled with much inspiration and recognition. Many things I'd wrongly believed about myself seemed to be magically healing. And there was an uncanny way that I was seeing many of my stories more clearly. They seemed to be automatically integrating into a wholeness or disappearing effortlessly while I listened to Gurudev's teachings.

On the sixth day when Gurudev arrived to sit before all of us, I felt the reverence when I bowed. The session opened as usual, but the topic moved from the psychological to the spiritual realm, and then came a lecture that went way over my head. He spoke briefly about the Divine Mother, a sacred energy or force, then began guiding us into another meditation. The phrase *Divine Mother* was acceptable to me, but I felt a flinch of rejection, as I had great difficulty stomaching any talk of the sacred feminine, goddesses, or symbolism of that ilk.

As Gurudev played the harmonium, he sang a chant, this time in English. It felt almost like a lullaby, soothing and opening my heart. It was simple, short, and repetitive. "Divine Mother, Divine Mother, I love You, Divine Mother." On and on it went. The music and chant were getting faster, and in that quickening, I was dropping into a meditation unlike any I'd experienced before. I was present and yet seemed very far away. Eventually, Gurudev began chanting, "Om, om, om, om, om, om, om, om …" It was seemingly unending.

Who knew how long we'd been in this meditative experience? I certainly didn't. And I had no desire to retreat from this deep state. There seemed to be a disturbance in the audience of students—a commotion of rustling bodies for sure—and a couple of voices shouting out. I had a thought to turn around and see for myself, but then it was as if the will to do so, or maybe the desire to do so, or maybe the thought to do so, faded away, dropping me into a personal silent cocoon. From off in the distance I heard crying, more shouting, and more rustling of bodies, and the whole while I felt myself rocking gently. When I realized I was rocking, it caught me off guard. I thought for a moment. *How long have I been rocking?* Then the thought dissipated as if it had never been thought.

Especially odd was that I was perspiring; my hands were perspiring. As soon as I noticed the wetness, I was gently, lovingly, connected to *the ache in my gut!* It and its lonely melancholia expanded and then bloomed into a deep never-before-experienced love. I had been escorted into my most sacred center. Hands, now dripping with sweat, began to dance, forming shapes and gestures. With eyes closed, I didn't know what shapes they were making, but they felt beautiful and graceful, fluid and magical. With attention on the hands, I then heard a whisper moving from my lips. The words were nothing I understood to be words, but my lips were intent on speaking. Paying attention, in an in-and-out sort of way, I felt and heard whispers of another language being spoken out of my own mouth. Although they were nonsensical to me, they felt intentional and clear. Before I knew it, my heart, this one's heart, was holding the sentiments of the utterings being spoken, and tears were streaming endlessly down my face. Though I could still hear many other things happening all around, my awareness was continuously drawn back toward my own center of experience by some force other than myself. The awareness was at times personal, as me, and other times detached and impersonal. As I listened to this mysterious language whispering through me, I couldn't comprehend the emotion connected to it. But there it spoke, as the hands danced, as the body rocked, and as the sacred center held me safe. None of these aspects of self that would normally be thought of as mine seemed to be so. They all seemed detached from ownership, yet their expressions *flowed through* this one, me, this being. The mind couldn't ponder for long; it simply watched from a distant place, yet resting in the sacred center.

"Divine Mother, Divine Mother, I love You, Divine Mother." Life was forever changed.

8

Arriving home from Colorado, I carried within myself gratitude and wonder, spaciousness and love. I was filled from the core in a way that I could not describe in words. Caleb was looking forward to seeing me and hearing about the journey. I was excited to share about the retreat with him. In relaying how many things Gurudev had talked about, things that both Caleb and I had been working with in our own lives, felt profound when introducing a new level of understanding. There was obvious resistance from Caleb when I mentioned the guru Gurudev and attributed much of the conversation to things he said. I didn't mind and figured he'd warm up to the message regardless.

"The day before yesterday, Gurudev led us in a Shaktipat initiation." I had been saving the most fascinating for last.

"Shaktipat? What's that?" Caleb asked.

"I can't say I know for sure. All of this is so new to me; I'm totally green! But from what I understood, it's an energy transmission that comes from an awakened master like Gurudev and sparks the spiritual energy in those around. It wakes up the Kundalini energy, which rests at the base of the spine. When the Kundalini's awakened, it begins to move more strongly through the body, especially the spine. I still need to read up on it. I mean, it was wild. I completely lost any bearing on time and where I actually was in some moments. Everyone in the room seemed to be going through their own personal manifestations."

Caleb was curious and a little something else that I couldn't put a finger on. Whenever he was experiencing unsettled emotions or self-consciousness, his cheeks and the area around his nose would become slightly flush. "I'm not sure I get it. This energy creates all these manifestations? And what about you? What'd you experience?" he asked.

"I don't know how to explain it." I paused. He gave me space to think. "Things just started happening, like my hands began moving on their own, and I was whispering some foreign language and crying. I think it's still sinking in. It was just unlike anything I've ever experienced. But it felt right, whatever that means. I can say it felt right."

I wanted to share more openly, more deeply, and more truthfully with him, but I always had a hard time speaking to anyone about my spiritual feelings. My spiritual feelings were my secret world, like a private, secret inner life.

Not yet a year ago in June, for my birthday, Caleb gave me a Krishna Das CD as a gift. I hadn't heard him before but had definitely been feeling a resonance with all things from India since that winter in 1996. We were sitting in the Love Room, celebrating my day, talking, listening to the CD, and eating strawberries. During one song, I just broke out in tears. The music alone sank me into the lonely ache in my gut. The only lyrics I was able to make out through the tears were, "Wander wild ... all roads lead to you ... laughing at the moon ... don't know who or what I am ... you kiss my face." There was no way I could've known how portentous this particular song would be.

"Sweetie, what's wrong? Why are you crying?" He leaned in and took me in his arms.

"I must just be exhausted still. Ya know, depressed, I guess, from this whole vertigo thing."

"Is that all? We were just laughing about the scene in that movie, and then you're crying."

I sat quiet, eyes looking down in my lap, feeling the longing ache and feeling at home within it. I didn't want to talk about God with anyone. I didn't want to say out loud the things about God that frightened me; the pangs of deep yearning I had for God; or what I felt it meant to me. I barely even understood it myself.

"The song" was my answer.

"What about the song?" Caleb asked. He thought this was one of the moments that would require his staying present and encouraging me to share—a little girl moment, a vulnerable moment, which he knew I resisted with all my power.

There was no way I could look at him and talk. This I knew. Too vulnerable. Too scary.

"I get afraid." There was a long silence as I stared at the pattern of pink, blue, and purple in the couch cover. He squeezed my hand. "I feel like I have this whole other life inside of me." This was new to him, considering there was nothing that he could think of that we hadn't shared with one another.

"What do you mean, a whole other life?" he asked gently.

"It's hard to explain. It's like there's a secret place where I hide how I really feel spiritually."

"But you meditate, and you talk about how you relate to the Universe, your lessons, synchronicity, trusting in God." He reflected what he knew of me.

"I know. But the deeper stuff. It all feels so private and personal, which I think is fine.

Sometimes I feel ashamed." I was now staring down at my hands as my fingers twirled and twisted the hem of my dress.

"But what are you afraid of? Maybe you feel private and ashamed because you were raised by atheist parents? Because it wasn't something they felt was true?" He was trying to bring clarity.

I was starting to feel hot. The sun was beaming in all the windows. I was starting to feel claustrophobic and anxious. This was a test in being vulnerable that he and I were always working on. Would I go further? I couldn't stand the tension building anymore.

"I'm afraid I'm supposed to be a nun or something!" I blurted out in tears. "But I know a nun is not really it, but something like that. I feel like if I really gave into what was inside me, I wouldn't have a normal life with you, with family, doing normal life things! I'd have to give everything up!"

The dam had broken loose. Caleb sat still and present, listening with flushed cheeks.

"How hilarious, huh?!" I laughed through a sob, "I can't even say a prayer out loud if anyone is within hearing distance. A nun … recovering alcoholic, nude modeling—well, you know, nothing extreme, artful and beautiful, but that's not nun material. Been around the block a time or two." Now staring into his eyes, feeling the intensity of my eyes on fire with this now spoken out loud secret, I said, "I've never gone to church, not that I feel that means anything for my path, but still! And I don't even know where I get this from. This deep longing in me just feels like it's trying to take me somewhere that I'm both terrified to go and yet I so desperately long to, need to, go." Looking back down into my lap, I asked, "What if I'm supposed to be a nun?"

I was done crying but felt embarrassed and surprised at what I'd revealed even to myself.

That was the last time I spoke about this secret spiritual place. Now, on the return from Colorado, I felt stirred even more deeply. I could talk out loud about the outer experience, but I wasn't ready to share the intimate details of my inner connection, and I was fine with that.

Both sides of my family were Seventh-day Adventists. My parents each attended Adventist academy in their high school years and at some point chose no longer to subscribe to the doctrine they had been raised with, or to any religious doctrine for that matter. That, coupled with the times I was born into, being the mid-1960s, and their being barely out of their teens, meant that there wasn't much place for religion or spirituality. Politics, yes. Social justice, yes. God, no.

Organized religion wasn't something that resonated with me and that spirituality hadn't entered my mind or life until I entered Alcoholics Anonymous. It was there that I realized how strongly the beliefs of my parents had affected me. My grandparents were Adventist, as were half of my aunts and uncles, while the other half's beliefs were more aligned with my parents'. Everyone knew where everyone else stood. Respect was given by each side. Yet I recognized that I no longer fit in either camp, and the chasm was only going to widen. Especially as my spiritual path deepened and its philosophy, practices, and experiential understanding took root, there was less to be said, it seemed.

9

I was grateful I'd given myself a week free from any obligations upon returning from Colorado. I'd been listening to the retreat recordings of Gurudev's lectures daily while relaxing in the Love Room. As I listened, I kept thinking that he was saying things that I could swear hadn't been said while in Colorado, but here they were. There was so much coming up in me that I couldn't absorb it all at the time.

Integration was needed after this event. I felt faced with a whole world I knew so little about, more accurately, this world inside myself. *Really? A nun?* I asked myself as Urisk offered me a short cuddle opportunity. Where had that come from? And Kundalini. I'd heard of Kundalini yoga but didn't really know much about it. It brought to mind people who dressed in white and turbans, like the teacher at the Kundalini yoga studio in Southeast Portland when I'd first entertained the idea. My mind felt consumed with all there was to learn along this new path unfolding before me.

I was now replacing the Bikram yoga I'd been practicing with the practice I'd learned at the retreat. It began with a prayer and a few rounds of sun salutation. The postures were to be done slowly, consciously, with a strong internal focus. I found that the practice kept me in the sweet flow I'd become accustomed to over the last year or so. This flow held the qualities of softness and open-heartedness and released me from the need to have opinions, all of which were opposite my tendencies. It also enabled nonattachment with ease. I had no drive to prove anything anymore. Unsure about exactly what I wanted to do or where I was going, I felt completely reconciled that I no longer had a desire to teach Nia. This had been hanging in limbo over these last months, but it felt clear to me now. I felt called to yoga. Its full scope was what I felt ready to explore. It was as if something in me knew dance or fitness was not my path.

About the second week into a home practice, I felt the chant Gurudev had been singing rise up from somewhere: "Divine Mother, Divine Mother, I love You, Divine Mother."

I noticed that the song effortlessly sang itself through me. As I attuned to it during my practice while coming out of half-moon to pause, I experienced my body returning to the position of arching to the right.

That's odd, I thought to myself. I straightened back to center, and as soon as I released an exhalation, the body arched to the right again.

"Whoa. This is really weird. Am I doing this?" I asked, talking to myself out loud. This time, I shook and jumped up and down a time or two.

I decided to enter a forward bend. I hung out for a couple of breaths and slowly returned to standing. Once I settled into center, the body twisted to the right of its own accord.

Baffled, I attempted another experiment. I struck warrior pose. I settled in, and when I released and came center, I left my feet wider apart, thinking perhaps my balance was off. And the body once again moved on its own. This time I remained still and left the body where it had put itself. I waited patiently, but nothing.

"Wow. Am I losing my mind?" I straightened myself back to center and exhaled, and the body moved into a twist—again!

There was no explanation for this. *Is it connected to vertigo? Am I doing this and for some reason am not aware?* I decided it was best to call it a day. I was feeling unnerved and a wee bit freaked out.

Experimentation of this initial sort followed the next couple of days. I was beginning to develop a sense of amusement along with confusion. But by the fifth or sixth day, something was very much afoot. I began to experience my body moving slowly but surely, spontaneously. On its own. Under its own will.

When Caleb got home from work one morning after his forty-eight-hour caregiving shift in a home for adults with developmental disabilities, I called him in to witness. Even though I didn't want to seem irreverent or dishonoring of the practice, I needed another perspective. Starting with half-moon, I came to center. "Keep watching," I told him with my eyes closed. Slowly the body arched back over to the right, leaned backward into another arch, then gently twisted so that the torso faced the floor. The body rested at this place for a moment and then released toward the floor into a forward bend.

When I rose and opened my eyes, I met Caleb's wide-eyed gaze. "You're doing that, right?" he asked.

"What do you think? What does it look like?" I wondered, since I hadn't witnessed it from outside myself.

"Well, sort of, but not really. It looks more like a breeze or waves are pushing you along."

"Oh my God! That's almost exactly what it feels like!" I was filled with wonder.

"It's kinda freaky, don't you think?" Caleb asked, scrunching his face slightly.

"I dunno. No. I guess from the outside. But from in here it's effortless and soothing and joyful. My body feels so relaxed even from just a couple of minutes of it," I explained.

From that point on, my practice of twice a day became a source of captivation and wonder. The initial spontaneous movement to the right gradually began to grow into a continuous flow of movements, some actual yoga postures I recognized, although many positions the body was put into were ones I didn't recognize. The body would flow and hold positions of its own accord for over an hour. And after a period of time, the energy moving through me would retreat, and I knew we—it and I—were done.

The emotions that accompanied this process moved from elation to fear in varying degrees as I cautiously surrendered to the inner momentum.

One day in the third week of my new practice, immediately following these first experiments within the laboratory that was my body, feeling much peace and wonder, I entered into one of the daily rituals, bath time. I'd started taking daily baths religiously after the vertigo and felt like it was paramount to helping me retain my calm disposition, as well as support my adrenal glands. The warm water added extra soothing to the nervous system and to the relaxation that my yoga practice was creating in my body and mind. Caleb's brother John and his girlfriend Ashley were going to be stopping by later, so I wanted to have this valued time before their arrival. I hadn't felt like socializing much in the last year and certainly hadn't felt like being around people since my return from the Colorado retreat. I was more than content to do my practice and read the new books, which were helping me to understand this new life. I'd always been more of a loner, but it was growing, even in my relationship. But tonight, we'd entertain.

Disrobing and sinking into the tub, I flipped the switch to the recorder. I continued to learn more and more from Gurudev's lectures, no matter how many times I listened to them. There were twelve talks, and I was reaching the end of them. Closing my eyes to take it all in, I seemed to recall this tape to be from the Shaktipat session. "Yes. This is it," I said under my breath as I heard Gurudev talking about Divine Mother. "Divine Mother, Divine Mother, I love You, Divine Mother." The words already were streaming through. *Who and what is the Divine Mother?* I wondered. *I'm going to have to reread what his book says about Kundalini …*

The harmonium was playing in the background, and I felt my breathing become quickened. Having no idea of everything that was occurring, I felt energy gathering in my hands and feet, an intense hot tingling that then began to spread through my body, creating the sensation of a stiff board. There were aches and pains, which again I was witnessing from a detached, watchful place. Above all, regardless of everything that was happening, if I were in my right mind this should have been causing alarm, but instead I had a strong desire to continue to surrender to what was put in motion. My hands stiffened up into a formation with arms bent in the position of a praying mantis, and my body, the body, was convulsing with the head arching backward.

Caleb arrived home to find me in this state. Though he was frightened, he had the intuitive knowledge not to try to interfere with the process. He let some of the water out of the tub and supported my head, which was banging against the tub wall. And there he sat patiently, fearfully, and fearlessly as I, his love writhed in stiff convulsions for about an hour. I was vaguely aware of his presence, of the ugliness and frightening spectacle that I must be. Simultaneously, a subtle vulnerability of feeling was exposed in my secret spiritual self.

Inside, ecstatic bliss was consuming me. There was a surrender and letting go that had only one desire, to keep letting go of all control. *Whose desire?* was a thought that floated through my awareness. I felt the spittle and drool and snot spilling forth. All the while I felt such an intense love, loving me and protecting me. As the convulsions slowed, my awareness rose gracefully to the surface. I felt the paralysis in my limbs and hands start to recede, leaving in its wake a deep, to-the-bone pain and tingle, yet it registered as only sensation. I *knew* for the first time that *this* was the Divine Mother. It was Her love holding me and purifying me. It was understood: Her love, Divine Mother's love, was both fierce and gentle. The pain and bliss were each Her doing and Her presence. I was in love with Her, and I felt a deep love for Gurudev. The love for both of them was immense, and the connection was rooted in the core of my being.

When my eyes opened, they were crying tears of joy and sorrow. There was laughter mixed with sobs bursting forth. I felt deliriously free and whole and connected to Love. Caleb was sitting by the side of the tub. The look on his face was hard to read. Blankness. Awe. Fear. Relief. It took a while before I could move or stand. My body ached, and I felt terribly weak. There were no words to say, no thoughts to think. Caleb helped me out of the tub, dried and dressed me, and laid me down in my favorite place, my perch, the Love Room couch. Gazing out into the sky, I too flew.

Needless to say, I wasn't the best company that night. John and Ashley arrived at the tail end of this deep cleansing. I experienced a tinge of shame and exposure creeping up to the surface when Caleb was getting me settled and I heard their voices. But the most prominent thought was, *How perfect that others should be present in one of my most spiritually vulnerable states, the thing I try to hide about myself no matter what.* An idea also flashed, recognizing that karma was going to come around a lot faster on this track. Inside I laughed, understanding the irony.

10

I had intense dreams over the next couple of nights. There were amazing mansions on high mountaintops, glistening in ethereal shades of color: gold, pink, and melon. There were voices speaking to me, teaching me, from some far-off land. My body began experiencing subtle electrical jolts of energy periodically throughout the night, only partially awaking me from the deep slumber.

I heard the familiar song to my now beloved Divine Mother. I felt Her heart smile as my own in response. I saw the face of Gurudev, from whom I was now learning more clearly what it meant to be a guru. In his presence I felt safe.

> I'm longing for You, moving toward You,
> The ache of surrender etching the way.
> Losing myself to find You, going deeper to be You,
> The ache of surrender etching the way.

Here it was again. This song had been following me. I wondered if this song had been leading me. As I listened, the song sang itself while I was in a half-sleep state. I felt it knew me. I no longer felt like this was a sentiment of unknowns, misunderstanding, imagination. Instead it was a truth being reflected. But from where?

And one morning as the sun was streaming through the sheer cranberry curtains, I heard a message from far off: "You must die and die again so that you may be reborn."

11

Weeks passed. It was as if I'd entered another world. Practice, which truly meant deepening my relationship with Divine Mother, Gurudev, and myself, held me spellbound. Changes were happening rapidly, that is, changes within. The external world, the world from which I had pretty much retreated, was moving along as usual, but my perception of that world was also changing.

What I was learning through direct experience about this magical force of Kundalini differed in many respects from anything I'd read in a book. I was a natural vehicle for this kind of experiential learning through the physical form of the body. The sensitivities all my life now seemed to be foreshadowing. However, I appreciated learning from the intellectual angle and felt like this enabled me to integrate everything that was occurring.

"The couple of books I've looked at so far," I was sharing with Caleb, "describe this energy as being inherent in all humans. It's what gives us the capacity to reach enlightenment."

"That means, then, that no one can become enlightened, whatever that exactly means, without this energy?" he asked.

"Right. It's more like the Kundalini *is* the force propelling and purifying us in order for us to wake up or reach enlightenment. It's called different things in different traditions, but ultimately it's the process of movement of spiritual energy, and it's rising through the energy centers and the spine in order to transform our consciousness. While it's traveling through the centers, we're in stages of awakening. When the Kundalini has cleared and rises to the crown, then a person becomes enlightened." I continued, while guessing out loud as I spoke, "But I have a feeling it's not at all that cut-and-dried or straightforward."

"Why and how does this happen, and to whom?" he questioned.

"What I've been gathering is that there are a couple of ways this takes place. Years of long, intense yogic practices and prayer. Or it can happen spontaneously, by the blessing or grace or transmission of Shaktipat, by a guru which was what happened with me, and sometimes by trauma. Karma definitely plays a role in its awakening as well."

Caleb was taking it in. "And what are the energy centers?"

"Chakras," I replied.

"The chakras? I know of chakras, but I don't think I've ever heard of their connection to Kundalini in this way."

"I know. I'm learning this is the yogic science, one of most ancient sciences, and it's really abstract in so many ways if you aren't plugged in, so to speak, energetically and experientially. You know how the chakras are vertical and go from the root to the crown? Well, supposedly this is how the Kundalini awakens, up through the chakras."

"Hmm." He sighed. "Very interesting."

"What's also interesting is the itching and weird sensations I was experiencing at the base of my spine when I started Bikram. I think the energy was stirring then. I think the energy started stirring with the vertigo. I actually think this Kundalini was somehow connected to why I was sick in 1996 and to the profound changes in the aftermath. I'm guessing it had already begun its wake-up back then.

I think the energy, the Kundalini, is intimately connected to the soul and that they've been working hand in hand." We just stared at each other, lost in our own thoughts on how to make sense of this in a logical, rational way.

The books were informative, but they failed to help me understand everything taking place. Nowhere other than in Gurudev's book was there a mention of the type of yoga practice I was experiencing. But even there, I hadn't understood what was mentioned until I began *experiencing* it directly.

Before long, my practice had become full-on spontaneous movements for an hour and a half, both in the morning and at the end of my day. I was lulled in beautiful swaying motions if standing. It felt like being seaweed at the bottom of the ocean or tall tree branches dancing in the breeze. These motions fed into other movements and poses. The body was twisted, turned, stretched, held stationary, and upside down. This force, this Divine Mother, literally felt like a nurturing mother. I felt so nurtured and loved. Peace flooded through me, and joy rained down upon me from inside my own heart. And that purple-blue glow! When I was held into the most relaxed states, when the body melted and the mind became silent, the purple-blue glow was intense within the mind's eye. It felt like it morphed and expanded and danced, filling my entire inner vision.

Through the spontaneous postures, I had the sense that the ancient rishis and masters had experienced this divine awakening through their bodies and eventually systematized them into the hatha yoga postures we know of today. These postures have healing and purifying capabilities, even if one is unawakened, because the origin of the movements is a divine intelligence. Its purpose is to awaken humanity.

I was becoming more sensitized to Divine Mother's ebbs, flows, and promptings. The sensations were sometimes very subtle, but when I let go of any expectations or judgments, Divine Mother's guidance would appear. Usually at the end of each practice, I would be lowered onto my back into Savasana or corpse pose. I often felt as though the mind was held suspended somewhere, tucked in some nook or cranny, because no thought would stir, only a sensation of consciousness, of awareness, of watching, of witnessing. And then, the I of any identification with personality dissipated into a silent, peaceful gap of nothingness, like a deep-sleep state. The time that passed from the beginning of my practice to the end felt timeless, as if I'd disappeared. The end was signaled by my eyes popping open. A deep breath would support my awareness in rising to the surface, and my body would be automatically free, like stretching. I was awake, I, my personhood, was back.

Both in and out of practice I felt what was becoming a very familiar inner pull or tug, which was the sensory communication that Divine Mother was using to call me inside, call me home. It was like being put into a deep meditative state from this inside force, like all my energy was sucked into a vortex inside of me as if I was going to sleep, only sleep wasn't actually the outcome. It was a call to let go, surrender, relax, and allow Her presence to take over. Meditation would take place spontaneously, or my breathing would take on odd rhythms for periods of time. Sometimes, my breathing seemed to cease completely. In other instances through my day-to-day life, it would alert me to what the body did or didn't want to ingest. Surrender was the message. I was being taught to let go of being the doer and to allow the doing to be done through me.

The words from the mysterious song that had been sung to me from some unknown origin were now being more understood by me, consciously. The path I was on was a path of surrender, at least for now, letting go of the old, of identity, of attachments and the mind. It was all about surrendering my trust to a force greater than myself. God?

Isn't that what ultimately we are called to offer to God? To surrender our will unto His? And this was the same, but I felt like I was surrendering my will unto Divine Mother. *Are they one and the same?* I asked myself on numerous occasions. I felt like I had glimpses of something larger knocking on my door, but I wasn't able to open the door but a crack as of yet.

Though I felt open, and though a deepening of inner peace and greater devotion was taking place within me, my external world was suffering. I managed to do the caregiving job effectively, if not better than before, as greater patience and acceptance had taken root. However, my intimate relationship was different. There were small rumblings, naturally so, from Caleb.

"Babe, can I just ask that when I come out of meditation, we not talk for just a while?" I asked exiting the Love Room after morning practice, when met with questions from Caleb. I hadn't addressed this at a neutral time like I'd planned, and Caleb felt jilted by the request. It was understandable that he didn't know that it was often challenging for me to engage in external interactions after being pulled so deep within. It took a while for my brain to switch gears into my communicative self. I often waited for a while before I came out of the room, until I felt all the way back into a grounded, present awareness. And even then, I often didn't have an inclination to talk. But today I hadn't taken that time, and the immediate interaction felt overwhelming.

He looked both hurt and frustrated with my request.

"Sweetie. I'm sorry." I went up and hugged him. "I want to hear what you have to say, but I want to be able to be present with it, and I just need a few. I'm sorry if I hurt your feelings."

"I just don't feel as connected to you anymore. I mean, you're in that room all the time, it feels like." I could tell some things that had been building were about to be released. "When we talk, the conversation always comes back to yoga and Gurudev. We're not even able to enjoy the same meals anymore, now that your food preferences have changed."

It was true. "I know. It's all changing. And I know this is my focus. There's so much going on, things I can't really give words to." I was in agreement with everything he was sharing.

Caleb and I had come together through an amazingly transformative course called Naka Ima, in which we spent a year in deep personal growth. The basic practices and teachings centered on identifying stories, releasing attachments, and realizing one's true center. The depth of processing, healing, and clearing was profound. We had come together with an electric passion, an immediate soul connection, and needs for healing in which we were perfectly fitted. We came together knowing that we had important inner work to do together with no attachment to what that meant long term. Consciously the relationship formed and grew, as did our love and respect for one another. And now, consciously, we would navigate the changes we were facing.

"I honestly don't know what to say," I continued as I took his hand and led him over to the living room couch to sit so we could talk. "I know we aren't connecting in the same ways anymore. Everything may be temporary, or it may not."

"We used to be able to have these great talks for hours," he said sadly. "And now, I feel like we hardly talk at all."

"You're right." I agreed again. "I don't feel like I can process in the same way we used to. It's strange to me too. But literally, I feel like some of my most obvious stories or things that I was super attached to, or triggered by, have simply vanished. Poof! There's nothing to process."

"And I feel you get impatient if I need to process feelings of what I'm going through," he added.

"I guess I do in some ways. Not always. But it's true. I don't know how to explain it, and I in no way want to discount what you're feeling, but it seems like more and more often, I can see it more clearly than I used to be able to."

"See what more clearly?" he asked.

"The baggage and how to let go. Not just for me, but for both of us. Somehow I can see past the story, even in myself. For instance, when Mom and my brother were over a couple of weeks ago," I started to explain, "remember that I told you after they left it was as if I had no buttons, no old triggers? All the past buttons that would normally send me into whatever spiral of anger, disappointment, or feeling discounted, all of it—it was gone, and very much to my amazement."

"Yeah, I remember you talking about that after they left," he acknowledged.

"There were a couple of moments in which I could feel one of my issues about not being taken seriously rising to the surface. I felt agitation building. I saw the old me, the old pattern of reaction, wanting to continue the conversation with Sam [my brother] in order to emphasize my point. To be heard. To prove something. But instead, I saw with a rapid flash of awareness to just let it go. I could see it was only going to be a matter of egos clashing. My story of feeling discounted just vanished. I saw it wasn't true, that it was just this noise trying to lure me into its static. Instead, I found that I wanted to just love Sam for who he was and accept myself along with our differences," I said, concluding the example. I hoped it was clear enough, as all of this was new to me too. I was hardly an expert at what was happening to my entire being.

"So is that how it is with us now?" Caleb asked, maybe a little insulted.

"Sort of. It's how it is with me and how that impacts us. I see that I can hook onto my crap, or I can choose to see that it is truly not real. It's a story I've learned to believe. It's no different from everything we went through and learned at Naka Ima. The difference is that now, with this ... grace, is all I can call it. I know this sounds weird, but I'm not the one who is experiencing this instant ability to just let go. It's as if it's being done *for* me, from some other level of me. The processing has become obsolete!"

"So you're saying, that you can see past the story and just let it go effortlessly?" he asked.

"For many things right now, I guess so. Things aren't getting under my skin in the way they always have. Will this last forever? I hope so, but who knows. Have I had to deal with one of the big wounds or deep roots that trigger the big hurt? No. So maybe that'll be different." I was winding down. "Right now, these days, the mind—and I say 'the mind' because it doesn't feel personalized to me—doesn't feel like it can hold a lot of noise in it. It, the mind, does what it can to remain in an empty state on its own. I know it sounds weird. This is why I'm not talking a lot. It feels like noise, and it's almost painful. It's not because I don't love you or don't want to connect with you. The mind will only take so much stimulus and activity." I tried to put it into words.

"Okay. I don't get it completely, but I feel like I have a sense of what you're saying. I know all this is new, and we don't know what it all means or what to expect. We'll just ride it out and see," Caleb said, feeling better to have talked.

"And I'll try to be more present with you in the ways you're needing. I know this isn't easy for you either. It's a lot of space that you're holding for me. I do love you," I said, looking into his big blue eyes, seeing him, being present with him.

"I know. I love you too. It's just scary sometimes," he replied softly.

12

As I sit alone in the still of the day,
I listen to the laughter outside my door.
The separation I feel in heart and head,
Wondering where it is I fit anymore.
Do I long for that laughter, the play, the race?
Do I mourn for the loss of the mask that covered my face?
Don't assume, as I sit alone, there's a lack of joy and contentment.
Because the secret is, they bubble up from inside
This very sacred, silent space.

I felt I was drifting farther away from the life I had known and from
those I loved. While love and devotion grew for Divine Mother, my
relationships with everyone else felt strained. Being with others,
with the exception of Caleb, was very uncomfortable, in particular,
family.

The challenge that presented itself was how to cultivate this new
way of being with those who have no understanding of or no desire
for understanding this waking-up process. How to resist patterns
that require dressing oneself in old, outworn garments in order to
validate the characters we all, as actors in life's play, have learned

so well? How to remain connected when all the familiar ways of connecting and being known are vanishing? And how to navigate the loss of what had been, even as the longing to embrace what was becoming entailed so much more of both fear and desire?

To return to that old costume of personality every time I needed to interact with people was almost unbearable. It felt as though I'd glimpsed the freedom of a bird that had escaped its cage. When I was with family, I could feel myself being shooed into the cage. Constricted. Trapped. My choice, at least for the time being, was to have as little contact as possible. I wondered if it would always be this way.

Just as my intuition had informed me before leaving for Colorado, my mother held the greatest challenge. My keeping my distance didn't go unnoticed, but I smoothed it over with small talk, keeping the focus on her. I felt much love for my mother and sadness that I was unable to share with her what was happening. I felt like the original fear I'd felt before leaving for Colorado was materializing. It seemed these changes in me were separating us. I recognized this as a story playing itself out, like some karmic knot with its own lessons that had yet to unfold.

For these first months of awakening, peace pervaded. However, almost one year later, there were stark moments of inner conflict that were like dark clouds passing through my mind. I started having fears of being possessed by this energy, Divine Mother, and Gurudev. Fleeting thoughts of Satan controlling me would roll over me, even though I didn't believe in him, or Jesus for that matter. The Christian concept of God wasn't on my radar consciously, but it was all over my subconscious. Cultural collective thought forms that I carried unknowingly still held sway in my mind. Inevitably, the mind would be harnessed by this divine force of Divine Mother again to reflect the states of calm neutrality.

These phases of paranoia were getting closer together. In the fearful moments, I'd fall into potholes in my mind. I began to imagine that in those moments when I grew calm, it was in fact a method being used by Satan to prevent me from thinking. My sanity would begin to quake, only to draw back into a calm, peaceful, witnessed consciousness. From that perspective, I'd recognize that my truest desire was for God. I trusted that this desire wasn't the act of the character Satan. I'd reconnect with the deep peace residing in me. I could recognize that my whole person was growing more loving and compassionate than it had been most of my life prior to this awakening process. The fear abated, that is, until the next purification and cleansing of those culturally programmed thought forms arose, like black storm clouds, once again.

The majority of the time I felt like I was held in a cocoon of love and protection while trust and faith took root, and part of that protection was the suspension of mind. This was also Divine Mother purifying and clearing the lenses of perception, which is a natural process of waking up. Regardless of whether or not I could make sense of it, it was and continues to be Her grace in action.

Divine Mother, or Ma Kundalini or Shakti Kundalini, as I had discovered this divine energy is also called, was becoming my spiritual Mother. It was in this Mother's bosom that I found transformation and new awareness on a daily basis. It was in solitude and silence that I felt most complete, in part because there was no one to coerce personality forth, to tease it with the possibility of desires, triggers, and attachments, which I felt protected from in the womb of the Love Room. For how long this could be maintained, I didn't know.

13

Honeymoon phases along this journey came and went. What started to become apparent was that Divine Mother is a force of nature, and as with all things that beat with life, there were cycles, ebbs, flows, deaths, and births. By fall 2002, this baby bird was being encouraged to leave the nest. All the grace that had been bestowed was now to be learned and embodied. Much easier said than done, as ego is a hard nut to crack, and always sitting in wait to play its role as our protector and stabilizer, as well as the resister of change and transformation.

I had received so much information over these many months. My perceptions had been altered, and I understood many deeper truths. And Divine Mother remained present. But that didn't prevent the me I'd known myself to be from returning.

It was time for a reprieve, or what felt more like a hard fall from an elevated state, and I wasn't pleased with the comedown. I had become accustomed to the experience of such freedom in a myriad of ways. I had hoped that the witness consciousness and nonattachment would be my new way of operating in the world. Even though it left a stark gap in my relationships, I felt more solidly connected to

God. Caleb was suffering most with the turn the relationship had taken. He had been the primary contact for me since my return from Colorado. As things stood, I was finding it impossible to communicate with most anyone else. He had been carrying the weight of my experiences, the effects of both the ups and downs on my being, the detachment from others in my life, including him, and the fears and irrational paranoia that silently crept in and out of my days and nights. He was relieved to have a more solid me back, and that solid me had come back with old triggers in place, only a shade less gross than they had been before.

As I reentered the world gradually, I resumed some relationships with friends, although they felt strained for me. I had a hyperawareness of my own opinions, judgments, and attachments and the returning stories. After a taste of amazing freedom from these characteristics, I found that to be dropped back into them was incredibly uncomfortable. I felt like I'd been put in some costume that was ten sizes too small. It was now up to me to work with what I knew to be true from the perspective I had been shown and had experienced. The judgments, opinions, and stories of the ego/personality had the potential to return me to old patterns of suffering. I had no shortage of characteristics for which I found the need to engage a conscious practice of releasing. The real inner work had just begun.

14

Falling back into old patterns was effortless, no matter how distasteful, and some patterns were stickier than others. I felt as if I was living two lives. One of these lives was in my home, in the Love Room, and sometimes with Caleb. There I had the freedom to be in the flow of whatever Spirit was dictating. The other life was of a personality that I felt I had little power over or choice about. The former was my preference, and just by having a preference, I allowed division and reactivity to sit in wait. The preference created suffering. Unless I was well rested, feeling connected to my center, and calm, I could be swept up feeling like an untrained puppy, with personality in the lead. Understanding personality is part of this play. My task of controlling it, rather than *it* controlling me, was part of the game.

Just as I had started to reacclimate to having my personality in full swing again, October brought my second trip to Colorado, for another week of being in Gurudev's presence. From the time of my arrival at the abbey, where these events were held, Divine Mother was strong and present. Waves of energy swelled up and swayed my whole being into moments of inner stillness and lifted my spirit into the state of Joy. So much had changed in the last months, and I felt like I was home.

There was a need that I felt developing upon arrival. I so wanted to share with Gurudev what I'd been experiencing. I was seeking validation and confirmation, and I craved person-to-person guidance. However, I didn't want to open up about all that I'd been experiencing in front of the group. My inner life felt very private and personal. And in truth, regardless of my past desires to teach Nia and the brief period of time when I taught Jazzercise in the early 1990s, I'd never been comfortable being up in front of groups. Even after many years of AA meetings, I could count the times I shared in meetings on two hands.

I found out quickly it isn't always easy to get an audience with a beloved teacher. The desire I had for this was forming into a stubborn attachment that was bringing me down.

I was able to witness how the attachment was forming and how I was creating my suffering. The obsession and clinging to what I was wanting was creating a division in my ability to really experience what was present. As frustration mounted, I began having an ongoing conversation with myself:

"I'm in a spiritual community of others who must be experiencing the same things. No one's going to judge me. I'm in the company of like-minded seekers and peers," said one voice in my head.

"Nope. Not gonna happen. That sounds great, and it's probably true, but I'm not there yet," replied the other. The secrecy of my spiritual life was not yet willing to be seen. The deepest part of myself was not willing to be revealed.

This conversation went back and forth for a few days. And all the inner noise was driving me crazy and making me cranky. Unfortunately, the voices wouldn't be quieted, because the attachment was strong. So, I needed to either be brave and raise my hand to share or to let go. I chose to let go.

The letting go itself was a struggle. I was still throwing inner tantrums until the matter resolved itself within me. The penultimate day of the retreat, I was in my room doing my practice, as I opted to continue in private rather than participate in the structured sequence hatha yoga classes. On the first day of the retreat, the energy of Divine Mother was amplified and very strong in this close proximity to Gurudev. I felt I needed to just allow Her to move through me unrestrained. And though I trusted I wasn't the only person who was experiencing this, I didn't see other students at the retreat surrendering so deeply in public. In the privacy of my own room, a deeper level of what is possible was about to reveal itself.

Opening with prayer and quickly sinking into the mesmerizing beauty of the inner seaweed-like waving of Divine Mother and the purple glow, I heard a voice speaking to me. The words were encouraging, regarding trust and faith. The voice was obvious, but could it be so? The mind was jumping from its quiet pool with some cautious thoughts, asking, *What's going on? Who is this talking to me? Am I imagining this? Is this really Gurudev? Is this really possible?* And then the mind quieted slightly to hear, "Quiet your mind and let go, because that noise will immediately take you away from trust and faith."

My hands began to dance similarly as in the first visit. Gestures of mudras danced spontaneously and organically along the chakras, beginning at the base chakra and fluidly expressing their mysterious secrets up to the seventh chakra. Gurudev's voice continued speaking to me, teaching me, although not all of it registered consciously. I felt as though I was being worked with directly. He was attempting to validate the very questions I'd been asking, so I wouldn't mistake his presence.

"Do not expect anything. Just deepen into what you are experiencing, and trust my guidance."

My hands were at the heart chakra, positioned, gesturing silently, and I felt receptivity down deep. It was the presence of faith *as a divine quality*, parting the curtains that were doubt and ego. There was a breaking apart and breaking away of fear and resistance.

"You don't have to see me in person, which is why it's important to establish contact in this way. I will meet you at the altar of your heart."

Again, all that was spoken faded in and out of my awareness. I was entranced with his voice inside my being, speaking to and awakening this one's heart. A question was posed, and I wasn't clear at first if it had come from me or him. I had to wonder if I was creating some kind of fantasy. I was in my thoughts and out of them at the same time. It was all quite curious. The question asked was, "Isn't it beautiful outside?" So simple and out of place. My hands continued to dance their sacred mudras, and I had an interesting sensation that I was looking *through his eyes*. It was as if his body and my body were merged. I could see his nose as if it were mine, as well as his hair along *my* peripheral vision. I felt an undercurrent of panic, while also hearing his call of trust and letting go of the thoughts running through the mind.

I was told: "Do not worry from where the guidance is coming. Just trust, let go, listen, and feel."

I felt my body being moved to a standing position and the momentum to walk coming through it. I didn't know where I was walking. My eyes were only gently opened. Walking in a meditative zone, I followed the body and trusted.

"Finish your meditation outside. Stay in meditation the whole way. You'll know where to go."

I was well aware of my thoughts as they were present in the recesses of my awareness. I realized I might feel very silly when all of this was over, yet how could I not explore what was taking place? I had been fantasizing on my way back from the meeting room that maybe I would be lucky enough to run into Gurudev, if it was meant to be, and then perhaps I could speak to him. After all, he was staying in a bungalow across the field from the dorms. It was possible. As I continued to walk, I was feeling a magnetic pull to the center of the field. I was sat down in a spot I'd been guided to by the gentle prompting of Divine Mother. My awareness and energy were drawn inward, yet I could feel the mind racing with questions, questioning reality, fantasizing still that maybe Gurudev would come to the field.

"Breathe. Relax. Let go."

The quieting of my mind was gradual as he guided me inward. I felt Divine Mother's gentle sway controlling my breath, calming the mind, and relaxing the body.

"Let go of all expectations, or you will miss the lesson you were brought here for."

Any thoughts still remaining were placed way in the back of my awareness, as if put on a shelf, and soon I lost all connection to them, or else they ceased to chatter. Instead I began to hear Gurudev's voice.

"Begin to feel yourself on the earth. Feel the sun on your face. Feel the breeze."

All of my senses became enlivened and intimately connected to the elements. It was as if my attention was guided into a widely receptive state and I became acutely aware of the sound of the dried leaves on the trees as they fluttered in the wind. I heard the barking of a dog off in the distance. There were a couple of different birdsongs being chirped all around me. The growling sound of trucks from somewhere far off in the distance and a horn beeping entered my awareness from off to my left side. All the sounds, regardless of how subtle or distant, felt loud and palpable and soon began to feel as a part of me. They were all perfect and harmonious. I felt from inside, not from a thought, that both the sounds of nature and those man-made were all perfect. There was an awareness that no wrong or right existed, no good or bad. I felt connected and one with all of them. I am that I am. The oneness of it all!

"This is how it feels to live in the altar of your heart. Now keep feeling deeply."

There was a smile growing across my whole face, not just the mouth. I felt my chest expanding with a gentle warmth, and I felt a tingling, stretching sensation widening into an openness that defies words.

"Let your edges merge, and feel yourself disappear into all that you are, all that is you. Feel the connection of all that is."

My body wasn't solid anymore. I dissolved into the wind, the sun, the ground, the sound of trucks. I knew the beauty and love for everything, just as it was. I felt the magic and grace of what was being shown to me. The experience of oneness was in me, was me, was God.

When I finally solidified back into the body, so did my normal state of being and consciousness. However, my face was still smiling, and divine ecstasy was still present. Gradually, my eyes effortlessly opened. The gaze remained soft as I slowly acclimated to the surroundings. Looking down, I saw I was sitting in a field of dried leaves that were all in the shape of a heart! It was as if I was literally sitting in the Altar of my Heart. I began laughing and crying, hardly able to receive all that had just been offered to me. I had no room to doubt the direct guidance of my experience, where it had led me, and the deepened faith and trust in Gurudev's love and guidance.

It didn't escape me that I truly could have missed the amazing gift and blessing because of attachment and expectations. *I truly didn't need to see him, in the physical form, because he in form was not the point. The importance was the embodiment of his teaching of Truth and the embodiment of receiving that Truth, which goes beyond the ego and personality bodies.* I left the weekend feeling blessed and aglow with love, gratitude, and humility.

15

Upon my return home, my practice took on a whole new depth and inner propulsion toward surrender. I began receiving inner guidance from Gurudev with more regularity. Though I had been blessed with such an amazing experience of Truth, and while I did feel trust and faith were growing, I still felt cautious at every new turn in this new inner realm. His guidance became a constant throughout my yoga practice. His voice was conveyed audibly to help guide my thoughts and teach me certain principles, such as, "Feel Mother, every small sensation. Feel Her loving and caring for you. Feel Her every guidance through you. Feel the subtleties, and you will know Her guidance. You will feel Her in your body. If you feel, you will know Her presence. Let the mind fade away, and listen to Her from the inside, guiding you and caring for you."

The blessing of his guidance was most often accompanied by a deepening of inner quiet and the presence of Divine Mother's loving energy circling here, opening there, massaging this, or pulsating that, stretching and strengthening. Quite often I was given guidance that I really didn't always comprehend, being at the stage I was. When I inquired inwardly what something meant, I would be told

I would know when it was time. I couldn't summon guidance on my own request. Usually, I would simply begin hearing Gurudev's voice in my mind; the direct contact was established from him.

I was again dipping back into the inner recesses. The temporary period of resurfacing into a "normal" life was once again being left behind. Caleb had appreciated the normal me that had peeked through for a snippet of time before returning to Colorado. And now on the return, he could feel me slipping away again.

"Why do you look so sad?" I asked one night at dinner, harboring a certain amount of denial.

"I feel like I'm losing you again," he said, looking down at his plate.

I was silent for a minute. "I guess it seems like I've reverted, huh? But you aren't losing me. I love you."

"No. I'm losing you. I'm losing you to God. You're changing in ways that I can't or don't want."

I felt a ping of panic. "I know you don't want this yogic lifestyle. I'm not sure that's what I've got going on or if that's where I'm going. I don't want to label it. I really don't know. But it's always changing. Let's just keep riding this out and see how it feels," I said as if to the air, with truly nothing left to say.

Most of my days were spent in the Love Room, once again, in practice or reading. Caleb and I had evenings together. With my changes in diet, it interfered with his love for sharing the bond we had once experienced through his cooking. Sexually, I was less interested. It didn't feel like I had much energy circulating in the lower centers. And our once long and lively conversations were something of the past. We'd had very similar communication styles and had the ability to process emotions and patterns together artfully. This had been a strong bond for us, as we were both highly sensitive and tuned into this.

My life was my practice, and if I conversed, regardless of the topic, my conversation invariably circled around to a spiritual bent. I studied whatever I felt guided to by a new internal compass and trusted whatever felt appropriate in the moment. Without my consciously planning or intending it, a solitary, reclusive life was forming from within me. My soul was doing its work, creating exactly what it needed for its evolution, through this body, me, as a sacred vessel of the divine.

16

One day during practice while receiving Gurudev's guidance, I was told: "You are being held in grace. Continue your practice and connection. You are cared for and being carried."

Hearing these words—really, any words from him—touched me deeply and often brought about feelings of unworthiness, as if I should be getting *it* better than I was. Just following the guidance, I felt the familiar prompt to stand and walk somewhere. With my eyelids gently parted so that I could see, I was told to keep walking and could feel an energy drawing me toward Caleb. He was napping in the bedroom. I approached him, and I could sense a different sort of consciousness holding my awareness in a zone. My head felt a thickness inside of it, but my awareness was crystal clear. My hands, or the hands that didn't seem to be mine, began to express themselves in sacred gestures, which I'd learned were mudras. They were dancing over his torso, at his heart, belly, and pelvis. The mudras were quick, continuing along the chakras and then up to his throat and third-eye centers. And then I was released. The thickheadedness and zone lifted, and I felt like me again. Caleb quietly received the blessings that had just moved through me without questioning.

I had entered into new territory, which I didn't always know how to handle. When too much newness entered in too quickly, I'd develop a knee-jerk reaction that would stabilize my sense of reality. It took the form of sweets or caffeine. My body had been rejecting certain foods since this journey first began. I reminded myself that it started in 1996, when I stopped eating meat after the mystery flu. Divine Mother made sure that my body was staying as clean as possible. The taste for many things I had really enjoyed previously, gradually or sometimes speedily shifted into a distaste. Sugar, sweets, and coffee were the biggies.

However, after those moments of intense otherworldliness, I could be found absentmindedly rushing to a coffee shop for double lattes and cupcakes, cookies, or whatever I could find to ground myself back into some familiar frame of reference. I wasn't too hard on myself about it once I saw the method to the madness. And though I accepted this in myself, similar actions would bring about a very quiet crying somewhere deep within. The only way I could put words and understanding to it was to say that Divine Mother was weepy when I ate or drank unhealthy things or participated in behaviors that were unhealthy or imbalanced for my system. There was a dance I was doing and finding balance in—or perhaps *something* was finding balance through me—to honor all that was taking place.

The first time I made a mad dash for the coffee shop was soon after I experienced the cleanse in the bathtub earlier that summer. I had sent an email to Gurudev, or his assistant, with details of what had taken place. I was curious. I'd felt moments of alarm following the event and desired clarity on what was normal. I needed some kind of answer and awaited a response.

I'd been sitting in the Love Room listening, again, to some of the tapes when the phone rang.

"Hello," I answered.

"Hello," said the familiar voice.

"Oh my God!" I exclaimed, knowing instantly who it was. "I can't believe you're calling me! I was just sitting here listening to the tapes from Colorado."

"Yes," said Gurudev. "I received a message that you had an experience. Please tell me about it."

I described the bathtub event and shared with him about how the spontaneous movements were consuming my whole practice now.

"This is very auspicious. Very good. I want you to continue to practice and allow Divine Mother, Kundalini, to move as She needs. Do not resist. But do not let Her hold you in any one position for longer than ten minutes, and don't let Her move for longer than one hour and a half."

"Thank you so much! I can't believe you called. I feel so much better," I said excitedly.

"You are protected. The masters are always with you. Please send me periodic updates as to how you are progressing. Keep practicing. This is very good."

"Thank you. I will!"

"Goodbye now." *Click.* He was gone.

As we hung up, the phone became filled with static, and my whole body started buzzing rapidly with what felt like electricity surging through my entire body. I was overwhelmed with the buzzing sensation, amazed that he'd called, and pleased that everything was great. It was too much to bear. I grabbed my purse, drove up to the coffee shop, and devoured two double lattes while I journaled in order to ground myself and get back down to earth.

Though Caleb was personally unhappy with the direction the relationship was talking, he was truly supportive in all ways. He was often as awestruck as I was with what Spirit revealed. Even as he was invited into the divine fold, and even though he felt gratitude when blessings came his way, that gratitude was simultaneously refusal and resistance.

Not long before this last trip to see Gurudev, I was sharing with Caleb about the hypnotizing and centering effect of the purple-blue glow.

"What is this purple glow?" He was acting odd, even though the question seemed simple.

"I believe it manifests at the sixth chakra, the third eye. I think it's sometimes called the blue pearl. At least that's what I gathered when I read *The Play of Consciousness* by Swami Muktananda."

Finally, I had found two books based on personal experiences with the journey of Kundalini awakening. *The Play of Consciousness* and one other, *Kundalini, the Evolutionary Energy in Man*, by Gopi Krishna, felt like lifeboats to my sanity. Gopi Krishna noted many similar details in his transformational journey that I was experiencing. Some were comforting, and some were disturbing, but overall it offered me grounding and assured me I wasn't alone.

"I gotta tell you something," Caleb said, cheeks flushing.

"What?" I asked. I noticed my heart had skipped a beat.

"Well, remember the first night home from your initial trip to Colorado?" he started.

"Yeah."

"Well, that night after we made love, I felt some buzzing through my body. And ..." Drawn-out silence.

"Babe, what? Would you finish, please? You're talking so slow. What are you nervous about?" I was anxious to hear and feeling impatient.

"And it went on for a long time. It was like electricity buzzing. Then I saw the purple light I think you're talking about."

"What?" I was dumbfounded. "What? And you're just now telling me this?"

"I didn't know then what it was. Even the buzzing. I didn't know it was connected until you started going through similar things and you told me."

"Do you still have sensations like that or see the light?" I asked, more with excitement than anything.

I could feel the resistance in him as he continued on. "Sometimes in bed I see the purple when I'm feeling relaxed and drifting off to sleep. I have only had the buzz a time or two since then. One of the times was after you were guided into the room when I was napping."

"I don't understand why you haven't told me. This is great. Maybe you should start to do some meditation with me?" I encouraged.

"This is why I didn't tell you. One reason, anyway. I don't want to mediate. I don't want this life for myself!" He was feeling emotional. "And I guess the other reason is that I don't want to feel like I have this happening to me. I haven't wanted to acknowledge it."

"Wow. Interesting." I wasn't sure which direction to go. "So you don't want to follow something divine that deepens your connection to God, the Universe, or whatever you want to call it for yourself? And it seems that you're ready for it if these things are happening, at least at some level."

"No. I don't want this path. Of course, I feel connected to the Universe, and I trust it'll grow. And I suppose it's good for me just as it is." He was clear. The conversation felt complete.

There was nothing to do but let go of my desires for his journey. I was acclimating emotionally, mentally, and energetically to the rapid expansion of my inner life. Caleb was accepting most of it supportively, even though he'd stated it wasn't for him. I was feeling confident and trusting in the guidance from Gurudev and the increase in devotion arising from soul, and I felt I had little control over its forward propulsion.

17

One dark cloudy day as I was lain to rest in Savasana after Divine Mother danced through my being, I heard a voice begin to speak to me. This voice wasn't Gurudev's. This voice was different, and I felt a different feeling or frequency, which seems an appropriate word, resonating within.

"Don't always expect the big sensations, because you will miss out on the truth that you are already there."

As if hearing my questioning as to his identity before I was even finished having the thought, he responded with, "I am your father. I solidify all that moves through you …"

I lost track of his words and only felt my face beaming with a smile, one infused through my heart.

Two days later, during practice, the hands were guided into various movements, rubbing together. This created tickling, itching, and burning sensations. As the fingertips were brought to barely touch each other, I heard the familiar voice of Gurudev.

"Stay present. Let everything fall away. Stay right here and feel."

The hands pulled away from one another as if playing with a ball of energy. Soon I could feel the ball as if it were physically present.

The reassuring voice continued to urge me to *stay present without labeling anything I experienced*. A slight panic began to rise up into my chest, expressing itself through my breathing and a sick feeling in my heart. Then a deep buried sorrow caused me to begin crying and sobbing as it rose from the sickness of the heart. It didn't even feel like me. My toes and knees began to curl, and mudras moved along the different places of my face, settling into prayer hands at the third eye. It was as if I'd become a foreign person. The curling body didn't feel like my own, and the expressions forming on my face didn't feel like they looked like me. Uncontrollable cries wailed forth as the body moved through various crippled-like postures. It was as if numerous deformations of times and lives past, were animating through my physical form.

The body was put to rest in Savasana, at which point Joy, a quality or state of being beyond emotion, began to spring up, into, and out of this one's heart. I heard the new voice, which this time I knew to be that of Gurudev's guru, my spiritual grandfather, or so it felt to me.

"You are done carrying that around. You are now free to open to more love."

I felt so in love with my lineage of gurus and Divine Mother. I felt deeply humbled and very grateful for these amazing blessings.

That night while I was sharing with Caleb what had taken place during my practice, he commented on the style of communication that was becoming more my norm.

"I've been noticing for some time now that when you talk about these experiences, you speak as if your body or mind are entirely different entities. It's as if they aren't a part of you."

"True. I remember feeling that back in 1996 when I had that flu/cleansing. That's when it seemed like I first started relating as if there were this differentiation within myself." I thought for a minute. "The way I've found to make sense of it is that the body does have a mind or consciousness of its own, particularly in these heightened states."

"It sounds like you feel separate from, say, your body's actions or its desires. For instance, now that you're not eating the yummy cakes I make anymore, you say it's because the body doesn't want them."

"Yep. Exactly. I don't feel as if I, my personality, is making that decision or even has the desire to discontinue certain things like that. But something has guided that to come to a halt. It was just like that when I stopped eating meat. The body said, 'No more.' Sometimes I think of it as soul's guidance. But ultimately I believe it's all connected." I sort of rambled as my way of thinking out loud.

"Do you feel like it's that place of watching or the witness consciousness that you're sharing from when you talk about it?" Caleb inquired, which was helping me to understand more clearly.

"Hmm. Sometimes, for sure. Other times, it just seems like I'm less identified with my body, thoughts, emotions, habits than others tend to be. I don't think I'm necessarily in a state of witness as much as simply becoming less attached to these aspects of being as 'me', if that makes sense."

The mind always wants to be able to understand or describe these different layers of consciousness or, one could say, different dimensions within our own soul or being. For me, it's been less important to try to figure out things that seem hard to really know for sure. Instead, staying connected to the direct experience and trusting that higher awareness will always reveal itself when I'm ready to receive that layer of wisdom is more important to me. My awakening process felt like there was an ongoing practice of surrendering the intellect to the guidance of the heart's experience.

18

With each deepening, I felt a growing desire to surrender even more deeply. It was as if this one's soul was on a fast track to merge and that the mind and personality were losing out on having a say. Not that I felt resistance, but I was becoming watchful of the quickening at hand. I also had an odd sense that other shifts were happening behind my back. It was like a surprise party was being planned by my closest friends, but mum was the word, or an invisible committee was instigating subtle changes in my life without telling me, yet there were subtle intimations that I couldn't put a finger on.

Meditation in itself had become a new experience since I'd received Shaktipat. Previously, when I sat, I relaxed and the mind became less obtrusive, although it remained chatty in the background. One simply learns not to give it attention, and sometimes it quiets, whereas other times it doesn't. Now, however, as soon as I sat, silence would emerge. No one was home on the inside. Achieving an empty mind was effortless, with the occasional thought streams floating by—then, once again, nothing. This emptiness made it easy to hear when guidance was present. From that void state too, when divine images or visions would enter into the mind's eye, it was easy for me to distinguish between the imagination and the mundane level of mind.

During a few practices in a row, I began to receive the ever so common mantra of "om" or "aum." The mantra sprang forth spontaneously and showered down from the crown of my head, vibrating through my entire body. The feeling of the vibration was accompanied by a deep sound of *om*. At times it vibrated as the short form of om. The experience of the vibration moved through all layers of my being, from gross to subtle. The emphasis would alternate and elongate on the three sounds. I learned the *a* carried the vibration for creation, the *u* carried the vibration of sustaining, and the *m* vibrated destruction—the sound of the cycles of life and death.

Wonderment once again filled me because what this meant was that mantras, in fact, carried a living consciousness, a vibratory, experiential, transformational power that came from a Divine Source beyond humanity. A symbol and a mantra is taken for granted and too often not fully experienced as a true divine force, and rarely is it energized to the full extent of its potential.

In quiet moments, oftentimes while I was in the throes of Divine Mother's presence lulling me into some humbled state, songs or poetry would play through the mind. I began keeping a pen and paper present for such moments. The moments had a tendency to dissipate as quickly as they arose. Their messages were always timely and painted themselves across my being as if a teaching from a personal oracle.

> Little did I know that listening to the voice, for many years called from the brambles, would lead me from this outerwear, feeling solid in my skin.
> Now looking into the puddle at my feet, of all that I have been, at last I am willing to let go of the bones as they hang, forfeiting their weight to merge with You.

As moved as I was by so many practices, I found myself being lovingly reprimanded at times. One such time began with Divine

Mother focusing on my breath. Her presence took control of my breath's rhythm and depth, while gently rotating my neck, helping me to drop into inner silence. A chant I didn't recognize rose up from the inner silence, being sung inwardly, which drew my awareness into the emptiness. From the emptiness I then heard Gurudev speaking to me in a much sharper tone than I'd experienced thus far.

"You are not listening to your calls and are not being present to the follow-through. ... You need to let go of your time perceptions and listen."

I asked if he was mad at me.

"I am only stating what is true and what is. Your openings will come and go, but you must be careful not to fall into elation."

At the time I wasn't able to understand everything that he was referring to. In hindsight, it became clearer, as he wasn't speaking as much about what I was or wasn't doing on a surface level as about how I was or wasn't integrating my teachings. At this time, though, I felt a little shaken by the tone I was perceiving and was not sure how to be with it.

Not long after, early in December, I felt grateful to receive more extended guidance from Gurudev. There was a brief period of time during which I felt a lengthened space of actual conversation taking place. At the time of conversing it always felt normal and I felt so blessed. However, I had an increase of anxiety in the aftermath of the experiences.

Inspiration was rising again. I longed to create something in my life, to find my dharma, my purpose. I had a desire to give back and be of service. Simultaneously, I was afraid of becoming obsessed like before, and I wasn't sure how to discern what was true inspiration versus ego's drive. The guidance I was offered was this: "It's all in the way you perceive it. You want to segment everything, and the fact is that it's all connected. You can be in yoga, practicing through every moment of your day. You turn to books to study, which has its place, but *all* you need to learn is in your practice and within you. You hold the truths, and they will surface. But you must continue to

85

surrender to the going inside. Books will affirm and give you more intellectual information, which is important but not necessary. It's all in the practicing, the going within, experiencing the essence and thread of truth that runs through all you study. You must match this with the experience of meditation and actualize it in all you do. You are still boxing yourself in, limited by your sense of time, your perceptions of how things, including your practice, should look. You are still holding much control that must be released."

To feel so seen and understood was amazing. I could feel karmic patterns being transformed and healed even as he spoke. I saw how correct the guidance was, and I also knew that I wanted more, more validation, more guidance. I wanted to be told exactly what steps to take. Even though I was receiving just that, there was a lag in the uptake. I wasn't yet taking in the fact that I was being given what I asked for. The still wounded parts of me inhibited the reception.

That same week, I felt more guidance coming through as I became more attuned to my spiritual grandfather's presence. There were qualities of tenderness and nurturing that filled me when he was present.

"Be well and at peace, for your path is golden. Although it may appear brown and dusty in the light and may shine through clouds, it is all in your choice of seeing.

"Be patient, little one. There's no hurry along this journey. You are held in love and caring, and you will do no wrong. We hear the song of your heart and the soul's call. Always that is you. How could we not love?"

Even his admonishments felt like love to me.

"You are like a child who has a new game, and then when you see no one wants to play, you immediately get up and walk away. You need a patient attention span, one that's able to perceive that you have blocks. But even people with blocks or more limited awareness succeed, simply because they just keep moving forward, wait, and persevere."

Practice with the beloved Divine Mother had evolved from spontaneous postures, which had a balancing effect and left my body feeling strong yet supple; to guidance from my lineage, with whom I was in love; to a constant flow of mudras. Deeper transformation was occurring as I was receiving other voices and guidance entering into my awareness. These felt like very different energies from those that I'd thus far experienced. Their guidance was accompanied with mudras and graceful whole-body dancing, which included the vibrations of other "personalities." It seemed that archetypal energies or deities were stepping in to guide me.

There appeared during meditation one day a new manifestation out of the purple radiance at the third eye, sixth chakra, the point between the eyebrows. As I was sitting in deep stillness, engulfed with the shimmer, it intertwined with a yellow glow. Soon the purple and yellow formed multiple triangles, encircled in one large boundary. But what engulfed my attention were the triangles. The geometrical shapes were hypnotic as there seemed to be triangles within triangles, all perfectly overlapping and proportioned, and they vibrated very subtly through my head. The color of purple offered shadow, and the yellow glow gave outline and highlight. It looked vaguely familiar but was ultimately foreign to me.

I found confirmation of this vision much later, as the Sri Yantra or Sri Chakra. Yantras are geometrical patterns or designs that represent the bodies of deities. One of the significant meanings of Sri Yantra is its representation of the cosmic mountain at the center of the universe, Mount Meru. But it is most widely known as the primary yantra of the Goddess and all aspects of Her worship, as well as Lord Shiva. On a personal level, this was foreshadowing the arrival of the Goddess into my consciousness.

There is no mistaking that many of the world's religious symbols and archetypes, have vast layers of meaning beyond what we see on the surface. Consciousness pervades symbolism with life vibrations, and when we become sensitized enough, expansive enough, and available to learn, the teachings are at hand. We need no books and no intellectual understanding, although it does help our human mind. It is the vibrations, the frequencies themselves, enlivening a direct knowing that is beyond the intellect. The Divine, God, Source, Spirit, is patient and awaits our awakening so that we may become receptive, step by step, stage by stage, phase by phase.

When not in my practice, which held me in the safety of Bliss and Peace, I was growing more anxious about what I was experiencing. Gradually, too, I was beginning to get strong creative inspiration coming through that seemed connected to my purpose. Peace was not a state I was experiencing in the outer world, yet Peace continued to call my consciousness inward, and this inward pull was growing and getting stronger.

There were three or four primary personalities, archetypes, or deities as I came to understand these energies to be, that were surfacing repeatedly. I began to embody their consciousness, their distinct dancing movements, and sometimes their facial expressions. The dances that spontaneously moved me were primarily fluid and graceful, always with mudras, and occasionally melodic toning would sing through me. At first I was intrigued but cautious. I felt protected by the lineage of gurus; however, my fear was slowly getting the best of me. Most of the guidance felt aligned to what I was being taught, even though the frequency of the guides, the deities, alternated. Soon a thread evolved, which at the time I had no understanding of its meaning.

As I felt a gentle wind winding around my heart inside this body, I was told: "Go to your heart and let your heart speak. Feel Divine Mother, how She moves and teaches. Study Her manifestations. Feel Chandika. Allow Her to resonate within you. Seek out Her energy of love. Don't expect big miracles; the small ones are just as glorious."

I had absolutely no idea of the identity or symbolism of Chandika. As if on a modern-day technological treasure hunt, I jumped onto the computer to begin the search. Goddess Chandika wasn't difficult to find, though Her qualities felt very alarming to me. The secondary alarm that was set off was the result of the title

Goddess. Walls went up immediately with my recurring aversion to
Goddess orientation.

Over the next few days, the guidance became conversations
of questions asked by me during practice, with clues given by the
"deities." They told me what to look up on the computer, and then
I'd return inward after I'd gathered the information, ready for the
next exchange. I honestly had no idea whom I was conversing with.
I felt like I was walking a tightrope, even for me, without more solid
knowledge of the energies I was connecting to. Most of the deity
energies that moved through me felt positive, as I was definitely
labeling them. The presence of Gurudev or my spiritual grandfather
would come and go, as far as I could tell, followed by the entrance
of another deity. All the while Divine Mother was gaining in Her
strength and presence.

At the tail end of this conversation or treasure hunt, after an
hour or so of dipping inward during a practice, followed by rising
to surf the internet, I was feeling giddy and anxious. In one of those
moments of researching the clues, and with continued amazement
at the fact that I was locating information that validated the voices
from within, my mother called.

"Hi! How are you? I haven't talked with you in a while," she
greeted me.

"Hi. I'm good. How are you?" I answered. Of all times, this was
not a good time to be on the phone with her. "Not sure I can talk
long," I blurted out before she could respond.

"I'm good. Just got home from errands. What have you been up
to? Are you in the middle of something?" she asked.

"I am. But I have a second."

"Whatcha working on?" she asked. Normally she would lead
and carry the conversation, which was what I was needing, but it
was too late.

With a rise in my voice and an out-of-control giddiness, I began
recounting the latest experience. "I'm doing some crazy things! I have
been getting all this guidance to look up a goddess and information

on her. I thought it was just some weird game with my imagination at first, but after I do my practice, where I receive the guidance, I look on the computer and find the answers!"

I was feeling out of control talking to her, which was fueled by deep self-consciousness to even be sharing this with her.

"I'm not sure I'm following you. Are you doing okay?" I could tell she was keeping a distance and didn't really want to know too much.

"I'm doing fine, I think. I mean, I do feel a little crazy. It's just wild how they tell me to look something up, and all the clues do in fact lead to valid information when I search online." I really needed to be quiet, but I just couldn't keep quiet. "I'm good. It's just not a good time. Can we talk later?" I asked.

"Yes. I need to go out for my walk anyway. I've been driving around all afternoon. I need to get some fresh air. Okay, honey. I love you! Bye."

"Have fun. Love you too!" And I hung up.

My body was full of jitters. The mind felt off-kilter. And emotionally, I was feeling a mixture of relief that the conversation had ended and a tinge of old stories that my mother really didn't care what was going on with me, in the depths of me. On another level, I understood this was too much for her to take in. Overwhelmed, and in light of sharing this event out loud, hearing myself trying to explain what was taking place, I began to feel frightened. I hadn't even told Caleb about it yet. Now that voice had been given to this odd phase, it felt like a break would serve me well.

It was confirmed by Gurudev in meditation that there was no reason for doubt and that the relevance of the experience would become clear as I progressed. I received confirmation that I was taken care of and protected. And so I continued to do my best to trust through my fears, even at times when I felt as if his voice was angry at me, which at this point didn't make me feel sad. Instead, it made me feel frightened and untrusting.

With the presence of Divine Mother growing and strengthening, and during one of my practices following the online hunt, Gurudev came to speak with my guarded mind.

"Your fears are distorting things right now. There is karma being worked out in your subtle energy bodies, including your mental body. Allow yourself to go deeper."

I was afraid to go deeper, and the fear was starting to prevent me from receiving direction. I was feeling confused. But as he spoke, I followed the guidance and felt my heartbeat. It was loud and deep. I was guided to feel it in my fingertips, then my head, then all over the body. It was as if I was literally inside my heart, and it didn't feel good. It felt like nausea in my heart, and it permeated my whole chest. It was thick and dense. I did my best not to attach to anything I felt, as difficult as that was. I held onto the affirmations and safety that had developed. Eventually the sensations lessened in my heart, and it returned to beating only in its proper places. Gurudev's guidance continued as the experience left me in Savasana.

"Allow your heart to become you, and you, your heart. But don't expect this to always feel good, because there is karma being released."

19

"Why would you continue?" Caleb asked later that evening, genuinely curious, without judgment of any decision I might make. The question wasn't easy to answer.

"The mind's definitely having difficulty holding what's happening," I replied, speaking from that detached place. "I honestly feel like this is the call of my soul. It feels as if it's desperate to dive deeper. I don't feel I'm the one in control," I answered.

"But you, 'you,' could implement control, right? If you chose to?" he asked.

"I guess so. And yet, my whole heart wants to surrender. It is longing to let go …"

"What are you letting go to? God?"

"Yes," I answered, "but it doesn't seem as if God feels so easily defined. It's confusing. Even though I've never been religious, I have to ask how all of this fits in with God as Christians relate to God. What about Jesus? I never believed in the Jesus Christians talk about, until now. I feel like he was a guru, like Gurudev, but clearly even more highly evolved and with a specific mission, obviously." I paused. "Really, though, I suppose it's Divine Mother I'm so in love with, and as much as I feel the soul is surrendering, I feel the Mother and soul are connected. And I want to be with them."

"So what about the deities? What about the fear and caution you have?" Caleb was playing devil's advocate. "I know how you are. I know your intensities, impulses, and inspirations that you are dedicated to following ..."

I cut him off midsentence. "But I think all of those are voices of soul. Now I get that all those big intuitive hits are soul! It's as if the cleanse in 1996 started this clearer connection to soul. Maybe even it was Divine Mother, but I just didn't have a reference for Her yet?" I quieted so he could finish.

"Great. I get that. That makes sense. But are all these influences at the moment soul? Or God?"

"I have no answer. I just want to trust that soul has led me to each door that has transformed my life, so why would this be different?" I asked. Normally, Caleb was a rock, reminding me that everything was okay. His questioning was shaking my very delicate root system.

We were both quiet. He was giving me space to ponder.

"I have to imagine ego is playing a role in this. I've read the cautionary notes about getting caught up in the fantastical experiences, rather than maintaining one's focus on God. Is that what's happened? Maybe," I confessed after contemplating for a moment.

"And you have been intrigued by what's going to happen next in your practice," he pointed out.

"You're absolutely right. It's all so amazing and unfathomable, at least to our limited intellectual mind! It's hard not to get caught up, I guess. You may have a point," I admitted.

I had an intense curiosity, which can be a danger on the spiritual path when there are many supernatural experiences at hand. It can be easy to forget God and become attached to experience. While I recognize that there was a "What's going to happen next?"

wonderment present, there were also more components at play. I was learning as I went, even if I didn't understand most of the lessons.

Talking with Caleb was helpful. I approached my practice afterward with more of a specific intention to connect to God with reverence, love, and peace. I felt like it was time to experiment with what I, ego, was creating, versus what God's guidance called for.

The intention didn't seem to deflect the presence of whom I referred to as the Stern One from appearing. He had a very significant signature pose that was embodied through me when he was present, which thankfully wasn't often. My body would become rigid, and the chin would tuck down into the throat. The mudras and arm placements were stiff and angular. He began to teach on the topic of control.

"There is no such thing as control, merely imagined protection from the unknown and a prolonged source of fear, confusion, misery, and tension. Feel it in the body, in its actions. Feel it in what is said and not said. Feel your heart open, and receive by the disowning of control."

There was no doubt that control, particularly attempting to control what didn't want to be controlled, caused stress, fear, and suffering. I could also see how control, in general, carried with it these potentials. I saw and felt control as constriction. Constriction is a natural opposite of expansion. Our very breathing cycles are created by these opposites. How to allow both opposites to merge into one cycle, constrict and expand, control and release? What is the balance on a spiritual path? Let go and let God. Thy will, not mine. These are teachings handed down and the ultimate request from Spirit, Source, God, to release our small selves into this Force. Yet the control that attempts to step in is ego, mind, and personality. Which to choose? Was there another choice I was not aware of yet? These were the questions at hand.

Even in my practice of conscious restraint and watchfulness, the guidance continued with my constant overseeing of reflection, accompanied by many mudras. From a deep space of emptiness one day, I felt Gurudev's presence but had only a vague recollection of what was spoken, as Divine Mother rocked me gently. His message followed:

"Communication from the heart must be free of attachment and fears. Listen to where you are speaking from. If your heart is not empty of these things, do not speak."

Expansion and love filled me. I realized that if I followed this guidance, then in my normal state I'd be silent most of the time. Unless in the company of a select few, I always had some attachment when I spoke. It often manifested as talking quickly and excitedly. Other times my tone was harsh and sharp with judgment. Rarely was it free, empty, loving.

It was during a practice after the Stern One had showed up, which left me feeling cautious, that a childlike energy filled me. She had a joyful grin, which expressed upon my face, reminding me of a little china doll. I was filled with a happy, innocent giddiness as she moved through me, sharing her wisdom and sacred mudras: "You will learn the innocence of a child and carry childlike joy within you, and it will grow. Know you are being given gifts, and one day you will understand them."

Immediately coming out of practice, I was feeling so free, carrying a wonderful sweetness within my heart. But as the minutes turned into an hour or two, fear crept in. Although I felt I always had a choice whether or not to stay in a surrendered state of being, and even though I believed I could impose *my* will at any time, breaking free from whatever energies were within me, doubt was being born. I was truly beginning to wonder if I was going crazy, and that scared me.

Everything I was experiencing was culminating in an explosion of mind. I was wondering where I was being led. What was becoming of my life? What was all of this for? Even my longing for God and what that meant felt confused. The guidance from all of these voices and the presence of deities continued to flow, whether I wanted them to or not. I truly began to wonder if this was what possession was like.

There were moments in which the fear building in me was persuading me to bring this adventure to a stop. Instead what I'd find within were prayers being sung from soul with such longing, swelling up from deeper than deep inside of me.

Sitting at the altar, this heart bows at Your feet in surrender.

The level of devotion, illuminating the depth of longing I carried within me, was a growing shock to my normal awareness. How did I have this much depth and desire for God, the Divine, and never before know it? Diving back into the abyss of meditation with the beloved Divine Mother, my fears would abate, melting away until they rose again. Onward and inward I continued.

As winter moved into full swing, the Stern One came to me in his ever so masculine forceful way. The whole time he spoke, the stiff mudras were active through my body. Although normally I felt nervous in his presence, this time I felt tears of gratitude flowing forth. The heart spilled over with beauty and acceptance, even though I couldn't remember all he'd said and did not have a full understanding of its meaning.

"You will need to make a decision and choose whether you are ready to progress further. Feel the subtleties of the heart. The softness of its energy needs to be in your awareness. The softness of the heart and its subtle levels ..."

The yellow flag of caution, which I kept watch for when the Stern One was present, turned to green, meaning to go forward. Although his presence was harsh, I felt the opening his energy created drawing me once again into expansion of my heart and surrender into who knew where. Choices were made.

20

Earlier in November the gentleman I had been caregiving for passed away. It had been a particularly challenging relationship, and I wasn't feeling ready to move on to another caregiving assignment. A friend of mine and Caleb's owned a cleaning business, so I asked her if she would be interested in having some help over the holidays. I had owned my own cleaning business years ago and knew she and I could work well together. It also seemed to be the perfect fit for my needs at the time.

Domestic work had proven to be good for me over the years, though it held its own dance of love–hate expressions within me. On the upside, I love to be of service and to make others' lives easier. Housecleaning had become my way of nurturing others. In the past it had suited my lifestyle in that I could work independently, make decent money, and set my own schedule. And I appreciated the physicality of it. On the downside, both housecleaning and caregiving had a low burnout threshold in different ways, one emotionally, the other physically. However, during these years, these areas of work enabled me the freedom to pursue other skills and alternative modes of learning, and I found I could alternate between the two as needed.

Cleaning at this juncture was ideal for me to remain in the meditative zone of practice while making a living. The joy of being of service sang forth while I worked through chanting and mantras. And it enabled the mind to remain empty, creating a bridge between work and the mystical home life I was living. I was finding that while I was cleaning, Divine Mother would flow effortlessly, occasionally bringing me to stopping points, drawing all my awareness within to the shimmering purple-blue light at the third eye for mini meditations. I became present and clear and remained connected.

On one such occasion as I was filled with Her presence and was guided through my work, Gurudev came to teach:

"This is how to do and be in the world. Stay present in what you are doing. Feel the rag in your hand. Feel the water. Stay at peace. You can stay connected to everything you do. Everything can become a sacred experience, a joyful experience."

Allowing Her presence to remain consistently this present also ran the risk that She had freedom to grow stronger, expediting Her mission within, and Her presence was becoming my norm. One day while working at a client's home, I heard Gurudev's voice coming into my awareness:

"When you love and move out from love, there is no winning on the other side. There is no beginning, middle, or end. There is only a constant stream. When you move out from ego, there is an end, because from the beginning there is attachment, fear, and insecurity of not winning in the end. One may win in the end, but there is always a price to pay. As soon as attachment sets in, the constant stream breaks. When you hold love close to you, there is little room for nonlove to fit. When you hold love far away, there is plenty of room for anger, fear, jealousy, resentment, and competition to take place."

As always, I was in complete awe and humbled when I would receive these visitations, which I considered blessings. There was such a fullness and loving connection as long as I didn't interject my mind into the mix and question what was happening and whether I was crazy. Possession was still a very real option for my thoughts to attach to, and yet the guidance was always filled with such love and cultivated more love in my being, rendering the fear nonsensical. But the rational mind wants things to make sense, wants to know, and wants rational explanations. Yet nothing about anything taking place in my life was rational.

One night my meditation became very strong. It felt as if the mind, any semblance of me, was about to disappear. I could feel all of my awareness and energy being drawn so directly into the third eye, into the center of the brain. The focus of the energy was almost painful and blissful simultaneously. The gaps of nothingness that I'd been accustomed to were now feeling like all of me was about to disappear forever. I began to feel frightened and called out for Gurudev. There was a desperateness growing. I was afraid my mind would be forever taken from me or that I would be taken over completely with no semblance of self-will anymore. No guidance was coming, no presence from the lineage. I was feeling completely alone, even as the energy lessened its intensity at the third eye. Mudras began dancing through my hands, and many other unknown personalities began rushing forth, but still no one was speaking to me, encouraging me, or making me feel safe. My mind flashed on past comforting words Gurudev had said regarding being held and protected. Now the mind latched onto the word *protected*.

Attempting to break the mind free from this hold, my own questions burst forth: "What am I being protected from? What does that mean? Is there danger? What are these strange personalities?"

Finally, with relief, I heard Gurudev's voice telling me, "There is nothing to be afraid of. What is coming out of you has been within you. You have been carrying energy that has not been needed for a long time. It is exiting you so it doesn't influence destructive habits or make you go down wrong roads. Do not be afraid of the mudras and energy. They are clearing. Cherish them, for you have been blessed, and hold them in your heart so you can feel their song. Allow what is leaving to leave, and don't contract around it with your thoughts. See with love and see with the third eye. Your other eyes have filters and cannot see Truth. As these other energies exit, you will be more prepared to love as the Mother loves and holds you."

Trusting and having faith was becoming a tedious discipline for me. Although I continued to practice, I knew I needed to lessen my time. Not that it seemed to matter, as my nights were filled with active dreams that felt as if I was experiencing past lives in half-waking/half-dreaming states. Bolts of energy shot through me randomly, waking me with startled reactions. Sleeping on my side was now the only position I could actually sleep in. Lying on my back seemed to lead me unintentionally into meditative states and other realms and dimensions. The fetal position was the safety, the comfort, that would allow sleep to occur. Day and night, night and day, required honed attention to master my thoughts, with *my own will*, if I was going to keep my sanity.

As the New Year of 2003 was rung in, I was on a course to harness the experiences and try to bring some of my own control into the picture. I had remembered reading somewhere that the Kundalini could be slowed and dampened if the energy grew too strong. I took that advice and began adding heavier food to my diet: pasta, cheese, more oils. And had I not already been a vegetarian, I would have eaten meat. I can't say this made much of a difference, but it made me feel like I was activating some of my own self-will once again, that I had turned over.

I began suffering headaches around this time. There was a thickness, throbbing, and pulsing, often at the crown of the head. Sometimes practice would help soothe it, but it wasn't without other sanity-testing risks of experiences that I could no longer process, even the beautiful ones. I was closing down, becoming less receptive, and contracting around anything that happened.

I desperately felt the need to talk to Gurudev. *Please! I need physical-world communication!* I called out inside my own head. I couldn't trust what the other realms were bringing me anymore. I called the number for his center and left a couple of messages. I emailed. I heard back from his assistant via email a day later. She said they would put me in the prayer circle. As much as I wished this to bring some solace, I instead felt more helpless. When I realized the chances for speaking to him were nil, panic began to flare.

The headaches grew into mini-migraines, and I began to experience nausea. Meditation was no longer bringing reprieve, but intensifying it. Divine Mother, whom I had felt such love and devotion toward, I was now referring to with disdain and distrust as "the energy." This wasn't a conscious shift in appellation. It was a direct reflection, sadly, of the turn of my mind's relationship to Her presence, a relationship of fear and distance. She continued to grow stronger, and I was begging for a reprieve. I needed time to get my head on straight. I was now certain I wanted off this train. I was feeling more sick, frightened, lost, and alone. Though I was grateful for Caleb's patience and attempts to calm me, nothing was working anymore.

I was referred a couple of cleaning clients after the holidays, but my ability to be responsible was being tested. With the headaches, there were a couple of times I had to cancel. This bothered me tremendously. In sobriety, I always prided myself on my reliability. In addition to everything else, I was beginning to feel a sensitivity grow over the right kidney. It came and went. Though it didn't feel exactly like a kidney infection, I couldn't figure out what else it could be. This new development was creating more distress. I'd always had a tendency to be an alarmist with matters of my physical health, and there was no knowing what could happen under these circumstances.

As I searched for ways to find relief, my practices were sporadic at this time, as sometimes they helped and other times they made things feel worse. One day of particular difficulty, I was hoping to find refuge within. I directed my awareness within my being and accessed a space of quietude. When I did this, my breath evened out, but my head began to scream in pain. I put my hands up to hold my head. It felt as if my brain was literally expanding. I began crying and begging for help. The crying seemed to alleviate the pain some, but my fears were looming loud. In the distance I thought I could hear Gurudev's voice trying to reach me, but I had built up resistance to receiving it. I was feeling panicked, crazy, and utterly alone. I could feel Divine Mother trying to calm me, when eventually his voice made it through:

"You are safe. We are with you and keeping watch. The energy has to move into areas to clear. It won't always feel good and may bring pain. You must let go of labeling the experience and sensations, as this creates more difficulty. Let the fear and the energy move through."

I could hear his voice continue to speak, and the pain did decrease a bit; however, the pain around the right kidney began to increase and throb. My focus then became attached to the lack of my own control and the sensations centering at the kidney and lower right back. I could feel the kidney literally being massaged and manipulated from 'the energy' within. The organ was being tugged and pushed. Energy swirled around it, and pressure felt like it was building up from inside of it. I was breaking into a sweat, and my stomach was feeling nauseous. Just the thought of this was impossible to comprehend, and the sensation of the energetic manipulation was making me sick. Everything Gurudev had just spoken to me flew out the window. The fear was too big, and the internal sensations were too overwhelming. I was afraid to stay in meditation, and I was afraid to end it. And I didn't know how I could let it continue or how long it would last.

Again, his voice managed to break through the inner chaos, even as the sensations continued: "Divine Mother is healing and nourishing the body. She is always present, moving subtly within you. She is the Life Force that allows your whole being to function and have life. This isn't new. The only difference is that She is waking you up on all levels, and now you can feel Her activities."

Something about his guidance made so much sense. It rang true. A peace washed over me. Her activity was still present but not as acutely, yet with his words, I could accept it and find space to stop reacting to it. I was able to take a step back inside myself, attribute what he said to the headache, and see that clearing was indeed taking place. His guidance had created space around the fears and reactions. I felt like bravery was stepping back in and that I truly was being supported and not left alone. Gratitude again entered into my mind, and I felt humbled and in love again with these amazing healing powers of Divine Mother and the presence of my guru.

I believe that lesson, along with Gurudev's guidance, resonated with what I trusted to be true. I knew clearing was happening. I was able to open back up and feel faith restored, if only temporarily.

Over the next few days I engaged in practice more affectionately again. This time Divine Mother created similar massaging sensations on my liver. This was also met with icky sensations that I was doing my best not to label or attach to, simply witness. The pushing and pulling on the liver, moving it toward the front of the body and the back, was a feeling that words can't describe. I had allowed the mind to surrender again with minimal caution. I could feel Her energy moving from the liver, to the kidney, to the intestines, and more to the head. I managed to calm the mind of any inner flurries that wanted to make a commotion, and at the end, I was prompted from within to lie down to take a long peaceful nap.

I wasn't feeling totally sane, but *I felt more in control of my reactions to the fear of insanity*. With semiclarity, over the next few hours I was aware of a slight irritation, I wondered if I was getting urinary tract infection. I started drinking extra water and potent unsweetened cranberry concentrate. This had worked in the past, if I caught the infection at the first signs, just as it seemed to be working this time.

21

It was at this juncture that I made a decision to share with my parents what was happening. I felt I needed some emotional support other than Caleb, and he could use the support, no longer be the only person holding me up. My mother in particular had had some questions of concern here and there, which were impossible to answer in a simple telephone conversation. And honestly, I was still worried about my mental stability and felt my parents should have some sense of the situation.

All of these seemed like logical reasons at the time, though Caleb cautioned me as to my expectations for the situation. On a deeper level, I felt the little girl inside of me, frightened, needing the safety and love of her parents. That little girl's need, along with fear, overshadowed the reality of expressing these circumstances to individuals who had no belief in God, were at best indifferent to religion, and had no frame of reference for what I had to share. I expected too much from the people who loved me and couldn't get outside myself enough to see they had no way to navigate what I was about to introduce to them. Because a long-ago, ingrained need of my little girl was seeking out healing, that shadow aspect of myself veiled any clarity and prevented me from knowing that this would not bring me what I sought. I was far off from any clarity.

My parents had been divorced since 1991, but had remained friends. We all met over at my dad's apartment one evening, my parents, Caleb, and I. The initial greetings between us and my parents were pleasant. Before long my dad was curious why I'd called this mysterious meeting.

"It's sort of a funny conversation that I want to have with you, but it feels important," I started. I shot a glance at Caleb sitting in the chair next to me, grateful for his presence and support.

"Is everything okay?" my dad asked. "You're not sick or anything, are you?" He and I shared tendencies toward caution and fear.

"No. As you can see, I'm good." I cleared my throat. "There are a couple of things I want to share with you though. As you both know, I've been pretty deep into yoga over this last year or so." They were both looking at me with expectant stares. "And, well, I'm not sure how much either of you know about yoga, but it's gotten pretty intense for me."

My mom sat quietly across the room. She, of course, had had some brief tastes of odd behaviors from me since this journey began but hadn't really inquired beyond what I had mentioned here and there. Dad was taking more of a direct approach to the discussion.

"You're going to have to say more about what you mean. What does 'intense' mean?" he said, encouraging me to be more pointed.

"Well. It's going to sound kinda far out, okay? But I've been feeling a little unstable. Not completely sane, but as you can see, I am. And my physical health is feeling precarious. To cut to the chase, though, I want you both to know I'm not crazy, if anything goes awry. You're my parents, and I need you to trust me and know I'm not crazy."

I was starting to feel emotional, and in part I could see now that this idea was what was crazy! Opening up this dialogue was crazy. I didn't even know what I wanted anymore. Now that the door was opened, the light bulb went on, and my little girl was wanting to run for shelter because she clearly wasn't going to get what she was seeking.

"Does this have anything to do with the night you came to stay with me, when Caleb was at work, because someone had been looking in your bedroom window? But you claimed it wasn't a real person," my mother said, recollecting an event a few months earlier. "And that when you mediate, things make cracking and splintering sounds through the house?"

"I'm completely lost," my dad said with concern. "What's been going on? Who was looking in the window? When did all of this happen, and why hasn't anyone said anything to me?"

"It was months ago," I said, feeling flustered. "That was right when I returned from Colorado. That phase has passed. What's happening now is that I'm getting a lot of guidance and voices in my head. It's all good, but it has me questioning my mental stability. Not that I'm insane, but more like it takes some time to get used to everything that is happening."

My dad now abruptly got up from the chair he'd been sitting in. "I'm not sure what's going on. And I don't know what you mean by voices in your head. What does that mean?"

I answered, "I have a psychic link to my teacher—my guru—and his guru. So they are able to guide me in my yoga practice and in life." I tried to speak confidently and calmly, but I was feeling the stirrings of old wounded stories on the rise. *No one takes me seriously. I don't really matter. They don't really care to know me. They don't see me.*

"How do they talk to you?" he asked.

"In my head. While I meditate and, now, sometimes at work." I wasn't even going to mention the kind of yoga I practiced, the spontaneous postures and movement facilitated by the energy of Divine Mother.

"And where are these, you said, gurus? Where are they?" my dad asked. I could tell he was trying to grasp what was being said.

"My main teacher is on the East Coast, and his guru, he's dead."
I cringed saying this. I couldn't even believe I'd opened this can of
worms.

My dad's face stretched from top to bottom and from ear to ear.
His eyebrows lifted, and he released a laugh, which wasn't actually
an expression of any kind of humor being experienced.

"And is this what you were talking about the other night when
you were getting directions to look things up on the computer?"
asked my mother.

"The voices are telling you to surf the internet?" my dad asked,
exasperated.

"No." I was about in tears. "Those are two different things.
There's guidance that I know belongs to my teacher—my guru—
and his guru. They are the main voices. They help me to learn along
this path."

"You're saying there's more than that?" asked my mom. She had
a tone I knew well. We shared the same quality of tone when we
experienced edges of resistance. It was a form of seeking control and
manageability of the unknown through judgment.

"Yes. These are what have had me worried and confused ..." The
tears started rolling down my cheeks against all my will. They were
sad tears, verging on angry.

Caleb grabbed my hand and stepped in on my behalf. "I know
all of this seems way out of left field. I've been witnessing all of
this for months, and it's been really challenging for me to navigate
through things I once believed too, or things I think I've known.
For the most part, she's done really amazing with everything that's
been taking place. Now, though, she's feeling worried. She's feeling
like she is losing control of things. And you're her parents. She wants
you to understand and needs some support."

"I wish I had some explanations that could make sense to you,
but I don't. I shouldn't have even come," I said, wanting to take it
all back.

"Have you talked to other yoga people? What about yoga teachers where you took the Bikram?" asked my mother, trying to be helpful.

"No, I haven't been back to the Bikram studio. I'm not going to find the help I need there." I appreciated her attempts, but my frustration was growing because there wasn't any way I was going to make her and my father understand.

"Have you tried to talk with someone who's connected to this teacher?" she asked.

"Yes. I've tried. No one's called me back, nor are they going to be calling," I replied.

"Well, there must be someone. You can't be the only person having these experiences." As this last statement was spoken, I felt myself shut down. I felt deeply unseen. Yet, the truth was that no one would truly see me, or anyone else going through this same process, without having this direct experience themselves.

"Of course, you're right. I'm not the only one. There are people all over the internet having Kundalini crisis awakenings. It's a spiritual crisis. I'm not contacting them, because most of whom I've found are not in any better shape than I. And I've tried to contact a Kundalini crisis center in another city, but they're no longer in business. Trust me. Most people in my position, at this stage of this, are *not* in yoga classes, and it's not an easy subject to broach with just anyone."

I couldn't discern whether what I was dealing with were my lifelong stories and the feelings of disconnection between my mother and me, regardless of how close we'd always been, or whether I was being oversensitive.

My dad interjected with a question: "Is yoga a religion? When you say gurus, does this mean you're in a cult? And I don't understand how someone who's dead or across the country can talk to you."

Before I could make any response, my mom, trying to offer a valid reflection, sealed my openness to further discussion.

"I hate to say this, honey, but do you think this could just be your ego fooling you, making you believe these fantastical things are happening?" She continued, "I remember when you were little. You had the invisible friends, and you always had great ideas about saving people, saving the world. Maybe this is just an exaggerated aspect of that."

I swallowed my tears and emotion, stuffing them down, and immediately erected a wall of separation. I felt cold and distant from both of my parents.

"Of course ego has everything to do with it, but not in the way you're inferring. It's in my nature to want to help others —or save the world if I could, for that matter. And maybe I really was talking to invisible friends. I think that could be a very valid thing after all I've been through."

"I don't know what you want from us," said my dad. He could see the tension growing in me. Though there was a deep love and friendship between my mother and me, we also had a history of a lot of tension, which I could see might be making my dad more uncomfortable, if that were possible.

"I know," I said, feeling vulnerable and defeated. "I'm sorry for laying all this on you."

"I mean, do you need a doctor, a psychiatrist?" he asked.

"No! That's the last thing I need, and that's been the point of this talk, so that I could get you to understand what's happening, so nobody jumps to uninformed conclusions. And as my parents, it would be important for you two to get what I'm going through. But it's a mistake. I take it all back. This isn't a cult. I don't need a psychiatrist. And I'm not suffering from some messiah complex." I knew I just needed to leave, immediately. "I think we just need to go. I'm sorry for all of this, but just in case you're curious, here's a book that is helpful," I said, handing each of them a piece of paper with the title of Gopi Krishna's book.

Caleb and I got up. As I reached for my purse, my mom came up to give me a hug. It was clear she wanted to be of some support, but we both knew she couldn't be. I quickly hugged her and my dad. Without verbal goodbyes, Caleb and I left the apartment.

By the time Caleb and I made it to the elevator, my pelvis was slightly burning. By the time we arrived home, twenty minutes later, I was bent over in pain. Not a dribble of urine was to be had no matter how much I tried to relax. He ran a warm bath for me, which I crawled into. I doubled over, and there I lay for hours. I kept warming the tub and received occasional relief when a drop or two of fluid would release.

The anger I was feeling was the anger turned to rage of suppressed sadness, of an entire life and multiple lifetimes, most likely. Any experiences, imagined or true, connected to my parents in which I had felt jilted, unseen, unsupported, invalidated, and unworthy were now all raging in the pelvis. It was hot and burning, contracted, and causing me to withhold any compassion that I might give to myself. As the night went on, I turned into a prune, and eventually my own tears began to flow. I continued to drink water and prayed for the morning, when I could get a round of antibiotics. This was something I tried to avoid unless absolutely necessary, but a bladder or urinary tract infection was one of those occasions of necessity.

It was absolutely clear that my own rage had triggered the regression in the infection. I knew energetically, through all I'd been learning and experiencing, that this was an accumulation of karma in full-blown activation. The next day, once I began the regimen of antibiotics, I was able to think more clearly. I was able to make notes of all the stories of grief and anger that this was connected to. It was healing. And when I was able to drop back into meditation within a day or so, I was simply grateful for the experience.

The event was of the first two chakras, which are the energy centers, that, among other things, hold the consciousness of these kinds of big emotions related to family, relationships, and security, to name a few. I realized I needed to stay very present in order to consciously clear this energy of past beliefs. The situation allowed me to gain more insight into the karmic beliefs I carried and to let go of unfair expectations I placed on my parents and myself.

We all come together, bouncing off one another, in ways that create grief or joy, based on karma. Our painful experiences, it has been said, are trapped in the energy centers, the chakras. Their presence, which is a vibration, draws situations, people, and places toward us, or vice versa, in order to be cleared, healed, so that our perceptions may be aligned with higher truths. This is the stuff of karma, the stuff that keeps us, soul, spinning on the wheel of time and returning through many incarnations in order to learn and grow out of these lessons.

Most often, we view our relationships through the lens of the lower center consciousness, which is a normal, reflexive view. As in the example above, I was seeing through the "glasses" of stories connected to rejection, self-worth, security, and familial bonding. On this level of consciousness, experiences are personalized. Ego takes these feelings very personally and becomes identified with the story: "I am unlovable. I don't matter."

However, when we raise our vision upward, perceiving through the glasses in the higher centers, we see the game of karma playing out with an opportunity to heal the past. When consciousness is raised above ego identification to soul learning, it loses the projections of blaming, right, wrong, and personal, or attachments of ego. Awakening allows us to raise our consciousness to these higher levels of awareness. In our mastering of our reactions to the stories, the past hurts, or the many versions of unlovability, the stories are starved of the energy that keeps them alive. The more we can be nonreactive and nonattached and not buy into our beliefs, the more those beliefs will fade and truth will be revealed.

22

I felt as if things were becoming manageable when I began urinating more easily. And there was only slight throbbing that came and went in the right kidney. Divine Mother's invisible hands massaged the kidney, and occasionally it felt as if gentle waves were rolling through my pelvis. I hadn't had the presence of any of the deities for a short spell, and my last connections with Gurudev had felt reassuring, even though I didn't get to talk to him in person. I had a new cleaning client scheduled to begin the following week, and January was quickly coming to a close. What a time it had been! I was thankful to be feeling some grounding and integration taking place and grateful that Caleb was also feeling a sense relief.

I was learning so much and realizing that my higher education was this life. This education was richer than any training or school I could imagine. Yet I was ready for summer vacation. One night at the very tail of the UTI while I was reading in the living room, I felt Divine Mother's presence gently pull my attention inward to meditation, as She did often. There I met the return of the Stern One. I was taken a little off guard, yet I felt strong enough in my mind to stay present. While the body went into some gentle spontaneous postures, in addition to the signature stiff mudras that came with his presence, my hands were directed into prayer position at the heart center, my chin tucked, as my stomach began to make a gurgling noise.

"Feel the fullness. It's full of undigested garbage. It must be emptied and excreted because all of it is poisoning you. You must let it go. Allow it to leave. Let the stink leave. It needs to be taken out. There is more in there than you know. Some of it is yours; some of it is not. Some has been necessary to draw to you, but you don't need it anymore. You need to make space. Do not push or force or resist. Simply surrender the poison."

My elbows were moved to gently press into the belly. It was slight, but my stomach began to make noises and started to feel nauseous. As I sat there, my elbows pressed more firmly, and all the while I was thinking about what the Stern One had said about not pushing. I was wondering if I was actually doing this, even though I could tell that I wasn't. The pressure was gentle but firm and not of my accord. Only by a surrender to the force within, the action happened *through* me. I started to feel as if I needed to vomit, and my lower back began to ache. At that point, I was frightened again. I didn't want to be taken on another scary ride. I interjected my will. I sat up and removed the elbows from my abdomen. I felt horrible. I had to go to the bathroom. I had a very large bowel movement, and the color was black and gray. The texture was flaky. It took a while before I felt emptied, at which point I only felt a fraction better. I was definitely not feeling well as I climbed right into bed, curling into a ball. My attention couldn't help but be drawn to the building pain in the lower back, with emphasis at the right kidney area.

Caleb peeked into the bedroom. "Sweetie, are you okay?" His voice was concerned.

"I'm fine. I'm just feeling like going to bed early. Thanks, though," I answered. I didn't want to worry him again. He walked over to me, bent down, and kissed me good night.

The miracles and nightmare of the next weeks intertwined in light and darkness. The culmination of all that Gurudev had been teaching me was brought to a new level of experiential learning. One of the drawbacks with this type of learning is that it's often impossible to find words that adequately describe many experiences and their nuances. Another challenge is that karmic lessons are deeply personal. Most often we are the only ones to really know the extent and significance of what we're learning. And for me, this is exactly why I believe so strongly in the practice of self-inquiry and self-reflection, and in the warrior-hood required to forming a relationship with one's sacred shadow. Though I already carried these qualities as part of the person I am in this incarnation, this period of time set the tone for a deeper way of interacting with these aspects of myself.

As I lay in bed that night, more awake than asleep, I argued with myself back and forth as to whether or not to go to the emergency room. Caleb, realizing things were not fine when he came to bed, said of course if I needed to, we should go. He also reminded me that the onset of this followed the guidance and presence of one of the deities. We decided that in the morning, if nothing had changed, I'd go to the doctor. Once again I was on high alert, which required I remain highly conscious. It seemed my life had become wrought with red lights, which I felt like I had handled like a champ, considering all the circumstances.

By morning, nothing had ceased. I had been up a couple of times with great discomfort to relieve my bowels, which were very active. I wanted relief. My assumption was that I had a kidney infection, but I couldn't be certain. It felt slightly different from what I'd been familiar with in the past, and once again, I just wanted all this to end. I was craving normalcy. There was mounting concern about my ability to take care of my physical world needs. I was worn out from feeling crazy or, at the least, trying to convince myself that I wasn't.

Painfully and thankfully I went to the doctor, though it was very difficult to move and walk. He didn't think I had a kidney infection, but he ran some tests anyway. He wasn't quite sure what the problem was and suggested a botanical and homeopathic remedy. He would call me when the test results returned. I was hoping the results would return with a definite yes, that I had a kidney infection. Knowing something with that certainty would feel comforting and would give me confidence that there was an answer. Even though I knew a cleansing was in effect, I wanted some semblance of certainty as to what to expect.

After I returned home and to bed that day, little did I know that I wouldn't rise from there for a month. The hours I spent in bed amid waking states, half dream states, meditative states, and sleep states were riddled with heightened awareness similar to that in 1996. I felt grateful I had read about *kriyas*, which means "actions." In this case, the actions were energetic shifts in the mind and emotions. Having this awareness helped me to stay somewhat rational. I had learned that the spontaneous movements and postures, those actions of the body, were also kriyas. In the throes of this cleansing I was able to discern that when the mind began to perceive memories or fears, those memories, or "actions of the mind," were kriyas. When the emotional releases flowed through, I recognized them as emotional kriyas.

I now had front row seats and a backstage pass to the greatest show on earth, the inner reality of psyche, the subconscious, and conscious levels of awareness. I couldn't always discern between what was me remembering the teachings I'd been given or what was Gurudev's presence coming and going with new guidance. I felt highly conscious almost all the time; however, there were few words to adequately describe what I witnessed.

I became acutely aware of the mental kriyas. I was able to perceive precisely how irrational my thoughts were, whether they were about the pain of the body, fear of my sanity, or the false beliefs I had about my/ego's control. Fears of death, my death, the deaths of those I loved, created scenarios in the mind that I watched like short movies across an inner screen, laden with the spectrum of panic and grief to match. And then it would all vanish and I'd experience a state of neutrality, nonattachment, and peace.

I was constantly riding the waves of pain. Especially in the moments when I was more awake, I felt queasy and repulsed by the sensations of the organs inside this body being purified. I could feel Divine Mother, who was on the verge again of becoming called, fearfully, "the energy," moving around inside me. She "handled" the kidneys, both of them, and the side that had more pain was incredibly tender to Her manipulation. But She was also waving like water through other organs, along with some places I hadn't even known organs were present in. What I became aware of was the mind's attachment and repulsion to the sensations, which were increasingly tactile. I could hear, or remembered hearing, Gurudev's voice reminding me to not label what I was feeling as pain or pleasure. *No worries about getting caught up in any feelings of pleasure here,* I saw myself think on occasion.

I heard these reminders: "Relax, soften the body, and breathe. Connect to the breath and feel its rhythm. Allow what is present to be present. Let go of needing anything to be different than it is, right here, right now. Be present with the flow of energy."

As I listened and practiced, the awareness that came to me was that *like all things, the cycles of nature ebb and flow. Life ebbs and flows. I could feel that the pain and contractions came in cycles.* There would be the pain of a contractive cycle and the release and relief of the expansive cycle. When the mind didn't interfere, perpetuating contraction and pain, there were moments of freedom from the pain.

Once I realized this reality, I honed my awareness. As the contractive part of the cycle came around, the mind had to stay present to the breath, nonlabeling and nonattaching. I found I could flow through it effortlessly, *and then the contractive sensation was no longer the enemy named "pain."*

In this state of surrender, I was able to open to new teachings that were taking place inside the body, reflecting the larger truths of contraction, expansion, life, and death. At one point I felt a growing heat along the right side of the lower torso. The heat radiated in waves, along the side and into the lower abdomen. It hung out over the large intestine, occasionally touching the upper quadrant of the liver, followed by sweeping waves over the whole belly. I felt nauseous and had an inkling to have a bowel movement, yet the bowels weren't ready to release yet.

The beautiful purple-blue light also ebbed and flowed at the inner eye. Its presence was soothing. As I gazed into it, the purple morphed into new shapes, some white, some yellow, all mesmerizing and stabilizing to the mind.

In states of sleep, I knew I was sleeping. It was as if *awareness* was always awake, present, and watchful. The dreams were vivid streaming colors that I had never seen before. Scenes of structures, nature, and animals came to life. In one dream I was at the end of a canyon, high up, overlooking some seemingly ancient structure. There was an awareness that I couldn't see through my two eyes. I couldn't open them, yet I was able to see anyway. There was a rainbow full of magnificent colors. In the dream, I was attempting to get Caleb's attention so he could see the beauty before us. From somewhere not too far off, I noticed a couple of very large, unfamiliar, almost prehistoric birds flying. Before I knew it, one flew so close to me that its wing brushed my face. The wind in its wake felt as if it blew me over, and I jumped into full wakefulness. The dream felt completely real. Even in my waking state, the brush of the bird's wing hung on my cheek. I had to ask myself, *Had I really been there? Wherever there was.*

When connection to the deeper consciousness within was lost, the mind would rush forth, seeing my vulnerability with accounts of madness and fears of dying. Then pain would grip the body. It didn't take long for me to realize I needed to stay vigilant and steadfast in the discipline of the mind. During these moments, connecting to intuition was challenging. I'd return to the very basic steps Gurudev taught me: *breathe deeply; let go of labeling something good or bad, or as pain or pleasure; merge with whatever sensations are present without resistance; and trust the space of inner silence.*

These foundations enabled me to relax and return to a state of peace and ease, and perception would expand once again.

It hadn't been a surprise when the results from the test came back negative on the kidney infection. It was becoming evident that these bouts of cleanses can mimic actual conditions or disease.

While lost in my inner turmoil, the very real worldly matters such as clients that I had to cancel and income I was losing, created another layer of turmoil in a number of ways. In the laboratory of my being, I had the opportunity to see all of the ways in which I/ego, the personality, clung to issues of survival and identity. It was clear how deeply programmed and on autopilot these fears and stories are. Just as for most of us, mine had been engrained within this lifetime, as well as during those lifetimes that remained a mystery. But in truth, *I only had to watch my reactions in the present to see glimpses of what I had lived previously through a different incarnation.*

Drifting into all the fuzzy zones, I found mind positioning itself to look at me. I wish I could make that clearer, although many readers most likely already understand this. More of you, I have no doubt, will at some point experience this.

Memories flashed through the mind displaying, perfectly, instances of fear. These fears were multilayered. I saw many ways in which I did my best to wield control in my life. There were ways I tried to control others as well as control others' perceptions of me. I recognized how control allowed a false sense of safety and security to envelop me. I felt humbled witnessing all the methods of control I'd hidden from myself as they rose up to meet me. I felt shame and embarrassment as my ways were revealed to me. There was an excavation at hand. I was more or less held captive and forced to let it all happen.

The anger that resided in me loomed large, and though I honestly hadn't been able to uncover its roots, I was shown how destructive it was to me and those I loved. There were reminders *to let go of judging* and to *practice nonattachment* to any emotions or memories floating through my awareness. This was put to the test when vulnerabilities and feelings of smallness began to surface. I had built walls of protection around myself to ward off feeling vulnerable and small, like a little girl. This little girl self carried feelings of worthlessness and insecurity that were too big and painful for me to even look at in the privacy of my own self. The pain connected to these hidden identifications is something that I'd tried to dress up in my adult "I can take care of myself" and "pull myself up by my own bootstraps" armor, which was rapidly being stripped away, exposing all of my wounds. I could hardly stand it.

The most accurate description for this experience is that I "browsed" through these feelings, pictures of myself and others, and situations in which I felt I was protecting these wounded aspects of a vulnerable little girl. I was shown enough to evoke emotion. The energy of the emotions, mostly grief and shame, rose to be experienced on the surface of awareness, then were escorted away with the teachings of *nonclinging. Let them move through. Breathe and let go.*

There were corresponding areas in my body in which these emotions were lodged. Although I knew this to be a fact, based on previous experience for some time, the ongoing flow of conscious release left absolutely no doubt in my mind as to the connectedness of all aspects of our being.

Our diseases and maladies are rooted in consciousness, as much as in the physical form. It's been said by Carolyn Myss, MD, that disease begins in the subtle energy layers of our being, prior to concretizing in the body. Complete and deep healing then requires work at all these layers of mind, body, emotions, and soul. In moments of clarity, I had great opportunity to bear witness to the "play of consciousness." Awe and gratitude filled me when I beheld how deeply this truth was being illustrated.

Truth is a funny thing. I refer to truth as having a lowercase *t* or an uppercase *T*. When I first got sober, it didn't take long for me to realize that what I called my truth would evolve with further learning into a different truth. Each truth was a necessary step to the next truth. So, for me, my truth at any given time was subject to my level of progression along an ever-evolving journey of personal growth. Today, I can't and won't claim to know many Truths with a capital *T.* The learning goes on. But that our emotions, beliefs, fears, and ideas become lodged in our bodies and create imbalance and dis-ease is a Truth I believe that applies to us in the physical form, in this material world structure.

From the kidneys and intestines, the cleansing moved to the respiratory system, stimulating symptoms of cold and flu, and then into the head. From somewhere in the recesses of my awareness I was told, *This is so challenging and frightening because of the attachment to the physical body and the physical world.* I was taken to edges of nothingness. This void carried a recognition of surrendering the body to a physical death. The entire body ached, throbbed, and pulsed. Fever came and went. The cough drudged up phlegm ranging from greenish-brown to yellow before it cleared. The sore throat eventually became laryngitis. There were days I could barely open my eyes. I was reassured that I was purging and was encouraged to trust the process. I knew intuitively this was true, I could no longer the voice informing me.

Although this phase was less frightening and comparatively less painful, my bottom finally fell through. My mind could no longer stay vigilant, and there were two last attempts where it felt clear that Gurudev was trying to reach me. But the mind was too full of static and fear, and I no longer had trust. I felt like he had led me down a path where I had no will left, and I shut out any of his attempts until there were no more.

Divine Mother lost and regained the status on Her pedestal many times. Eventually, She took on a new, darker image in my mind. Her energy was relentless. I hadn't been able to meditate the whole time I'd been bedridden, yet Her purple-blue light was always on. Occasionally it had changed to a deep red glow, always returning to Her purple shimmer. I had recognition that the red glow that appeared was the physical earthly center purifying the first chakra. She moved this one's body around the bed in various positions, reminding me of the frightening images from *The Exorcist*. All my fears of possession were coming to a fine point, and all the teachings and higher consciousness I'd expanded into had crashed head-on into body/ego identity. Images, thoughts, and memories billowed up in front of my mind's eye. Past experiences, people, and situations I had long forgotten rose up, filled with sorrowful emotion or yuckiness, which made it clear karma was being released.

Passing before the inner eye for a period of time was a parade of eyes staring at me. All shapes and sizes—kind, evil, demonic, angelic, human, and nonhuman—were staring at me, laughing at me, and I couldn't wake up from the living nightmare I was trapped in. I was in fits of fears and tears, watching the mind attempt to cling to control, only to recognize its need to let go. There was no control to be regained. I felt completely lost in this inner world, and I felt very far removed from the outer world. Dreams had gone from ethereal colors and otherworldly beauty to frightening characters attacking, tiny dwarf-like figures sticking their fingers in my third eye, and snakes biting, thrusting me awake with a racing heart and feelings of doom closing in on me.

Caleb played nursemaid as best he could. He was overwhelmed and tired from all of it. He played caregiver at work and then took care of me on his days off. During his shift I was terrified to be left alone. My mother stopped by once or twice to bring some food and wanted to help. I knew it was hard for her to be so much in the dark, but after our last time together it felt too stressful to me to try to explain any of this. There was no way she could comprehend what was taking place. I appreciated her desire to help, but I really didn't want her with me. Caleb and I had arranged to have our good friend Sandra stay with us while Caleb was at work, although there really wasn't much that needed to be done, since I was asleep or in my own world most of the time. But just knowing I wasn't alone brought me great comfort and meant everything to me.

23

Then came the day when I felt strong enough to get up out of bed. It was heavenly to walk the whole thirty feet or so across our little bungalow to sit in the living room. My body was really sore, quite weak. I'd lost weight and was still on the tail end of cleansing. Soft food was beginning to sound good, like white rice. My eyes were puffy, and my head was still thick and full, but none of that mattered anymore. It was all relative, and as far as I was concerned, in comparison, I felt great. I hadn't been out of bed for the last month. All I wanted to do was sit on the couch like a normal person.

Everything had been surreal for some time and continued to be so in those first couple of days up and out of bed. The me I'd known myself to be felt dramatically different, and I wanted desperately to find that old life again. The recovery phase was slow but steady. I enjoyed baths again and started taking short walks down our street. I could only make it past a house or two at first, but I knew that would change.

I expressed to Caleb that I was done with yoga. I felt mournful about all I'd taken for granted. I wanted our life back again. I had witnessed more clearly that the intensity of my past drive for a career had passed on to yoga, and I was sorry. He was happy to hear this—and cautious.

While I felt done with yoga, yoga wasn't letting go of me very easily. The energy, Kundalini, Divine Mother, remained very present when I relaxed too much. There now was more of a propensity toward emptiness within. From all that had been released, I felt light and empty. *Vacant* is the most applicable word for the state of mind I was in. And in the vacancy, She would enter, rocking me, gently moving my head, limbs, etc. Only this time around, I resisted. I interjected my will. I became willfully active of my own accord. The purple-blue light was still shining at the inner eye at night every time I closed my eyes. Instead of losing myself in its draw, I made sure I lay on my side and kept my mind occupied with thoughts until I could sleep. As I'd discovered early on, lying on my back would drop me into a meditative state at night, so to avoid that level of consciousness, I continued to roll onto my side or stomach.

The mind still held more expansion than ego consciousness could handle. I had an awareness of the mind. I was able to sit back and watch it barricade itself from too much thought, particularly any analyzing of what it'd been through. There were visceral reverberations of energy shifting into new positions. I was shielding myself from the intense level of consciousness demanded of me, day and night, all those numerous hours while lying in bed. The mind felt like a dangerous playground that was off-limits without a parent's supervision. I had too much to contemplate, to integrate, and to feel, and not enough courage, trust, or perspective. So I held on tightly to my sanity as I disappeared into escapism.

My method of distraction and control became television. It seemed at every turn, Caleb was as challenged as I, just in different ways. We weren't TV people. More honestly, there was anti-TV sentiment in our home, especially on his part. We had a TV set only because we enjoyed movies. However, as I was gaining strength back, I employed television shows to occupy my mind, to absorb my brainwaves. Silliness, like reruns of *Friends*, *Seinfeld*, and *Dharma &*

Greg, became my babysitter. Whatever channel these shows were on, I turned to, playing them over, and over, and over. And I watched. As long as I stayed engaged in the shows and didn't relax or "space out," I was okay. This kept the energy from settling into my awareness, and I felt safe. I felt in control again. I was putting on my old clothes of personality, opinions, judgments, and preferences. Pretty soon, I was walking more, fully dressed in more ways than one, and ready to leave the house altogether.

I was completely humbled by the raw power of the previous year, especially culminating in the last months. Running away inside myself, from Her presence, thanking Her yet dismissing Her, I didn't want to be reminded of all that had transpired, not even the iridescence of Her purple-blue shimmer, its beauty, that at one time held me transfixed and mesmerized. In the end I closed my eyes tighter against it, wishing to blacken the screen before me, inside of me.

Each day brought trepidation of Her cleansing. I prayed only that I would be well and move on from Her movements, Her intelligence, Her will. I didn't want to fool myself or bring about false hopes, but I wanted this to be true. I questioned, "Is She done, finished for now? Will She just subside back within the depths of my being, working effortlessly and silently? May I be well and gather myself back, straighten the perceptions and thoughts in my mind that today haunt me? Will I return at some point in time to a place of innocent wonderment and gratitude for all I've experienced?"

Caleb and I were trying to focus on real-life, material world things again. Although the topic I'd introduced was too big to explore when we'd last met, my dad supported me in the best way he felt he could and offered some financial assistance for the work I'd missed, for which I was grateful. That was a relief for both Caleb and me. Neither of us made much money, and I was becoming quite an expense.

I was excited to be preparing to head back to work. Miraculously the new client whom I had yet to visit had patiently waited for my recovery. I was so happy to hear that, and felt supported by the other clients who had wished me well and were looking forward to my return.

With a firm resolve to end my yogic journey, I packed the altar into a box, clearing space in the Love Room, and put away books and the photos of my teachers. I felt sadness, loss, guilt. I felt confusion about how I felt toward Gurudev. I felt abandoned yet was aware that I'd been playing in a realm of spirit, uncertain as to where accountability was to be placed. I only knew the door was to be closed if a new direction was to be taken.

24

On my first big day out, Caleb and I decided it would be fun to go downtown and run around. It was a drizzly day, which isn't that unusual for a Portland spring. The clouds, the rain, the breeze, it all felt fabulous. We went to a Greek restaurant, and I was feeling so excited to be feeling alive again. How much time I'd lost. I was grateful for all Caleb's support and was wondering if our relationship was going to survive. But for the moment, I was going to embrace it all.

Once seated in the restaurant, both of us, damp from the rain, realized we were famished.

"This feels so good!" I almost shouted. "And I'm even loving the rain. I truly have missed you." I was feeling young, free, and playful.

"It does feel good. It's been a long time since we've been out together," he said with a smile. "I honestly wasn't sure how much longer I was going to be able to hang on."

"I know." I felt sad. Without too much discussion, uncertainty about the relationship hung in the air.

"And are you going to eat some of our favorite foods—with garlic?" he asked, laughing, since garlic was one of the foods my body had no longer been interested in while in the presence of the Kundalini.

"I want lots of garlic!" I replied.

We had a great day. Affectionate. Laughing. Playful. Intimate.

A few days after our outing, one of my clients had given me a Deva Premal CD, *Love Is Space*. When I arrived home from work and finished showering, I put it in the player as I fixed some lunch. The first notes of the chant were sung, and immediately my heart started to ache, opening once again. As I stood in the kitchen feeling the sorrow, Divine Mother began to sway like a gentle wind through me. Tears streamed down my face. I longed for Her. I longed for God. I longed.

> I'm longing for You, moving toward You,
> The ache of surrender etching the way.
> Losing myself to find You, going deeper to be You,
> The ache of surrender etching the way.

The lunch was put on hold, and I sat in the living room, in the middle of the floor, and cried. I felt so confused and fearful. I was terrified of losing control again, and yet somewhere within, I wanted to lose it. I felt like I belonged to this path, but I didn't know what that meant anymore. Talking to an empty room, I asked, "What about this promise I'd made to Caleb and my commitment to him?" I knew I couldn't go back to Gurudev. And I knew I couldn't go it alone. "Where will I go for support?" Like I'd told my mother about my searching for help online a few months ago, I saw that many of the accounts of people experiencing Kundalini awakenings were at least as bad, if not worse, situations than mine. In a twisted, selfish way, that had brought me comfort.

At the time I didn't find anyone who seemed to be engaged in this way of living while being seemingly balanced and sane. I felt at a loss. And, again, there was Caleb. I loved him. He had made it clear this wasn't how he wanted to live his life. He wanted other things that we might be able to have together, but not if my life was going to center around my spirituality in this way. I didn't have any answers. I had longing and concerns. With all my will, I remained calm, made no decisions, and chose to wait and see how I felt as time went on.

The resistance was short-lived. The heart and soul knew the path was mine to follow, regardless of the risks. "Perhaps I could play both sides of the fence?" I wondered. As much as I loved having the presence of Divine Mother fill me, I decided to play a very conscious game of control and surrender. No more spontaneous postures, and I only meditated sporadically, as long as it was free of any other experiences. It all felt under control. When I informed Caleb that I was simply opting to return to a basic meditation practice, he was accepting but had little comment.

We both shared the desire to support each other in the direction of our highest good and for our growth. There was recognition that this was something that I needed to let run its course. My intention was to remain in this world, in the relationship, and still be present with a spiritual life.

"I realize you need to follow whatever this is, but it's not easy for me, and it's confusing. It all feels unpredictable," he said.

"Yeah. I get it, all of it," I concurred. "I'm sorry."

25

Shopping the next week at New Renaissance, a spiritual bookstore in Northwest Portland, I saw an ad on the community board for a temple and fellowship out in the suburb of Beaverton. They followed the teachings of Paramahansa Yogananda. I had loved *Autobiography of a Yogi* and felt like they could help me. I called and made an appointment with one of the ministers. I told Caleb that I was seeking some assistance and that I was looking to find out how to move forward in a balanced way. This brought relief for him to know that his role of sole supporter would end.

When I arrived on the day of my appointment at Ananda Mandir, I felt excitement and hope. I talked with the minister, and he mentioned that he knew of Gurudev and that the path I'd been traveling was very dangerous. He explained that under the guidance of Yogananda, Kundalini energy is not invoked as strongly. He invited me out to service on Sunday and said I may be interested in their comprehensive course of teachings. I accepted the invitations to both. There was an experience of feeling held, and my whole being felt relieved.

As I was driving home, I had a subtle awareness that my vibration or frequency had jumped up a couple of notches. I could feel the presence of Yogananda very much with me. It felt like I was being taken under his wing, that I was being adopted so to speak.

I began going to service on Sundays. The course wasn't scheduled to start for a few months, but I was ready to sign up. As much as I appreciated opening to this community and felt an affinity for Yogananda, I knew this wasn't my path. But I also felt with some clarity that he was available to help me and lead me to where I needed to be. I felt that it wasn't necessary for me to be a disciple of this lineage in order to be taught and guided.

It was only a matter of time before Caleb and I knew we were nearing the end. Although he was open to seeing where things went when told I was no longer pursuing a yogic path, now, with my return, he saw where I was heading. While I'd been sick, he'd been letting go. Letting go of me. Letting go of us. Letting go of the life we'd once had. Grieving and releasing. Our paths were diverging. We were both aware that this sometimes happens when we allow one another the space to grow and evolve.

He was feeling called to travel more, which I had no interest in. He was interested once again in exploring polyamory, which he'd been involved in when we first met. I knew I wanted monogamy. He was more of an extrovert and wanted to experience more in the world, while my introverted ways had increased with my practice and I was more drawn to connect internally with God. My returning to a yogic life made each of our paths more clear and enabled us to bring closure to our romantic ties, but our friendship remained strong.

The transition of relationship was clear but gradual. We remained living together for a period of time until he found a new roommate, at which point Urisk and I moved in with my mother temporarily. The change of relationship had its pain, yet there was little confusion about whether or not separating was the right thing to do. I was able to remain in the higher centers of awareness, recognizing that change, separation, and transition in relationship carries pain, and I held the emotions I moved through, with minimal crashes into the stories I'd been programmed to feel about loss.

Those emotional crash moments dropped me into stories of feeling unlovable, that I didn't matter as much to him, especially when I saw him moving ahead effortlessly. While I knew intellectually that he'd had plenty of time to prepare for this, my heart and ego felt hurt and easily discarded. Fortunately, I had the ability to see the changes in perception for what they were, and I didn't get caught in the web of false stories for long. The consciousness and friendship we'd cultivated helped the split to be unlike any other breakup in the past, and I was truly grateful for that and to him.

Experiences of Kundalini awakenings are becoming more and more common. One problem remains: many people waking up don't know what's happening. Spontaneous awakenings can wreak havoc in a person's life. They are often misdiagnosed as mystery illnesses, mental disturbances, or emotional breakdowns. They manifest differently in everyone, depending on karma, readiness, spiritual orientation, and toxicity of the body, to name a few factors.

This phenomenon is known throughout the world's religions and spiritual traditions by various names. Even in India, where it is most easily accessed, it has been misunderstood. The science of yoga revolves around this process without directly speaking of it. It's the secret teachings of direct experience by the esoteric and mystical practitioners of old.

Kundalini lifts our ability to perceive beyond the material, mundane world. She offers a direct connection to God's grace. She spiritualizes our being and guides us along the path necessary for our soul's journey, back to Source.

In short, the rising of Kundalini also known as the Holy Spirit, is to lift us as human beings to our highest potential and awaken the spiritual qualities that lie within all of us—qualities of Love, Peace, Compassion, Wisdom, and Divine Creativity. It purifies our minds and hearts of that which holds us in fear and ignorance. It is the great evolutionary force in humankind, and it is in process, before our eyes, whether it's visible or not!

PART II

PART II

26

By June 2003, life's edges from the previous year had smoothed out. I was integrating all that had come before, relishing the pleasant simplicity. I had a base of cleaning clients that was growing and had returned to dancing on a regular basis at the Body Moves studio downtown. On Sundays, I attended services in Beaverton at Ananda Mandir, where I appreciated the fellowship and disciples of Yogananda. The new meditation technique they taught was proving to be balancing, and I was planning on taking the yoga teacher training affiliated with Ananda in Northern California later in the year.

I was taking everything slowly, feeling the grace of Yogananda's presence lifting me into spaces of love and gratitude. Not long after moving to my mom's, after I'd moved out from the home Caleb and I had shared, I was still feeling cautious. One evening after meditation, I was feeling uneasy. Much to my surprise, I received the presence of Sri Yukteswar, Yogananda's guru. I could feel his frequency, and his image popped into my mind, letting me know I was safe and protected. I hadn't necessarily felt a connection to him previously, but there he was. I felt his presence until I fell asleep.

It had fallen over me peacefully, and I felt good knowing he was standing guard.

By the end of June I was thrilled to move into my own abode, back in Southeast and enjoyed creating a sacred nest for Urisk and myself. Dancing again brought me into like-minded community, and soon I was creating new friendships. The people whom I was drawn to and those drawn to me, it turned out, had also had their own Kundalini awakening experiences. It was as if divine guidance was at work, leading us to one another, introducing us to kindred spirits, letting us know we weren't alone.

One new friend had done a ten-day Vipassanā meditation retreat that sent him on months of some similar experiences I'd been through. He too was just recently resurfacing in the world. Two other women had experienced less intense trial and tribulation, but they, too, had been through great transformational processes, setting their lives in new directions and leading them to follow their deeper call to Spirit. It was a great comfort to have peers who understood and could support me in the mysteries of my learning. I found too, that dancing was a way to be present with Divine Mother in a new and expansive way. With the safety net of Caleb no longer present, I felt too vulnerable to allow Her to flow during practice at home.

The safest outlet for me was the Deep Wave Conscious Movement class. This class was a wonderful container for revisiting the body's intelligence and dabbling again with spontaneous movements of Divine Mother. With the lights dimmed and the music deeper, mostly slower and rhythmic, the fifteen to twenty-five of us would find our own inner connection and allow a soul song to move through us, free and uninhibited. I knew from the past year that Her presence truly did magnificent healings for the body, kept me close to God, and cleared karma, so I didn't want to be completely without Her. I felt nourished experimenting and testing the waters again. I was taking care of myself and trusting after a time that She and God understood this.

Discussions revolving around spirituality, the various paths, dos and don'ts, were hot topics among a couple of my friends. Conversations of God, religion, spirituality, transformation, experiential learning, and exploring karma in our lives were all invigorating and stimulating for me. I had never done well with small talk or surface chatter, always drawn to the meat of the matter and then into bone. That was more my style.

One of the things I loved most when I first entered AA was that people got to know one another intimately and quickly. There was a rawness and realness that fed me. I could be real about my hurts, my quirks, and my vulnerabilities because most of us were sailing in the same boat of feelings. Perhaps it was a part of my dysfunction, bonding with another's pain, or a lack of proper boundaries, but aren't the desires to hide or subdue one's suffering or rawness simply protection mechanisms? In some cases, I believe so.

My communities of friends and the topics that fed me changed over the years. But over the last couple of years of isolation, I didn't really have friends. Spirituality was paramount in energizing my life now, and I processed everything through spiritual filters. One of my new friends from dance, Marie, had been through a Kundalini awakening experience, which had left her sensitive to boundaries and led her to question what she felt was right and wrong as far as a teacher's responsibility goes.

As we sat enjoying tea after class one day, she was feeling particularly triggered by Pierre, one of the primary movement facilitators

"I don't feel that it's right for Pierre to be setting a tone for unsuspected awakening to occur," she said.

"I'm not sure I'm following you," I noted. "He's simply opening with exercises to relax us and open us to the music and dance."

"Exactly. But he's aware that the opening breath work has the potential to spark the Kundalini. Not everyone is ready for that. It's irresponsible of him."

"But isn't it true that teachers introduce techniques and yogic breathing exercises all the time, in all sorts of classes?" I countered. "If the fear is that this divine force is going to spark, then so many exercises and techniques would be off the table."

"That'd be extreme, and I'm not saying these practices shouldn't be introduced, but in conjunction with the conscious movement practice, it's a fire waiting to be set." Her point of view was clear to her.

"I feel like I understand what you're saying. You feel like more caution should be used." I began to share my experience, knowing that each of us had awakened unexpectedly, and that fact alone held a charge.

"I remember feeling really frightened during the time when I couldn't get any response from Gurudev when I was in the thick of crisis." I continued, "At the end, I felt abandoned. I felt like it was wrong to thrust this process on unsuspecting people."

"That's precisely what I'm saying. It was irresponsible. And it's dangerous." Her stance felt solid.

"But here's the thing I've come to see. I believe that the teachers/gurus, whatever you want to call them, are functioning from a level of awareness and understanding that we don't have. I believe they recognize that they're only a vehicle for *potential* awakening, but they themselves don't determine the level of potential," I explained.

"But Pierre isn't a guru, ya know. He facilitates dance," she added.

"I know. I'm not saying he hits the status I'm referring to. The point I'm getting to is that it's the individual's soul, karma, desire, and devotion that determines what level of potential is going to be expressed, and then how will it be cultivated and nurtured. That's another chapter of the same story," I ended, hoping I sounded clear.

"When I was awakened, it was in dance, up in Colorado, and I had *no* idea what was happening for a long time. I tried to talk to the teacher, but neither she nor anyone else had any information to help me. And I see the same dangerous possibilities here." She clung onto her fear.

"Marie, you're preaching to the choir. I get where you're coming from. What I'm saying is that you received a blessing, just like I did. It was your time. It wasn't because of the person facilitating the dance. It was already in you, waiting for the moment to spark awake. And now it's up to you, to us, to unravel whatever that blessing holds as we continue on the awakening journey. I try not to be a victim to it, which isn't always easy. Do I feel scared sometimes? Of course. Does my mind think it's going to break whenever some new and different experience takes place? Yes. Do I get uneasy at times if the energy running through me feels too strong for my nervous system? Yes. But more than anything, I know that it's the path to God, of God. And, though I have no idea what that means really, I believe that Power is ultimately in control. Not my teacher. And unfortunately, not even me. Maybe we had to wake up without the kind of support ego would have liked because it's part of our karmic blueprint. And this is just an opinion, not *the* truth. Just what this little me, from a neophyte perspective, understands at this time. It could change." I'd completed what felt like a lecture. Unfortunately for some, I had that tendency—to say a lot in all my passion.

"So you don't think Pierre is doing anything wrong? That he's being irresponsible?" she asked.

"I don't. He's facilitating a class, incorporating techniques he's learned. I know some of us in there are living with an awakened Kundalini. Did it happen in there? Maybe. Do some people have issues we don't know of? Maybe. But no, I don't think Pierre is responsible. I hold God and the soul responsible," I said, smiling.

"You mentioned earlier that you didn't want to be a victim to the energy. Do you think that's what I'm doing?" she asked thoughtfully.

"Listen, I haven't known you all that long, so I don't want to jump to conclusions. I'm not passing judgment. I just know how I have felt at times. I hear the fear lingering from the past, and I recognize that feeling from when I felt trapped in the worst nightmare as I perceived it *at the time*. If you're feeling something resonating with that simple statement, then sure, I think you should examine it. See if there's a story connected to it, and see if you feel victimized in other areas of your life, past or present. If you do, then maybe there's a theme karma's teaching you." The conversation ended, and we felt closer for it. We knew our kind were not always easy to come by, and we appreciated the camaraderie.

In my work, cleaning houses continued to be a vehicle for guidance to chime through. The cleaning zone was easy to drop into. Getting into the groove, like meditation in motion, I found that the movement cleared the mind. I held the intention of being of service in the forefront of the mind. While chanting what I was learning at Ananda services, my vibration lifted some days into ecstatic blissful love. This high vibration that flowed through me blessed the homes I cleaned. Some clients commented not only on how nice the physical clean felt to come home to but also that there was a palpable wonderful feeling they experienced. I knew what they meant, even if they didn't, and felt grateful that a gift like that could be imparted through me, this vessel.

In talking with new friends, I came to understand that different people had strengths in what could be called psychic sensitivities. Some have precognition gifts of knowing future events. Some could see what most couldn't, the gift of clairvoyance. My strength and connection seemed to show up mostly as clairaudience, the ability to hear guidance from the unseen or unperceived realms. Previously, I thought it was only because of the Shaktipat, which connected me to Gurudev and his lineage, that I was able to hear him. But as it turned out, this perception wasn't limited to only him. *Kundalini sensitizes higher and subtler vehicles of perception.*

Now, I received Yogananda's guidance most often, at one house in particular. It was the largest home I cleaned. It took most of the day, so I had plenty of time to be in the zone. It was then I began carrying around a notepad and pen. I could sometimes remember what guidance was given for a short period of time, but often it would slowly fade away. In the midst of many changes while navigating this new life, feeling fear and uncertainty, I received this from Yogananda:

"You are not in fear. Fear is how you are labeling your experience. However, it's only unfamiliar and unknown. If you label the energy 'fear,' then that is what you will create. You need time for integration. All of this is new and not tangible in the way you have known your life to be. But it is not fear."

At another time when I was feeling confused and apprehensive, faltering in commitments to my practice and feeling like a disappointment, reassurance came through: "We are patient. We know beyond what you know. Your heart, your commitment, your love is known. Your path is known beyond what you can see. Time is allowed."

Divine Mother was definitely a presence held in deep devotion by Yogananda and at Ananda. The disciples held it, Her, Kundalini, very differently than I had learned previously. Though some of the experiences in my past were still *perceived by the mind* as harrowing, I greatly missed allowing Her presence more fully. And I often missed Gurudev. There were instances in which I witnessed some of the disciples during service "jump" from seemingly invisible jolts. I knew She, Divine Mother, had sparked in them. Sometimes I saw sways fill their bodies. But there were no spontaneous mudras or postures, at least not that I saw. This didn't mean that it didn't occur in the privacy of the disciples' own sacred space, but no clues were visible outwardly. As distance grew between the instability of the past and the groundedness I felt growing, I wanted to invite Her back into my practice. This was never difficult, since the challenge had been implementing control so as *not* to allow Her to lull this body or mind.

I was living just a few blocks from where I'd lived when I moved to Southeast Hawthorne in 1996 when my life took its first transformational turn. This time I was a mile south toward Division, in a basement apartment. I imagined the new abode was assisting with giving me the grounding I needed. I loved the new space, and Urisk had his own special entrance, the window. I kept it open so that he could go about as he desired. Being as solitary as his mother, he was happy to have a home again, free of other furry friends. My mom had a cat, which Urisk was not too keen on. He always stayed close to the house, and just as back in Northeast Portland with Caleb, he always came in for the night.

Emotionally and mentally I felt stable. The new routine, friends, and physical world direction supported my sense of security. The services at Ananda had more of a Christian feel than what resonated with me personally and were inclusive of Jesus in the lineage. Gradually I opened to this and found the willingness to release my resistance to the Western religious overtones fairly easily. I felt protected and held by the lineage of Yogananda as I invited Divine Mother into my heart more fully.

I established a new altar in my home. This time, it held photos of Yogananda, Sri Yukteswar, Lahiri Mahasya, and Babaji Krishna. I opted out of including a picture of Jesus. Even though I felt more open, I just didn't feel that kind of connection. Before every meditation, and in the invitation I was extending toward Divine Mother, I invoked the protection and guidance of the lineage.

Inviting Her in to meditation felt right and true. Divine Mother moved gracefully and gently. Her sway enabled me to drop into a deeper meditation than I'd been in, in a very long time. Silence. Emptiness. Even the soft rolling of the head and neck I surrendered to once again. For the first couple of mediations I maintained a calm mind and short periods of surrender before I interjected my will to still Her energy. All was well.

I was experiencing greater moments of love and compassion moving through me. My days felt in perfect balance of doing and being in the world and in my own personal space. There was acceptance and grace that carried me effortlessly through my days, my relationships, and my alone time.

One day while driving home from work, I noticed a homeless man standing by a bus stop as I sat at the red light. While I looked at him, I wasn't aware of any particular thoughts other than a normal expected compassion for him and for the large homeless population in Portland. Before it could register, I felt my hands raise up, facing the gentleman in a gesture I had seen Yogananda do in photos. It was as if a blessing was flowing through me. I was caught off guard, since this felt like an unfamiliar context. I was in daily life, just driving along, and this was a complete stranger. But I was left feeling blessed with a greater love—impersonal, but love nonetheless—for my brothers and sisters in the world.

27

Caleb had invited me to go with him to the birthday celebration of a member of his family in July. It had been some time since we'd hung out, and I was looking forward to spending some time together. While we drove, we chatted about work and his romantic interest Amanda. Amanda was his manager at work. I viewed her as a taste of my own medicine, a karmic return. He had been experiencing an attraction for her, and she for him, since before he and I separated. I'd been in and out of feeling all the ego triggers of insecurity and jealousy in the beginning of the infatuation. Amid the triggers and stories that crept forth, I had enough awareness to know I was reaping what I'd sown when Caleb and I first met.

When Caleb and I first met and became friends, we had a strong mutual attraction, and Jace and I were struggling in our relationship. Though Jace did his best to respect the intense bond Caleb and I had, he also saw it, as he so eloquently put it, as "the big Mack truck speeding directly toward us." He was right. And the truck made an impact. We were all involved in the Naka Ima community. At that time there was a growing exploration of polyamory within the community. Caleb was actively in the exploration circle, while I knew myself to be monogamous. Our new connection was challenging my ideas of what monogamy meant to me.

Caleb and I had a strong chemistry and powerful heart connection. When we first began spending time together, we'd sit for hours sharing some of the most intimate parts of ourselves, cuddling, and feeling the chemistry build. All the while, I was still with Jace and was honest with him. It was an interesting position for me to be in. I had become the pot calling the kettle black. I was a walking judgment of what I had placed on so many others regarding fidelity, emotional or otherwise. I'd had an emotional affair with Caleb, though out in the open and with full communication and disclosure with Jace. Until Jace and I split.

On New Year's Eve heading into 2000, Jace gave me the ultimatum to choose. I chose Caleb, the Mack truck.

Moving forward into a romantic relationship with Caleb, though I wasn't interested in multiple partners, I was conscious of the choice I made. I knew I'd be in the fire of healing some of my deepest fears. I knew that this relationship would bring up fears of abandonment, my insecurities, my self-worth and lovability issues, as well as those issues around trust. The truth was, I was on a path of healing into wholeness. I was willing to walk through these fires to release the programming.

Three months into our relationship, Caleb went off to a monthlong gathering to explore further for himself if polyamory was the path he wanted to continue on at that time. I stayed home and went through my own fires of initiation into self-love. That month I faced those fears head-on. At the time of his return, I'd moved into a new awareness of unconditional love and freedom for us both, based on a coming home to myself and falling in love with myself first and foremost. Much of that month wasn't pretty, nor was it graceful, but in the end it was all worth it.

When Caleb returned home from that month away, he chose a committed monogamous relationship with me, and I chose that with him. The three years we were together weren't free from continued tests of strengthening what I'd learned while he was away that summer. However, the consciousness and rigorous honesty of our relationship made this inner work truly inspiring and was a true bond facilitating our love and acceptance for one another.

In the end, Amanda and Caleb gave me a tiny glimpse of the pain I had caused Jace. I felt greater compassion for Jace. There were many decisions I'd made at the end of that relationship that I'd like to think I'd do differently if the opportunity arose again. The outcome would have been the same, but how I handled it could have been more sensitive. I had been given the opportunity to wear the other shoe as my and Caleb's romance ended, when Amanda entered the picture.

That day as Caleb updated me regarding Amanda, the emotional charge had dissipated. He and I had surpassed the energy of romantic relationships that had the potential to trigger a threat to ego. I was an impartial listener, offering objective feedback.

Talking and riding west of the city, we entered into wider-open spaces—more nature, trees, and fields. It was during this period of time something in my eyesight changed drastically.

"Wow!" I interrupted him.

"Wow what?" he asked.

"Sorry for interrupting, but look at these trees," I said.

"Yeah. They're nice."

"Not just nice. Look at the leaves. It's like they're lit up!" I saw him slightly tilt his head forward to look out the passenger window. "And the details of the bark on each approaching tree I can see from here! Each detail of the tree, all of it, all of them, completely detailed and radiating some kind of light!" I was captivated.

"Hmm. I don't think I'm seeing the same thing you are," he said.

"And look at all the blades of grass," I continued as my gaze fell to the passing green below. "How can I even see those blades? We're moving quickly. This is crazy beautiful ... and oh my God, the flowers over there!" I pointed to a garden as we drove down the side street toward his mom's house. "Every petal is perfectly unique. And those colors!" I had no words.

It was as if everything around me had become enlivened with a glow, a light, a radiance, a sharpness of detail. And each detail of Mother Nature's artistry was brought to the very surface to be admired. It was like my eyes were playing tricks on me, showing me nature's true shimmer and glisten, if only with graced eyes to see through. Life was pulsating everywhere. My eyesight was electrified just for that short time, but I held it as a blessing of the transformation taking place in my being.

These states of heightened awareness were not my doing. Grace enters in on its own accord to reveal to us when we're open to receive—the blessings of Yogananda through me to a complete stranger. The moment of encountering the true splendor of Nature's beauty imprinted on my being. The Divine Presence, whatever we choose to call this Power, this intelligence, it's alive and waiting for all hearts and souls to awaken to the call. I felt as though I was just beginning to see that this journey unfolding mysteriously before me and within was intended for everyone—eventually. The teachings of the masters, including Jesus, or Divine Mother, aren't limited to one but can be attributed to all. And the guidance I received confirmed just this: "My child, see through the eyes of Love. You must look with eyes of Love which see with the Heart. Remember to see beyond the forms in front of you but to see the Love that is in everyone."

28

That summer, I met a most special man.

A friend of mine, Eddie, was having a party for one of his housemates, Byron. Byron was moving out to Cornelius, to a small organic farm where he'd be living and working. I arrived with my friend Sandra to see him standing on the porch. He caught my eye with his thick and long auburn hair, red beard, John Lennon glasses, and big grin. But as we walked up the porch stairs, I also noticed he was young. Caleb had been ten years younger than I, and I felt like I needed to return to romances with people who were my own age, so I dismissed any inclination toward attraction. Even though Caleb carried himself with maturity, and although I tend to be young and free-spirited for my age, I felt like it was time to return to my age bracket.

The party was fun. I felt social and connected with people I hadn't seen in some time. I wasn't a night owl, so as the dancing was about to begin, with an intoxicated Byron DJ'ing, I called it a night.

There was a month in between that first meeting with Byron, which was brief, and our meeting again. We met the second time at a street dance on Southeast Division, which gave us time to connect and dance. Although he was younger, he felt grounded, mature, and present. He was also lighthearted and courteous, and his big laugh hooked me. There was an attraction that felt deeper than I could explain.

Our connection felt easy and comfortable. He was nicely balanced in his masculine and feminine qualities, and I appreciated the more dominant presence of the masculine. I felt like I needed more masculine energy in my life. I had noticed that during the initial cleansing and emptying processes of the year before, I had been left with some stark realizations about my own masculine edges. During that period, I had softened into humbleness and vulnerability, which were qualities of being I craved. It felt challenging to regain that softness again, as much of my survival, independence, and control had set back in, along with my tendency toward sharpness. The yang qualities made it harder for me to remain in the heart center. I felt like I needed a strong male partner to hold that yang energy space, enabling a softening in my being. As uncomfortable as it had been, I had a desire to rekindle the raw pink skin.

It was then another month before Byron showed up one Sunday morning to ecstatic dance. After dancing, we went to have tea and get to know one another a little more. I loved that he journaled, asked questions, and was very open in sharing. I would consider that one of our first dates.

Being that Byron lived out in the country, he came into town on the weekends now that we were dating. We had our standing weekend date. He'd come calling with bags of fresh produce from the gardens, and we'd feast. He was a gentleman with some old-fashioned values, which I truly appreciated. I could tell from our conversations that he was introspective, spiritual, and not prone to whimsy. He was a poet and writer. He had enough experience to know better, but not so much that he carried heavy baggage. I appreciated his open-mindedness. Byron was eleven years my junior, but I suspended judgment. We were both open to exploring the blossoming of this relationship.

We weren't sexual immediately. I wanted to share with him more about my spiritual life, but not right at first. If and when it seemed like we felt called to move toward the next level of intimacy with some commitment, then I would talk with him. Within a month or so, we discussed that we both wanted to be in a monogamous relationship and go deeper. I knew then that the subject needed to be brought out of the closet.

Broaching the topic of Kundalini awakening is a funny conversation to have because really, no matter what is disclosed or what is said through words, it can't do the actual personal experience justice. I wanted him to have as full of a picture as he could before we moved to the next level. Caleb and I had already been in a serious, committed relationship before this journey began, and he had every right not to want to travel along with me. I wouldn't begrudge him that, nor would I want to lead Byron into a relationship that could be overwhelming.

The night we talked about the journey I was on, Byron listened intently. I let him know that I thought the worst was past and that I'd changed my ways of practice, but there were still elements of unpredictability.

"I feel like a big difference at this point is that I don't feel as if I'm being propelled on a soul level beyond what I have the capacity to hold on to at an ego level. Does this make any sense to you?" I asked, checking in.

"I don't think I'll know for sure until I witness something for myself," he replied. "But if you're wondering if any of this changes the fact that I want to spend time with you and continue to get to know you more, it doesn't." He kept things super simple.

We talked about his relationship with God. He'd grown up with religious parents and a Baptist minister for a father. I inquired about how they would feel about my path, if he and I were to grow into a more serious relationship.

"Years ago it would be much harder on them. They used to be much more conservative than they are now. I'm sure they'd have some feelings as well as questions, but overall, I think they'd be fine."

"Do you feel you have a Christian view, spiritually?" I asked.

"I would say yes, in that I feel a strong connection to Jesus."

It was nice to feel that we could each have our own views, our own ways of connecting, and move further into whatever our relationship was meant to be. While he had spent the night on his weekend treks into town, this night was to be the first time we made love.

It took Urisk a while to get used to having to share bed space, especially on the weekend mornings. Normally during the week, he and I had our morning cuddle-fest time before I got out of bed to start the day. He slept at my feet during the night, and in the morning he moved up to cuddle into the position of my spooning him. We'd come a long way, and the joy it brought was mutual. On the weekend mornings, however, when Byron was present, I'd awaken to see Urisk sitting about three feet out from the bed, staring, glaring, and waiting for Byron to get out of bed. At the point at which Byron got up to go into the bathroom, Urisk would make his move. He'd crawl into bed with me, and there we'd have our cuddle time. Eventually, he warmed up to Byron, but our morning routine remained valued for us both.

Within a few weeks from the time Byron and I first made love, we shared a moving, sacred experience together. As he and I were entering into a deeper relationship with each other, Divine Mother rose through this one's heart and body with an unexpected force while he and I made love one night. It was as if I was catapulted back into the full throes of Her presence. The heart grew into an expansive state I had not experienced prior. It was as if there were light radiating through the heart center. Mudras once again danced my hands gracefully in the air in front of the heart, then spiraled down to Byron's heart and danced new, foreign gestures; then my hands glided up to his third eye. Tears of joy and ecstasy spilled forth, interceding any thoughts to stop it, but the beauty of the surrender was overwhelming. Byron, below me, gazed wide-eyed, and then perhaps when it was too much, he closed his eyes. At the end there was elation and wonderment. Our hearts merged. And with closed eyes, he too began to see the purple-blue light dancing in his inner sight. Awakening had begun.

In the aftermath, while I felt shaken by the experience, Byron's response would set the tone of grounding for our journey together. He felt completely blessed by the mystery that unfolded before him. There was no fright, no resistance. He had felt amazed but didn't question anything that happened. He didn't feel the need to understand; he just had a steadfast knowing and acceptance of the blessing bestowed. I wanted to take it in this nonattached stride, but I had all sorts of familiar stories animating in my mind again. I didn't know how this could happen. I thought I was protected. Wasn't I now practicing on a path where these kinds of events didn't occur? I was baffled and nervous.

This dynamic would play out in a myriad of ways in our relationship. He became the stabilizing force to my flitting to and fro, spontaneous nature. I had great appreciation for this balance, and over time he recognized that my spontaneity brought levity to his pragmatism.

Throughout the rest of the summer and fall, I played a little more freely with Divine Mother's presence in my practice. I saw that it didn't matter that I was practicing a different technique, or that I was connected to a different lineage, or that I was doing a structured hatha yoga posture sequence, which was a part of a three-month course at Ananda. It seemed this soul knew what kind of path was mine to follow, how it should manifest, and the lessons I had to learn from it. No matter how much control I intended to impose, She was still always waiting just outside the door, patiently waiting for me to invite Her in.

How often do we think and believe we are in control of our lives, of life's twists and turns? When we enter into the spiritual realm of trusting and surrendering to God and Spirit, when we engage in true surrender, it becomes unpredictable. I believe the more we listen to the guidance of soul, the more we are actually listening to the path of our destiny unfolding. We indeed have self-will; however, in the game of surrender, that self-will is sacrificed.

My mind held concepts with boundaries that were continuously shattered. Knowing the way of Spirit, I found it impossible to know what the path would hold as I let go. "In my Father's house are many mansions." And perhaps we each get to traverse one entire mansion while others get to spend time in a room or two, while still others explore the many mansions.

I had much appreciation for the teachings in the three-month raja-yoga course at Ananda. I felt like so much light was shed on traveling a yogic path. It clarified so many points I hadn't yet strung together. When Byron was with me on the weekends, he joined in doing the Energization exercises they recommended at Ananda, at least in the morning. My daily schedule was such that I was able to do energizations, yoga postures, and meditation practice somewhere in the day, even if I couldn't accomplish them all in the morning. Going to classes two nights out of the week, I wasn't dancing as much, yet I was still able to make the Conscious Movement class, which was a favorite at that time.

29

What I was learning confirmed much of what Gurudev had talked about regarding yoga in the West. There are many paths of yoga, and eventually they all unite, even though we each may have natural draws to a specific limb of the whole tree. It was validated again that true yoga is far more than merely exercise via hatha yoga postures. While the benefits of calm and more peaceful states of being, better health, and reduced stress attributed to the practice of postures are highly valuable, they are laying the foundation for the depth of yoga. In conversations with friends, I found that this point could be one of contention, although I didn't see that it had to be. Yoga is great for exercise and to get through the day-to-day better. It's good as a healthful practice, and for many that is all they require. As Gurudev used to say, "This is good because eventually they will be ready for the real yoga." But for one to actually follow a yogic path, there is much more involved. As I had been finding out for the last year or more, true yoga is transformative of one's entire life and being, mind, body, and soul.

Though I was feeling that I was very much in the right place, I knew I wasn't "home" at Ananda or with this great master

Yogananda. The vibration was indeed quite high, and love and light radiated through the fellowship. Affirmations and joy were the expectation. Why would that not feel in alignment to me? I wanted to belong and accept these teachings as my path. But while I wasn't planning on returning to Gurudev, I felt that many things I had experienced, and the teachings I held closely through him, weren't going to fit in this path.

For example, I knew that the *connection to the physical body, to go beyond the body and its energies, was a powerful means of allowing higher realizations of consciousness to occur.* When I tried to approach this with the minister whom I dearly loved, his perception was one of caution about attachment to the body and suggested I not give too much credence to sensations. As I tried to explain my point and offered an example, it was apparent we weren't going to see eye to eye.

It was a lesson in respecting that each individual is called to different ways of learning. We each have unique karmic tendencies and a soul's guidance that leads us to what is needed. Some people are called to Christianity, some to Islam, others to Judaism, and still others to Buddhism, and so on. Each tradition offers what each soul needs. There need not be a right or wrong, division, or prejudice. The call I was receiving was different from what the Ananda path held.

At the end of the three-month course, I had the option of continuing on to receive disciple initiation and learn the secret and powerful Kriya technique. I debated within myself because I desired to rest in the lap of Yogananda's safety and move forward peacefully. The clear half of me knew this wasn't where I was meant to lay my head. I wasn't his disciple, and I had the notion Yogananda knew this too. Reconciliation was made within. Discipleship and initiation wasn't part of our plan together. After the course ended, I still continued to go to service. It was a nice common ground for Byron and me, and we really had a fondness for some of the members. The incorporation of Jesus and the Christian influence resonated with Byron, while it held enough of the Eastern vibe, with chanting and meditation, to resonate with my being. We both felt fed and nourished.

As winter approached, Byron's work at the farm was going to be ending. We discussed options, both logistically and romantically. We decided that he would move into the cozy basement and could help me with some of the housecleaning accounts. If he decided to return to the farm in the spring, it would be a move that could be done with ease. Just a couple of days before he took off to spend Christmas with family in Indiana, he made the final delivery of his belongings to what was to be *our* new home.

30

For the next week, except for the holiday celebration days of Christmas Eve, Christmas Day, and New Year's Eve, I answered the call to dive back within my own being, as guided by soul. I willingly surrendered with deep pleasure into the abyss of silence.

Learning to read Divine Mother's guidance took me to ever new levels of energetic sensitivity and understanding. Her reminders were never harsh, but when I felt the soft whimpering in the core of my being, I knew I had transgressed a boundary. With the months I had put in between Her all-encompassing presence in the not so distant past and the balanced approach in the present, I still often felt I was dancing on the razor's edge. The time with Gurudev had been incredibly profound and vibrationally transforming. Mother's presence never left, only my relationship to Her changed. I was gradually allowing Her to lead the way again, only with a deeper sense of awareness as to my limits.

During the week of Byron's absence, I had a feeling of catching up with myself, reviewing my feelings about the relationship, what I'd learned in the raja-yoga course, and doing basic integration. I didn't spend much time with friends except a short visit for New

Year's Eve, ringing in 2004, at Caleb's party. The majority of time I spent in solitude, reading, doing my practice, and lying flat on my back in deep spontaneous meditation.

The first day or two of the Christmas break, I thought I just needed to nap. Putting on quiet music, I'd lie on my back on the couch or bed, not asleep or awake, but present to a silent inner direction to just be. It was similar to the practice of spontaneous postures in that after almost exactly one hour, my eyes would pop open and I was done, released, energized, and ready for whatever the next thing was, which was usually reading.

By the end of the week, this was taking place a couple of times a day. I recognized it to be somewhat like the yoga nidra meditation, yogic sleep practice we did once or twice during the second trip I'd made to see Gurudev in Colorado. However, that had been a guided meditation with specific instructions, so I wasn't certain. *Could this yoga nidra just have happened spontaneously?* I wondered.

Often while in that state, I'd feel my body buzzing and vibrating slightly, or I'd have amazing awareness of being completely merged with a great emptiness yet still felt full. Moments of epiphanies visited me, revealing the Self, thrusting it into conscious awareness. Every now and again I would have a distinct feeling of disappearing into a black hole of nothingness. I only realized this gap in which I had disappeared because I had returned from it. At that point I'd create some kind of movement or inner distraction that confirmed I was really there, present.

Samadhi has multiple levels of unifying, merging, becoming one with God. During mediation, and particularly the spontaneous bouts of yoga nidra, when we are completely absorbed into the nothingness of the void, when one's identity vanishes for a time, is when samadhi occurs. The initial stage merges consciousness into the gap and then releases it back to the world of the senses. Eventually, at the highest levels, consciousness remains merged with God, even as one is in the world.

Paramahansa Yogananda: "That state when you are totally absorbed in inner awareness of God, no longer conscious of the world, is called sabikalpa samadhi. It is 'partial dissolution of the world.'"

The days were serene, my needs were minimal, and the mind was present in each moment. By the time Byron returned, I felt refreshed, relaxed, spacious, and at peace. While he had stories to share about his time back home, my report was brief and uneventful.

We began our new life living together, merging our individual rhythm into that of a couple. This transition was effortless and nourishing.

31

Winter was smooth sailing and uneventful. Byron and I found our flow with one another. Both of us were avid readers, and he was appreciating the time to work on his writings. We lived simply and quietly. Our personal space and quiet time was of equal importance for each of us. Living in a small, one-room apartment, we found that if one of us took turns going to the coffee shop for a few hours a day, it was helpful. I felt a growing comfort in my practice, protected by Yogananda, and Byron's groundedness added to the safety I'd been longing for. He also began a mediation practice, and now with the spark of awakened Kundalini, he too was experiencing the spontaneous postures. As I expected, he took it all in stride.

Although there was nothing I felt the need to change at the moment, and although I didn't feel a creative urge or desire, I knew I didn't want to keep vacillating between cleaning houses and caregiving for my life's work. Since I had decided against the Ananda yoga teacher training, I was unclear what was next. I did, however, find an anatomy course at one of the nearby yoga studios in Southeast Portland, just down the street from where we lived. With a natural inclination toward the body, I found that this felt useful regardless of what direction I was led in. I was in study mode and content to do just that.

Spring 2004 arrived, and Byron decided not to move back to the farm, choosing to continue cleaning houses with me. He appreciated the free time and was happy to have the chance to sink into his passion of writing with less distraction. Between the two of us, we were fine financially, as long as no unexpected emergencies showed up. This wasn't optimal, but it was the "in the moment" manner that we both were comfortable operating in.

The anatomy classes were two evenings a week, and I loved every minute of it. Coupled with studying for class, Byron had suggested I read the New Testament. We'd had a conversation in which I told him I'd never read it. He was surprised. I explained there had been times when I first got sober that I'd attempted it, but each time I tried, I had horribly scary dreams. Oddly, it had felt like some force had done its best to keep me from exploring that text, and succeeded. I thought now it was appropriate. I felt protected, and I was warming up to Jesus as a part of Sunday services.

It was decided: the New Testament was next on my list. The first responses I had once I began reading, I must admit, were quite reactive. I could feel the resistant and angry energy of my parents toward Christianity, which became more apparent to me when I stayed conscious enough to witness the level of reactivity I had. Not all of my feelings were my own. I didn't fault them for the feelings they carried. I could understand the frustration of organized religion, of any denomination, since I shared the sentiments of my own accord.

On the flip side, to my joy what I found was how obvious it was, in my new perception, that Jesus was a yogi. He was a master, and what the New Testament reflected to me were yogic teachings. I grew in excitement the more I read. Questions arose that I wanted to explore further. From my perspective, I saw *that all of Jesus's teachings were meant to awaken. However, what was lacking, at least in the text, were the practices, the actual keys needed.* What I would shortly come to learn was that *Christianity did have the experiential keys; they just weren't found in the mainstream, exoteric religion of the canonical books. The esoteric inner traditions were where the jewels were hidden.*

Though Gurudev had talked briefly about the Holy Spirit being the same as Divine Mother, the energy of Kundalini, I hadn't fully registered what that meant because I'd never read any Christian writings or the Bible. As I read it now, I felt completely absorbed in the text and resonated most with the book of John in many ways. Not only were passages illustrating Jesus displaying the same abilities as great yogis, but also, from a yogic perspective, Divine Mother/ Kundalini, as the Holy Spirit, was given life.

The passages regarding the Holy Spirit filled me with excitement and recognition. I was awestruck with John, chapters 14 and 16. Jesus speaks of the Counselor that will be sent to aid the disciples. When I read 14:6, there was a familiar statement I'd heard throughout my life but didn't know its origin: "I am the way, the truth, and the life. No one comes to the Father, except through me."

Jesus introduces the Counselor in 14:16: "I will ask the Father and he will send another Counselor to be with you forever—the Spirit of Truth. The world cannot accept him, because it neither sees him nor knows him. But you know him, for he lives with you and *will be in you*" (emphasis added).

In 14:26 the text reads, "But the Counselor, the Holy Spirit, whom the Father will send in my name, will teach you things and will remind you of everything I have said."

And it follows up in John 16:12, where Jesus is explaining, "I have much more to say, more than you can now bear. But when the Spirit of truth comes, he will guide you into all truth." And in John 16:15, He continues, "All that belongs to the Father is mine. That is why I said the Spirit will take from what is mine and make it known to you."

In my perception, the necessity of the Counselor arriving meant that the disciples could be taught from *within*. Bells were sounding in both my heart and mind. I felt I understood the intimacy of what was being taught because the learning from within that Jesus spoke of was experiential direct knowledge. That the Counselor or Holy Spirit was masculinized, whereas this force in many other traditions has a feminine expression, didn't feel like a deterrent.

And while I could see where such statements as "I am the way, the truth, and the life. No one comes to the Father except through me" could be divisive and alienating, I instead understood it from a perception of consciousness. The Holy Spirit or Divine Mother *is* the spiritualized life force. This life force awakens our consciousness from the mundane worldly plane, lifting it to the higher perceptions of divine consciousness, where God can be met and eventually merged with.

I could personally attest to Its/Her/His teachings within this being, purifying, guiding, and illuminating. Kundalini, Divine Intelligence, is said to open the doors of perception, which allow the untapped faculties of consciousness to spring to life. Through these doors of perception, heightened awareness connects us to the Presence of the Divine in all its manifestations. This heightened, expanded consciousness is 'the way.' It isn't limited to a person, a single teacher, or guru. It is inclusive of all that are uplifting humanity into awakening.

To me, I was simply reading another language, a sacred text from another tradition, of another divine being, attempting to lead us onto a higher path. This didn't discount or minimize Jesus's mission in the world to me personally. However, I also didn't have prior religious indoctrination that required my mind to jump hurdles in order to accept or explore other angles of understanding. I was wide open, ready to receive whatever I could, and my mind began desiring to know more. With so much yet to understand, so many questions, I had never really considered myself a seeker until I began reading the New Testament.

It was amid this seeking upon the first reading of the New Testament that my heart began its opening to Jesus. The Gospel of Thomas, and all its sayings, some of which sound nothing like the Jesus of the Bible, yet more like a yogi, ignited more curiosity. The Gospel of Philip threw my mind in a scurry, with the claims of Mary Magdalene as the companion of Jesus, and the one "he kissed often on the mouth." Once again, I had become a sponge, soaking in all this new information. Some I understood, some was out of the mind's reach, but the body, heart, and soul responded with a mysterious affirmation. A whole world opened up as I realized Christianity was very rich. This richness for me was in the discovery of the Gnostic texts, and the growing desire to keep learning was ripened when I delved headlong into the swirling theories and stories of Mary Magdalene, both as she stood alone and as she stood in relationship to Jesus.

32

In the midst of school, work, relationship, and my own personal studies, my practice shifted. There were familiar sensations returning that I was becoming accustomed to again during meditation. Divine Mother was illuminating to me the importance of the spine. Not only the physical spine but also the subtle spine, the Sushumna. This subtle channel had been introduced to me by Gurudev in meditation, but at the time I was told I'd learn more about it at a later date. Sensations of energy tickling its way upward through this channel came and went. The trickles of tickles were primarily in the lower vertebrae, rising a bit and then receding in accordance with the inhalation and exhalation, the energy rising and falling, eventually working its way upward and toward the brain and crown chakra. Those sensations were easy enough for me to accept, but there were other sensations, such as feeling as if a steel rod was installed in the center of the spine, that were harder to accept. This steel rod lengthened and grounded my being and awareness. The solidity was more than I could bear, but I couldn't say why, other than that it was new and unexpected. At the first experience of this, I sent a call out for Yogananda. His presence was felt, and his voice stabilized me:

"Don't become attached to the body and fear. Bring it up to your heart center. Transform it into Joy and raise the vibration. If it stays stuck in the lower center consciousness, it is the vibration of fear and apprehension."

Every new experience sent me into a whirl. I called out for support and felt a reactive story, a karmic story of victimization that was hard to shake. In the aftermath, it would be clear that I was fine. Invasion, psychic takeover, or whatever it was that the mind of ego was terrified of happening never manifested. Without any concrete memory of the victimization that was spurred, I felt like I was on the hamster wheel of rote reaction. Contrary to the fears, the following instances brought an experience of spaciousness or love, infused by Divine Mother. My interpretation of it became "creating space for grace." With the support of Yogananda, I was finding the courage to continue deepening my walk on the path of spontaneous postures and the guided bodily sensations that Gurudev had initiated me into.

I had a need for things to make sense logically, so I created an inner division through linear thought processes. I couldn't understand why Yogananda encouraged me to do spontaneous postures when none of the teachings I was familiar with, either through Ananda or even Yogananda's book *Autobiography of a Yogi*, talked about them. Nor were they approved of by any of the ministers. Needing answers, needing sensibility in the mystical realm, I tended to set up roadblocks to my growth.

The reality I lived in, though it was becoming more familiar, was often bizarre to me. One day while working, I noticed there was a conversation taking place within me. I'd been questioning, for the umpteenth time, my sanity and the reality of Yogananda's presence. Yogananda's voice rose inwardly and explained with patience, "You must remember, things are not black and white, this or that. You want this or that path and expect a particular look. I come to all in the ways they can receive me whenever they are ready, to whatever extent they are ready. I come to you when you are open and able to receive me. Your channel has been opened. You have surrendered enough for me to enter. You have awareness that it is possible and know how to allow me to flow through you. There are those who are primarily existent on different planes. There are so many levels. Your guru and many others who have moved beyond physical form commune in me, in many ways you cannot understand, just as many do not understand you, nor will they believe you. I do not come here to prove anything to anyone. I am here when I am ready to be received. Each traveler has their own time. I am a beacon to show the way home."

Always with a notebook on hand to write down the teachings I was blessed with, I found there were few words to express my ongoing gratitude for these gifts. Incorporating them into all fibers of my being, integrating them into the wisdom intended—that was the trick. Continuously I felt slow, thick, and dense. I learned not to judge this but simply to accept that the pace of my learning wasn't up to ego's expectations. That in itself was laughable.

Images began to fill the inner eye during my practices. They felt random and disconnected and would be seen sporadically. I had learned not to hold on or attach to any manifestations during practice; however, sometimes they seemed to be etched into my mind. The *quality* of the images and scenes seemed to have an *aliveness*, in conjunction with a *feeling-sensing quality*. There was some distant knowing, remembering of something so out of reach, that was quite different from the random pictures that sometimes drifted across my inner screen.

The first ones to make their appearance were from a time far off, in some distant past. There were long pieces of paper spread out on a surface that I couldn't see. The walls themselves were lined with these papers, rolled up and slid into crevices in the rock. There were rows and rows of these crevices, sort of like shelves within a cave, like some ancient library.

The next one, I felt as if I were in underground caverns. The caverns looked as if they'd been created to be little rooms connected by tunnels. There was a dim light source from somewhere, but I couldn't say exactly where or what the source of light was. I say that 'I' was the person, even though I can't be certain. It felt like some form of 'me.' I was stepping down into one of the cave-like rooms. The walls were a brownish, red canyon colored rock. Both of these visions carried a vague sense of doom and anxiousness, though nothing seemed wrong on the surface.

There was another scene that played out before my eyes, of another 'me.' Though I've never been to a Catholic service, it seemed a scene of Catholicism to me. There was a man in white with a beard standing before me. Something was said that couldn't be heard or understood; however, the real me, sitting in meditation, began crying with a desperate longing, as the me in the vision lay down, completely prostrate in front of this man. The physical me, in meditation, was crying and confused because it was hard to differentiate between the vision and myself, here and now, while simultaneously being there and then.

Through the visions showing themselves inwardly, it wasn't hard for me to connect the dots to all the Christian studies I'd been undertaking, whether I understood any of it or not. However, the quality present reminded me of many dreams having a similar surreal connotation to events or images that I knew as past lives. The past dreams were experienced in the earliest stages of waking up. And now, experiencing vivid imagery in this way, in meditation, was new to me.

A few weeks after these inner scenes had shown themselves, while sharing them with Byron, I found them to remain perfectly clear, in layers of detail of what I'd seen and in the emotional state of the visions. But more interesting was recognizing that patterns were taking shape.

"Have you seen images like this often?" Byron asked, after I'd shared with him.

"Not really. Right after I got home from the initial trip to Colorado, in dreams I saw images or scenes that I felt viscerally.

Usually they woke me up. Sometimes it felt like they involved some incarnation of me. Others felt like they weren't personally attached. In one dream, for instance, I saw an old-fashioned car with the look of the 1920s. I knew it was outside our house in Northeast Portland, but there were no other homes in the dream. It was surrounded by fields and trees. The car was completely full with what seemed to be a family and their belongings. I had a heavy feeling from it, maybe somewhat desperate. As the dream ended or I woke up from it, I saw the face of a little girl, four years old or so. She had her face pressed up against the car window and was banging on the windows, crying. I woke up with a jolt of deep sadness and desperation. It's that quality that I've gotten to know, not that I can explain it, but it's always a visceral feeling. And whatever the images, they never fade."

"And that's how these are feeling?" he asked.

"Yeah. But the other thing I'm noticing is that these events go in phases. For example, the previous visions appeared in what was a really active phase. There are numerous 'seeings' that occur. When I'm sitting in meditation, the inner experience is that I feel deeply centered, but there's a lot of visual activity. Now, a few days later, they've stopped. Internally, stillness and silence reign. I'm aware I'm just clear and empty. There may be a floater or two across my awareness, but it's connected to the present day, here and now. Then it floats on by," I explained.

"That's interesting. So the phases come and go in cycles. I guess you get time to integrate or ... who knows, huh?" he responded. All of this was new to him, yet he took it all in stride.

As enthralled as I was in the studies of Jesus, I couldn't really think of Him as the same kind of energetic presence as Yogananda or Gurudev, for instance, nor the lineages of either of them. Jesus felt untouchable and completely otherworldly, even though I believed Him to be a yogi. He was, after all, Jesus. I had never heard of anyone "meeting" Jesus, unless of course we count saints, but they seemed more naturally predisposed to such an encounter. I, however, was content here with Yogananda. Even though he wasn't my "home,"

I had gotten quite comfortable with him. I was about to glean an important lesson for myself, which would take a couple of years yet for me to really grasp. The saying "That which you resist persists" was becoming my motto of life. Each step of the way, if I was paying attention, those things that repelled me have ultimately been a destination along this inner journey.

33

Jesus was the initiator of clearer seeing of the depth of resistance I had to the plans of Yogananda, God, or the Universe. Yogananda was insistent, in an ever so gentle but firm way, to introduce me to Jesus. I was greatly confused and exerted much digging in of my heels at the prospect of this introduction. *How do I really know this is safe? How can I tell if it is Jesus and not some demonic form in disguise? Now I must really be crazy.* I mean, who was I to communicate with Jesus? I wasn't even Christian!

I had a deep-seated story in both my conscious awareness and the subconscious. Fear loomed from somewhere unknown to me. Each new transition of experience sparked fear. At every twist and turn I had tremendous caution. I didn't blame myself. I actually thought it was normal. Wouldn't anyone be worried about the intentions from unseen and unknown energies? Of the many experiences that I'd had, I honestly didn't receive them lightly, or in fun, or for the sake of "spiritual adventurism." My desire was for God, for the purity of my soul evolution. I wasn't interested in astral traveling, past life regressions, channeling, or any of the popular explorations. I was in it to transform myself into the highest expression of being, even if I didn't really know what that meant. Most of the other areas made me uneasy and very cautious. Witnessing Byron's reactions, however, evoked envy in me. He remained always trusting in God, rarely reactive to my or his otherworldly experiences with anything other than gratitude for the blessings. He had an innate faith and trust, while I had innate fear. This would take many triggers and peeling of layers to reveal the source, which resided not in this lifetime.

Yogananda, with great patience, love, and compassion, eventually helped me with the transition to allow Jesus into my energy field and then my heart. The vibration or frequency of Jesus's presence was subtle and gentle, yet strong and Light. What I found transpiring was a deep well of love and devotion for Jesus. There hadn't been such emotional outpouring in my spiritual journey thus far. I felt the smallness of myself as an innocent child with him. I couldn't help but be humbled and submerged in a deep well of reverence. This was the kindling of a fire that dated back to eternity, and I felt it on the soul level.

During one meditation, I was blessed with the experience of Jesus in my heart. The heart gently stretched, burned, and ached, to reveal Him within. A Love that was in no way a personal love, but the higher quality of Being Love, filled me. The Sacred Heart. I sat and cried tears of both joy and loss, from where I didn't know. But I felt like I had walked away from or closed my eyes to this love in some other time and place, and now I was being welcomed back into His majestic arms. As I came out of this meditative blessing, soul bellowed forth its devotion and joy: "When a symphony rises up from this heart to the Lord, how can I not let my being be moved?"

My entire being was filled with a lightness and tingling. The head and neck began to circle, the body slowly lulled with a gentle rocking motion, and I felt flooded with His divine Grace. I was rendered speechless. Empty.

My time with Yogananda lessened. It seemed that as soon as I was able to accept Jesus in my life and heart, He became my path. Just as I missed Gurudev with waves of melancholy, I also missed

Yogananda. Because I was still in the habit of perceiving these beings linearly, it felt very either–or, black-and-white, this path or that path. Even though I had received a teaching about this, the deep knowing had not integrated into my being.

34

Over the summer months, I continued to attend occasional services at Ananda, and Byron began attending service at a little Methodist church a few blocks away. He had taken his parents there during one of their visits and really liked it. The minister was liberal, and politically and socially oriented, which fit Byron's activist spirit. I went with him every so often, but for me, I craved a more internal worship style.

The body was signaling another transition at hand, and that concerned the pain that was accumulating in my right shoulder. The repetitive motion from cleaning was wearing out the rotator cuff, and I could see the end of this work not too far ahead. With perfect synchronicity, there were two invitations I received to teach private yoga sessions. Of primary concern: I wasn't a certified yoga instructor. The only people I'd led through hatha postures were my mother and another friend. This was casual, and there wasn't an expectation from them or from me to be any kind of teacher. Intuiting that the door was opening for a reason, I walked through.

While it was true I didn't have yoga teacher training under my belt, I did have the series of anatomy classes I'd taken the year before, some anatomy background from Jazzercise, which I taught in the early 1990s, and Nia. I had been studying a fabulously detailed book, *The Anatomy of Hatha Yoga*, by H. David Coulter. The hatha yoga taught at Ananda was coupled with the sequence from Gurudev and Bikram practices. Aware that none of this gave me the education of an instructor, but with my depth of body and energetic awareness, I felt comfortable saying yes to these specific requests. Neither person had any medical issues or injuries. I knew that was a whole other can of worms. This was a perfect opportunity to discover if I had a desire for a future in teaching.

Working with these two women ended up being markedly different from the previous sessions I had led with my mom and friend. In the time that had passed since then, much more intuitive interaction had taken place. My hands felt spontaneously drawn to soothe, relax, gently press on the muscles, and support the body during the session. Years earlier I had been involved with learning an amazingly nurturing method of bodywork, Breema. What seemed to be coming through me was very Breema-esque at times.

I had put together a gentle sequence, and the results for these women were quite moving. Both of them were going through stressful, emotional life transitions. Through the postures, the touch and support, they not only dropped into states of deep relaxation but also were able to release emotional energy they'd locked into areas of their bodies. From my own practice and energetic openings, I was able to intuitively sense where they were holding tensions or emotions in their physical form. I offered just the right support of release while postures automatically and intuitively moved through me. The process was meditative for them and me. Each time I spoke, the voice that came through to guide and soothe felt like an intimate stranger to me. My true voice was speaking forth, and I was starting to sense an aspect of my purpose. This purpose, I had an inkling, wasn't about teaching yoga, but what it was, was still hidden in the shadows.

A specific energy had become familiar over the last year or so, when abrupt change and transformations were at hand. My emotions would feel internally explosive and raucous, coupled with an actively restless energy. My whole body would become anxious and agitated. The first time I experienced this had been just before Caleb and I had decided to split up. At that time, I chose to sleep in the Love Room for a couple of nights in front of the altar. I called on Yogananda and prayed to God for assistance to be in His will. I felt I needed help. I felt something needed to "break down" so that I could get clear.

The morning after the second night, as I worked cleaning a client's home, I continued to pray out loud, asking to be shown God's will. There was a tangible blindness I was experiencing, something I wasn't seeing. Not literally blind without the sense of sight, but more like something that needed to be seen that I was unable to see or afraid to see. The inner tension around the blindness kept mounting, and an explosive force of emotion from inside was building. I felt scattered, one could say on the verge of hysteria, although I knew that wasn't accurate. The buildup of energy and angst, on the verge of losing control, was dependent on me to let it go, let it pour through.

As the tension and prayers increased, an emotional breakdown, or breakthrough, ripped through any control I thought I had over my life. I fell to the floor crying and sobbing. In those moments I saw clearly. I knew without a doubt that I was going to follow my spiritual path. The commitment was made in that flurry of sight, of soul's decision, and I knew it meant the end of Caleb and me. I called him in the midst of the breakdown, crying, admitting that I couldn't and wouldn't resist it any longer. My spiritual path, God, was my life journey. By the time I was finished cleaning, all the fears of loss rushed forward and an attempt to backpedal took place in my mind. But the veil had been torn. The truth was revealed. This was the clear seeing both of us needed to know we were no longer aligned in a romantic relationship.

My right shoulder was to be the second thrust of truth, and the showdown wasn't any more graceful. One of the most interesting things about these breaks was that they always occurred at the same client's home. The energy of this family, though awesome, was also fairly chaotic. So, in some ways this "house of chaos," was the perfect container for dismantling.

I was on the fast track to learning how to surrender to a benevolent destructive inner force. At the time I would have run for cover and been terrified by the identity of the inner teacher who dismantles and destroys what no longer serves the soul's evolution. Had I known that this aspect of the Hindu goddess was the one stepping forth from the many of Her energetic expressions, my caution would have sprung back into a roadblock. But alas, little did I know, since it wasn't time for me to face head-on one of the most frightening forces, even though She was instigating the demise of one life so that another could be born. Her grace is both fierce and loving, we understand once we know how to relate to Her power and presence. This the soul intimately knows: true surrender drops you to your knees, painfully casting out all that is false, while simultaneously filling the heart with blissful freedom.

I had glimpsed the gift I had to offer, yet I wasn't sure if it was to be accessed at this time. I wasn't sure if I *could* access it at this time. My body was definitely getting tired again, the shoulder was in pain, and it would only be a matter of time before I'd end up circling back around to caregiving. I was tiring of this cycle and wanted to move forward, but I wanted to do it with more presence than the previous attempts.

There was resistance to moving forward into an unknown direction. Thrown into the mix with this desire for forward movement was fear, confusion, and many layers of self-doubt. Again, I felt I couldn't see something that should have been clearly right in front of my face, but steps were being taken. The shoulder had begun to radiate a numbing pain down my arm over the course of a week or so. I didn't see how I could make a living teaching without the proper credentials, and I couldn't afford at that moment to undertake full-on teacher training. And besides, I didn't really feel called to teach mainstream yoga, as would be implied through committing to that kind of sizable investment. "I feel trapped." This was a feeling whispered from a distant place.

Our Southeast Portland basement apartment had a second room that we asked the landlord to use when Byron moved in, which we made into a large make-shift closet and Byron's space for writing. The altar was in the large main room, not too far from our bed. Privacy was undeniably out of the question, but I knew it was time to enter the sacred space of the altar for the night. I stretched out on the floor in surrender, seeking a higher guidance than my own.

I prayed to Jesus for the blindfold to be removed, to help me see beyond the veil of the karmic blocks and fears that seemed to be raging inside of me. And so for two nights I lay and prayed. I did my best to be a blank slate for God's purpose to be written upon. As if the symbolic blindfold had been waiting for the day of cleaning at the house of chaos, once I was there and in the zone, the illusions began to crumble. My fears of financial insecurity loomed with doom. It had taken awhile to get back on my feet after the initiation of this yogic path. It had taken awhile to merge myself back into the physical plane of self-sufficiency, and how did I know I could even be of service in the ways that were calling to me?

What the women I'd been working with were receiving was beyond the "exercise" of yoga, as would be seen in classes. But I had no way to articulate it or to promote it, nor the confidence to stand tall in what I was sensing to be moving through me. There were levels of insecurity, fears of being seen, of being judged, and old wounds from a little girl hearing in the background, "Who do you think you are?"

But the breakdown was on. I had full rein now and was clearly seeing both what was holding me back and what was whispering me forward. And the pain in the shoulder and arm intensified. This force was relentless. I was beginning to feel an unknown form of Divine Mother being ushered in. The stripping away of the false wasn't for the weak of heart, mind, or spirit. Soul reveled in this fierce presence I was experiencing. Sometimes soul had soft, subtle ways that could easily be overlooked or misunderstood, but nothing about this presence was meant to be misunderstood. This force had a name, a distinct mission, and purpose. The breakdowns were becoming familiar and trusted. She who breaks down the old would be known by name in the future, and I'd call on Her directly when I needed to die.

It was done. The decision was made. Just as before when I'd called Caleb, now I called Byron full of emotion and energy.

"I can't do this anymore. I'm done!" I cried.

"Okay, honey. I don't know exactly what's going on, but I trust you." Cool as a cucumber, he grounded me. "What are you done with?"

"I'm done cleaning. I don't know how I'm going to make a living, but my arm is letting me know, something has to give." I felt very dramatic next to his composure.

"Good. Let's figure it out when you get home. I think it's great!"

"Really? I think it feels scary," I replied.

"Well, it doesn't have to be. Let's discuss it when you get home."

The arm was finished working. I felt like the body was once again helping to guide me on my path. Later that evening in our discussion as to what would come next, we decided Byron would take over all the cleaning clients for me, and in my normal rush of inspiration, I made the most logical plan to move forward. I set a date that week to talk with my mother and propose to her a deal that would entail moving into her condo.

35

Byron, Urisk, and I were slated to move into my mother's condominium in North Portland by the end of March, the next month. We were responsible for a portion of the rent, and we would care for her cat, Ruby, and the house, since she spent most of her time at her boyfriend's home anyway. The condo was large enough for all of us on the rare occasion she was around. Byron and I had our own bedroom and bathroom. And I was able to use the empty third bedroom on the first floor as a meditation room and for sessions with clients.

I felt a sense of relief and forward movement. True to our own individual dynamics, Byron and I moved at very different paces. I had loved my apartment in Southeast Portland during the time I'd been there. It had served as a nourishing, grounding, and sacred environment. Urisk continued to blossom there, and we were each feeling a new sense of wholeness. It had been a cozy abode for Byron and me to become accustomed to living with one another, working out our space and energy dynamics.

I was ready to move on the instant I had the revelation of the next phase of transformation. Byron, on the other hand, liked to take things slower. Even though we had the option to move sooner, as we were in an informal house-share situation and the owners had a new tenant who would be happy to move in as soon as possible, he wanted to take the time to process the goodbye of the old and the hello of the new situation.

Having moved around all my life, I'm an uberefficient packer and mover. I'd traveled light most of my adult life; therefore, I can be out and into a new place, completely settled, in forty-eight hours or less. This was no different. Granted, more time could've been taken, but dragging it out felt stressful and scattered to me. I was thrilled to be moving and grateful for the support my mother was extending. Even though there were some perks for her, it was truly we who were reaping the many rewards. Urisk had lived there before, as we'd stayed at my mom's briefly in between leaving my and Caleb's home and finding this last one. The cats had been acquainted, which meant they would be fine once they had more time to settle in with one another. As for me, one of the highlights was to have the luxury of a bathtub again after this last period of time with only a stand-up shower. It didn't take me long to find my new groove.

Though I had been seeing the first two women privately in their homes, I was looking forward to seeing clients in the space I was creating at the new home. I had placed a simple ad in a small healing and health magazine for my private sessions. The first call I received was from a man in his mid-thirties, Thomas. I explained on the phone that although I utilized some hatha yoga postures, my process facilitated greater wholeness, self-awareness, and spiritual connection, rather than being a yoga class. Our time together began similarly to the other sessions. I had a gentle sequence and supported the openings and lengthening with touch and verbal cues.

Usually there were a couple of opening floor postures, then standing, then returning to floor. During his initial two or three sessions, we didn't move from the floor. He began releasing emotionally immediately. There was energy of wounding moving through him, releasing past trauma. I worked with him very intuitively. My hands were energetically drawn to just the right places to support whatever he was in need of in the moment. We worked with the principles I had learned from Gurudev. All of the inner guidance that had been given to me was now helping this man. I could hear myself reciting Gurudev's guidance. "Feel the sensations. Let go of labeling pain or pleasure. Don't resist, don't push, just allow the body to open. Stay connected to the sensations and the breath ..."

In the beginning, the sessions with Thomas lasted up to three hours. I allowed whatever time it took. I was fortunate to have space that felt safe and private, and not a full schedule, so I could be available for his process, rather than a constrictive time constraint. There were times he needed to be held while he cried, and other times he needed a pillow and throw blanket as he gathered himself together, integrating at the end of the sessions.

I felt so grateful for the time I'd spent in the conscious community of Naka Ima in the late 1990s. It was there we all learned together, as peers, as teachers, as guides, how to hold space for one another's healing process. It was completely unconventional; none of us were trained professionals, which I know makes some people uncomfortable. But what we found was that nine times out of ten, we can be supportive witnesses to another's unfolding, to another's emotional or mental breakthrough, which first tends to look only like breaks. We learned that we could listen and be present and aware of our own needs or someone else's and respond accordingly, which is a gift to all involved. We also learned that when support is available, we each have the inner strength, fortitude, and intuitive knowledge of how to heal. That community, with its intention for conscious awareness, personal growth, and spiritual growth, illustrated to me a new level of valuing myself and others.

Naka Ima was how I'd learned to live my life before I opened to yoga, and yoga was a catalyst to deepen those truths. This was how I lived in relationship with Caleb and what our healing work together had been. And now this consciousness was a part of my relationship with Byron. I was deeply moved and excited to see that it had evolved into being instrumental in allowing me to be truly of service to one in need of catharsis, without stories and dogma, and to help others.

As I suspected, the more Thomas cleared emotionally, the more grounded and centered he became. Before long we progressed to the standing postures. Though we were doing hatha yoga postures, I was clear that my intent was to guide his awareness inward to connect with the energetic wisdom of body and soul, to find inner alignment and peace. And those were part of the new awareness he gained.

Maybe a month into our work together, I began to see clear signs of what I sensed to be the awakening of Kundalini. I felt confused and was uncertain whether or not I wanted to proceed, whether it was in his best interests, and if I was the person for this. I talked with him about it, letting him know this was what I believed was happening, and saying he could decide whether he wanted to continue. I told him I couldn't guarantee what it would look like. He was intent on deepening the process.

He'd felt like his whole life had been changing since we began working together. He was feeling more whole, as well as closer to God. So we continued onward. Divine Mother, Kundalini, was predictable in Her initial areas of movement. We monitored Her strength and his personal experiences, with a focus on connection to God.

Moving into this new arena, I thought again about my past conversation with Marie. As I reflected on my responses, I saw it was easy to hold the more detached view when I wasn't the one feeling directly responsible, no matter how much of an illusion that was. I didn't feel a burden with either Byron's or Caleb's awakening. I felt those were spontaneous occurrences. And although they may have been influenced by being in my sphere of energy, the understanding I had formed was that it was because we were intimate partners. But now with the work with Thomas, I was feeling more watchful, curious, questioning and cautious.

During this same period of time, I received two other referrals, and a pattern began to emerge. The Kundalini energy was waking up in each person I worked with, within very short amounts of time. I wasn't clear whether they were guided to me because their Kundalini was already awakened and on an intuitive soul level they were drawn to me because they were on the verge of Kundalini surfacing, or whether this was happening *through* me.

In the big picture it didn't matter who, when, or why. This was what was being brought to my door. What I recognized was that I was able to assist the awakening to whatever degree each person was ready to accept. All of their experiences were individually unique and also shared some commonality. There were two primary principles I stressed, one of these being opening to their connection to God, Spirit, Source, whatever that power was for each of them, for that is ultimately the goal.

The second task of importance was developing intuition, which meant connecting to the voice of soul, their soul's song. It's that voice that I believe is in direct communication with Spirit, where the guidance we need shines forth.

The work coming through me became my teacher, along with those I worked with. I found that as I went deeper into my own heightened sensitivities and practice, the intuitive guidance that came through me strengthened. The work became two-tiered. Assistance was available to those who were in early stages of opening and healing their fragmented selves. I had the ability to intuitively tap into appropriate bodywork and energy points and to clear any residual energy of emotional release. The second tier was teaching them to hone the body's intuitive guidance, Kundalini.

Personally, of course, just as always, I encountered struggle and resistance. Though I felt truly aligned with what was coming through me, I also felt cautious. Dealing with things that couldn't be explained or seen was challenging not only because those with whom I was working weren't necessarily exposed to a subtler realm but also because I felt a sense of responsibility for those who came to me. The last thing I wanted was for anyone to go through what I had gone through. And I can say that in all of the years I've been doing this work, no one has. There was only one client who was opening up and surrendering with a sense of inner urgency that did usher in some times of imbalance. However, because of my own personal experience, I was able to make suggestions that supported a new level of harmony.

Resistance chaperoned every session I scheduled. Enthusiasm in the days before spiraled into sleepy heaviness the closer it got to the time of the session. Once the session began with a check-in, I would wake up and feel inspired to begin. My enthusiasm peaked throughout the session, yet my legs felt weighted and tense. By the time goodbyes were exchanged at the end of each session, new energy would be filling me, but my legs remained quite sore and achy, which I attributed to both my resistance and need for grounding. Being a vehicle for this work brought a sense of wholeness. It felt aligned and natural. I was grateful to be of service in this way and was always amazed at the intelligence that came through me.

This resistance went on for years. I learned not to take it seriously and eventually brought the light of consciousness to the underlying causes, stories, and fears that stagnated Spirit's flow with that undercurrent of heaviness. Karma brought itself to my attention as I witnessed the consistent themes and stories that threaded their way through my life, just as it speaks through all of our lives.

I will give one such example to illustrate just how inhibiting our past can be to our evolution.

The irony of being called to work with others spiritually meant I could no longer keep my spiritual inner life, my private secret life, separate from what was manifesting outwardly. This pushed my edge at every turn. I didn't speak to anyone outside of Byron or Caleb about this part of my life. And if anything needed to be said to others, it was always very cryptic and vague.

Interestingly, the actual light of my purpose, Spirit's presence, was my shadow. My resistance to this sacredness through me was a relationship requiring healing. The shame that wound around the legs, at the least, one could say, went back to choosing to incarnate in the care of atheist parents. However, there's little doubt it also stemmed back beyond this lifetime.

Many healers, mystics, and psychics have a sense that they were persecuted in past ages, perhaps even burned at the stake for witchcraft during the Inquisition. This leaves an unknown scar, laden with rooted fear that can be challenging to uproot. Especially if one isn't fortunate enough to have a memory, the invisible memory becomes a silent partner of blindness and inhibition. I had a sense that not only was I most likely persecuted, but also I may have caused harm by accident or through darker actions.

Regardless of what unknown lives I've lived and what took place, the present journey has been a long karmic road of healing, a chance to rise into the truth of this incarnation without apology or hiding. I can say that as these past energies cleared and the shadow found integration through deeper awareness, ease with my purpose became more fluid. And I'll also say that it's still in process. Even today, the little I, the ego self, is self-conscious about saying prayers in the presence of others.

Shadow aspects of our being are the key to coming into our wholeness. The shadows are those parts of ourselves that we judge, feel shame about, or dislike. They are the hurts and fears that we keep tucked away in internal closets, cracks and crevices, hoping no one, not even we, will see them. We ourselves do what we can to avoid them, and many of us succeed in ignoring and repressing these parts of ourselves. When the shadow is in charge, we are fragmented, unable to be authentic. The shadows are projected onto others and hidden out of fear of rejection. They often create angry or judgmental personalities. These are the aspects that are labeled bad, shameful, or wrong. We all struggle with shadow issues; however, the more light we can shed on them, the more compassion we cultivate for ourselves and others, and the more at peace we feel in our own skin.

My work continually grows and changes as I do. It hasn't been an easy road, nor has it been comfortable. But each step of the way, I take heed of the alignment, energy, and deeper learning, and I am sure that being of service in this way comes as natural to me as breathing. God moves me through the obstacles in this incarnation, and I submit, over and over and over, because that's what it takes.

36

Jesus filled my life during this period at my mother's. I had free time to study, practice, and see the several clients I was working with, and life had a spacious flow. Mary Magdalene had become a constant presence in mind and heart, for both Byron and me. I was intrigued by the many theories I read circling around her and her role in Jesus's ministry, with similar pagan rituals predating the time of Christ and having similarities to His and Magdalene's story.

I found I was amazed by her pervasive presence after her relocation to Europe. Her exaltation as a saint and illuminatrix again revealed the commonality between the path of yoga and Gnosticism. Upon finding that she was an illuminatrix, the knowing for me was that she was an initiator of Shaktipat, the spark to awaken the Kundalini or Holy Spirit. Under normal circumstances, some of the theories may have seemed far out. But with an experiential knowledge of "depth yoga," as my grand-guru called it, its science was applicable to many questions that I had regarding Jesus, Magdalene, and Christianity.

This first summer at my mother's, I'd been struggling with constipation. This wasn't a new issue, as I'd struggled with it most of my life. However, it was now becoming a greater concern. There were days on end when my bowels weren't showing any movement. It often helped to do an abdominal massage, but that was failing. The squatting position was also fruitless. My hydration was adequate, and the diet that had always helped to manage constipation was consistent. I could feel Divine Mother's energy focusing on the intestines, trying Her best to move things along during practice, yet nothing was proving of benefit. Particularly as I lay in Savasana, Divine Mother could be felt acting on the colon and intestines, and at one point I was able to experience, through the sensitization of the Mother, the rectum literally expand, releasing tension it had been holding! It never ceased to amaze me the depths to which the body carries constriction and stress.

I'd done quite well at not allowing reactivity to grab hold regarding the comings and goings of the body's seeming abnormalities. This, though, was starting to get to me. The midnight hours, when the energy of the night is the densest, were prime time for my consciousness to slip into the center of fear, anxiety, and doom-filled imagination. I woke up one night in that realm with stories of colon cancer taking over my mind. Years ago my grandmother had colon cancer. She and I were both Cancers, which are famous for having stomach/digestion issues, and we both had the habit of internalizing and personalizing the emotions of others. After nights of being assailed by fears of disease and death, I was becoming exhausted. On one such night, sweat was beginning to mist my skin. My heart was pounding in my head, and fear gripped me. I tossed and turned. I did my best to engage my breath consciously, so that it would deepen and slow its shallow, quickening pace. But the hamster was on its wheel, and the turning couldn't be interrupted. My thoughts were glued to doom.

The inner questioning began. *What am I afraid of?* I asked over and over, getting answers such as pain, surgery, expenses, and, *Oh my God! I'm going to die!* Ah, death! The great root of it all.

Death had been a great fear of mine most of my life, even though I'd never had anyone close to me die, nor did I lose my first grandparent until I was in my twenties. My initial death experience involved the first woman I did caregiving for. I loved her very much, and her death greatly changed my ability to be present to the feelings of loss surrounding it. But, as is the case for many of us, the fear of death continued to hold a powerful sway over my consciousness.

I'd always had a whispering belief that my death wasn't going to be from an accident or something outside of myself, but from some form of cancer. For a good part of my life, I couldn't even say the word *cancer*. I remember watching Shirley MacLaine and Debra Winger in the movie *Terms of Endearment*. There's a scene at the dinner table when the cancer conversation comes up, and everyone at the table whispers the word. I loved that and could so relate. That is the only movie that I had been able to watch that deals with that topic, and it was a kind of medicine to my fear. I wailed and I sobbed each time I saw it. Yes, I saw it numerous times. Debra Winger's character gave me a much desired strength, and at the same time, I was able to experience my feelings around the death of an illness from a safe distance.

This night, lying in bed, having escaped the hamster wheel just long enough to see the fear of death clearly, I succumbed to the fear. I stopped trying to run from it and felt the fear completely. I allowed the heart to race, the body to sweat, and the breath to be shallow and quick. The panic signaled clear and present danger. No more fighting it. I received it. Rolling from the protective fetal position onto my back, I opened my arms and heart and said, "Okay. I accept that if this is my fate, so be it." As the night moved toward morning, the hamster wheel had stilled and I rested in an acceptance of death. I had surrendered to it and to all the sensations that stirred panic in my body because of the fear.

There was no more panic; there was only peace. I had seen and experienced too much over these past couple of years to doubt that if that's what God had in store for me, I was in compliance with His or Her will, not my own. I called on Jesus, and indeed felt His gentle rays simply present, nothing more, nothing less. *There was an experience of freedom, especially a freedom from the torture and suffering caused by the mind.*

Not only by accepting death, the inevitable fate of all life-forms, but also by accepting what was present in that moment—not fighting it, but surrendering to all the energy of fear that was stirring—I had a clearer view that cancer was probably not the case at hand. But I had to accept it for what it was in order to quiet the inner noise, in order to gain a clearer perspective. These had been the teachings of Gurudev's. How powerful the teaching, and how grateful I was that his wisdom was still helping me.

I died into death's peace in the wee hours of the morning. I made an appointment to see the doctor, not out of fear, but because it was a logical next step, because I had done all I could do on my own. I was able to get in the next day and felt even more relief.

The doctor I usually saw was a primary doctor at the National College for Natural Medicine in Portland. I loved NCNM. I appreciated the students and the doctors. I felt well cared for. I felt confident in knowing that a number of minds, ideas, theories, and experiences went into helping whatever ailed their patients. I received a technique from the doctor that I could do myself to help the ongoing tendency toward constipation. With some special tricks of the trade, it didn't take long before the bowels were moving along appropriately. Well, appropriately for this body.

My last bout of constipation, though milder than the one that led me to NCNM, was just around the corner, and it brought with it some interesting synchronicities. Byron had gone back home to Indiana to visit his parents. While he was gone, I was enjoying the extra space.

What must be said as a part of the constipation issue, from an energetic perspective of the body, is that all illness is connected to the chakra system, our body's subtle energy system. For the short time I had been hearing about chakras, I interpreted them more as a helpful concept or diagram from which to gauge insight. However, when I began on this path of awakening, I learned from an experiential level that these energy centers are indeed literally centers of power and consciousness in the body. In a discussion one day with a client, Andrea, I attempted to explain this to her.

"When you talk about the chakras, you talk about their color, where they are in the body, and that they're centers for energy, but I'm not always sure I understand completely," Andrea stated. She too was suffering from some problems with her digestion and bowels.

"If it's too hard to take it all literal, that's okay. You'll learn more as you progress, but for now, let's keep it simple," I began. "You've seen the diagrams, I'm sure, of the colored circles, ranging from red and orange to purple, and oftentimes gold at the top of the vertical images."

"I have seen that at the yoga studio," she reflected.

"Great. These basic colors tend to be the norm, but they do fluctuate in some artwork. Right now that isn't important. What is of importance is that each center is like looking through a particular pair of glasses, so to speak, and each center is connected to various organs and systems in our physical body."

"What do you mean by 'looking through glasses'?" she asked.

"Well, in each center resides our consciousness. For instance, right now, you're having some life issues concerning a change in job and a new home of your own, and there's a struggle with your mom. Correct?" I asked Andrea.

"Right."

"On a most basic level, we could say that the grounding in your physical world is shifting and feels unstable. Does that feel accurate?"

"Definitely. It's really stressful right now," she added.

"Our grounding comes from the root chakra. It's usually depicted as the color red. It connects us to the earth and gives us a sense of stability."

"Which I don't have at the moment!" Andrea said with some emotion.

"Right! Not only does it connect you to a sense of security and stability, or in your case instability, since you're not particularly connected, but also it houses all of your thoughts, stories, ideas, and experiences relating to your feelings *about* stability and the like, including your feelings and views on family and community and even any ethnic, religious, or nationality belief. *These perceptions of these subjects are the glasses you see through.*" I was breaking it down as simply as I could.

"So considering giving up my business right now and moving into my new apartment by myself, and feeling stressed and insecure about the changes, is all being worked out in that red center, which is ..." She was positioning her hands to mirror the placement I'd shown her earlier, down at her crotch and the perineum.

"Exactly," I said, holding myself between the legs and telling her to press at the perineum, which is the skin between the anus and the vagina.

"And," she continued, "my mom's opinions about my choices are also here."

I shook my head, acknowledging *yes*. "Now let's take it one more step. We're going to add the other issues connected to all of this. You've been going through a breakup in which you feel your trust was betrayed. Correct?" I asked. She nodded, her eyes reflecting the surfacing of her sadness. "Which also affects how you feel about yourself, your self-esteem, and your own feelings of power in the world. Am I correct in how I've been hearing you?"

"Oh yeah. I guess I have a plateful."

"You do. So, not only is your root unstable, but also your relationship perceptions of betrayal, loss, and anger reside in your second chakra, the orange one." I began adding an expanded view as I rested my hand on her lower abdomen.

Andrea thought for a minute. "And your analogy is that the perceptions and all the feelings I have about my relationship are 'the glasses,' or the consciousness, or the perceptions I have regarding what I'm going through?"

"Yes. But the second chakra also includes energy about money, sexuality, and how safe you feel emotionally. All of this is up for you.

You're in the middle of big changes and some deep lessons. Let me just add one more level here." I could tell she was able to take it all in, so I continued. "Last but not the least, the self-esteem and self-empowerment aspects of your being? All of this is held in the third center. This energy center is usually seen as yellow. And don't forget, closing your business in order to pursue something new, well, that challenges your whole self-identity. Ego is going for a big ride now!" I laughed in excitement for the transformational period she was in.

"I'm not sure if I feel better or worse after looking at all of this in such detail," Andrea said, exasperated.

"It's okay. Because however you feel about it, it's going to change continually for a while. You're establishing a whole new way of being in the world right now. The consciousness in all of these centers is evolving, and you'll be wearing a new pair of glasses for each of them by the time you've made this shift."

"Wow. You make it sound so exciting, but I feel really overwhelmed," Andrea confided.

"Of course you do. Who wouldn't? Do you see why? 'Cause you're going through major growing pains. *The more conscious you can stay with it, the more ease you will find in the process.* And let me add, because these three centers in particular are going through big shifts, you should just take a minute and reflect on the problems you're experiencing with your body functions."

She sat quietly for a minute. I gave her space to soak it all in and explore a little deeper.

"I'm thinking about how crazy my digestion has felt lately and the constipation problem."

"Yep. The third chakra regulates your digestion; the second, your reproductive organs …"

Andrea interrupted excitedly, "And that's why my cycle has been more painful and sporadic!"

"Yes! Isn't it awesome when you can start putting all the pieces of the puzzle together?" I was excited too. I loved it when people really felt how big and important it is to be conscious and awake and to realize how we are energetic, physical, and spiritual beings. "And let me finish with two more things. One, your constipation is also connected to the first chakra. You may be unable to let go easily right now 'cause you don't feel like you have solid ground beneath you. Second, the soreness in your legs is no doubt another piece of that. Perhaps a clinging for safety and security, a need to use your physical body to compensate for the energetic shifting at the moment."

"I think I'm getting it. So what do we do now with all of this?" Andrea felt inspired and supported in this new understanding. Grounding was already beginning to establish itself.

For me personally, the constipation grabbed on once again as my personal identity continued to shift. I felt challenged in this growth. I wasn't having much luck even with the special technique I'd learned from the doctor. I knew I was in flux in the root center. There were subtle constrictions connected to creating a new foundation for myself. *Would I be able to do it?* I was as of yet unsure.

I was also noticing I wasn't feeling hungry at all, which wasn't usual for me. After a couple of days of not really wanting to eat and not having success in the bathroom, the body spoke loud and clear, craving a large salad and brown rice. That was it. So I obliged the guidance. Morning, noon, and night, I ate the salad and rice. The next day, I had a BM. This time came a new potentially alarming occurrence. The stool had blood in it. Not much, but it was noticeable. What in the past would have rung a whole choir of bells and whistles was met only with curiosity. I wasn't in any pain. The blood appeared one or two more times over the next couple of days that I could see. The body continued to want only brown rice and salad. And my bowels were moving better than ever. I trusted that whatever was happening was perfect. Perhaps there was a hemorrhoid? Perhaps something was clearing? I really didn't know, and I found it interesting how unattached I was. My past acute fears were presently abated. It wasn't that I didn't care or wanted to be irresponsible; it was that I really trusted that there was a greater wisdom at work, and I trusted *it*.

Two days after I'd found blood in my stool, I encountered some wonderful synchronicities. First, I picked up a local health and wellness magazine, and to my pleasant surprise I found an article about Mary Magdalene. In the magazine was an interview with a priest from a tradition I was completely unfamiliar with, the Essenes. I was enthralled with what I read and very excited to see that in the next couple of days I'd be able to attend their Sunday service. It turned out that this priest and priestess were from a spiritual community down south by Eugene, and they drove to Portland to provide a Sunday service and potluck once a month. They revered Jesus and Mary Magdalene, and taught that she was Jesus's primary disciple, wife, and co-teacher. After Jesus's death, she went on to begin her own order, through which she continued the line of Jesus's secret teachings.

I didn't know what to expect from the day. The service was really cool and quirky, and the priest was incredibly charismatic and funny. Though I had hoped to hear more about Jesus and Mary, the service was actually more of a lecture, encompassing esoteric teachings, quantum physics, and vegan / raw food diet. My mind felt like it was receiving downloads of information that I couldn't readily understand yet I could feel, viscerally, as truths registering in my body. The information felt more intellectual, but there were energies in connection to what was being shared that were alive and restructuring something in my mind and body. Personal experiences that previously I didn't have a way to explain were being revealed. The understanding and workings of Kundalini were also talked about, which felt reassuring. It had been quite a while (since I'd left Gurudev) since I had been in an environment where people discussed this intelligent life force energy, the life force of all that exists, in a way that I had known it and experienced it in my own life. I appreciated that they understood the Kundalini as a teacher in its own right. They were on the same path, more or less, and they understood the yogic component to Christianity, which lies in the mystical and esoteric teachings.

I was on cloud nine! I felt energized and inspired. The second synchronicity was that they believed in a raw food diet. I hadn't heard of raw foodists before this, nor did I understand the raw diet, but I was very curious. What I did understand was that my body, at that present time, had been guiding me more toward raw foods. It began with the salads and rice, which cleared the constipation. And in the last few days, my body's intuition was guiding me to more fruit and especially other vegetables. Raw. I wasn't necessarily eating them because I liked them. It felt boring, but it felt right, so I didn't question it. A state of wonderment embraced me.

The alignment and the perfection of the guidance I was receiving was undeniable. For days, my being was in a state of expansion, joy, and awe. In one word, I was high. My awareness felt wide open to higher vibrations. The heart was overflowing with love. And I felt the presence of Jesus regularly in meditation. Nighttime was filled with dreams that I couldn't quite remember, but they involved images of circles of people in white. These figures in white were both gathered around me, and I was also a member of the circle. I felt I was being given teachings, but I harbored no recollection of the knowledge upon waking.

The third synchronicity involved my friends Caroline and Sebastian. One day while visiting them, I was sharing about the food choices I was being called to and the Essene service, when Sebastian walked over to a bookshelf and handed me a book.

The Essene Gospel of Peace. I read the title. "Wow! So you're familiar with the Essenes?" I asked. "And what a book!" I exclaimed as I randomly read: "Happy are you when you come to know her and her kingdom; if you receive your Mother's angels and if you do her laws. I tell you truly, he who does these things shall never see disease. For the power of our Mother is above all." I skimmed as I turned a couple of pages. "Purify, therefore, the temple, that the Lord of the temple may dwell therein and occupy a place that is worthy of him."

I looked at Sebastian wide-eyed with excitement and gratitude. "Go ahead and take it," he said.

"Really? I can borrow it? I'm just in awe at the timing and how perfect this looks!" I exclaimed.

"It's yours! I want you to have it." He was beaming as much as I was.

"Thank you so much! I can't wait to read it!"

I devoured *The Essene Gospel of Peace* that afternoon and evening. As soon as I got home, I took it into the bathtub and began reading it, and I finished it while stretched out on the bed, facing west, soaking in the afternoon sun from our bedroom overlooking the Willamette River and the green hillside.

The book recited spiritual fasting teachings by Jesus. Fasting was supported by the aid of the Angels of the Earthly Mother and the Heavenly Father. As I read, my whole being felt softened and quieted with a peaceful presence. The read was soothing and resonant. I gained clarity on the religious concept of our body being a spiritual temple for Jesus, or Christ Consciousness, or Divine Presence to reside within. I saw that not only does Jesus live in our heart, but so does the presence of the Divine Mother, and what honors the body, honors them. The always evolving sacred path I was traveling made it certain that the body as a temple of God, which many may see as a metaphorical statement, is in fact a literal teaching. It's a teaching of embodiment, surrender, and reverence of the divine within.

Sources claim that in 1928 Edmond Bordeaux Szekely (pronounced "say-kay") first published his translation of *The Essene Gospel of Peace*. This ancient manuscript was discovered in the Secret Archives of the Vatican and "came to fruition as the result of limitless patience, faultless scholarship, and unerring intuition."

When Byron arrived home from Indiana, I was elated, high, vibrating at a higher frequency, and excited to share with him all that had happened in his absence. I was so excited for him to go to the Essene service with me at the end of the next month. I filled him in on some of what the service entailed and, more importantly, what I'd been finding in my research on the Essenes.

Byron was intrigued by what I was sharing about the Essenes, and we both were finding resonance. He was less excited about the food aspect. He appreciated my experience with the guidance around the food and constipation issue. He too was in awe of the intuitive movement toward raw food, followed by the synchronicity of the raw food teaching of this group. However, he made it clear that he was not in the least interested in exploring this diet for himself.

When Byron and I first met, he was a big eater. He ate anything and everything. He respected that I was a vegetarian, just as he respected that some of his closest friends in Portland were. That didn't, however, prevent him from getting into debates with others about his belief in eating meat. I rarely entered into those conversations. My diet transition to vegetarianism was something that happened overnight, after my sickness in 1996. It happened organically. No philosophy or dogma, no judgment or shame. It was only afterward that I began to study more about it or understand any ideology around it. For me it was a very personal transition, based on the guidance of this one's soul communication, which allowed a trust in that process for others.

In our relationship, it wasn't a big deal for me that Byron ate meat. In 2005, awareness was beginning to dawn on him that he had patterns of food addiction. As he became more aware and allowed himself to see these patterns, there were changes he was making. He began attending FA (Food Addicts Anonymous) meetings and was feeling less interest in meat.

When the end of the month arrived, off to the Essene Sunday service we went. I loved it. I was fed and nourished by every word. Byron found it interesting and felt a connection to what was said, but he felt overwhelmed by the lecture. He isn't as interested in a lecture format, with a lot of intense information, over a couple of hours' span of time. His temperament is very different from mine in that way. One of the best finds of the day, though, were some CDs that the priest was handing out. We heard a sample and were sold. The CDs were by a musician named Shimshai, and his music would be a catalyst for the spiritual deepening that Byron and I each would undergo.

August found us at our first National Essene Gathering at the community in Triangle Lake, the home of the Essene priest. The whole weekend was filled with eye-opening lectures on raw foods and the assistance it plays in one's spiritual awakening. The speakers ranged from doctors, to elders in the raw foods movement, to nutritionists, to those speaking from the wisdom of personal experience. The evenings were filled with uplifting, high-consciousness music, and Shimshai was one of the performers. Classes for yoga and meditation, herbalism, and essential oils were scattered through the weekend schedule, and the land that the community called its home was beautiful and serene. The entire menu of raw foods just amplified the vibration of the weekend. Though neither Byron nor I was quite ready to jump on the raw foods train, education was at hand, our eyes were opened wide, and our hearts were uplifted with gratitude that weekend.

There was something extraordinary about meeting people from all over the world and from different communities, leading many variations of alternative lifestyles, who were also followers of Jesus and Mary Magdalene. To recognize that to follow Jesus one didn't have to be a Christian felt liberating. And the fact that there were many followers of Mary Magdalene moved me at a core level. How could such a powerful, prominent, and revered woman such as she still be so in the closet in Christian teachings? Even so, I felt freed from many of the judgments or opinions I had about mainstream Christianity. I no longer felt trapped by being misunderstood or by potentially being seen as harboring some kind of rebellion whenever I spoke of Jesus and was asked if I was Christian, to which I'd always reply, "No." I wasn't sure how to explain it to people, and they didn't know what to do with it. There was mild confusion on both ends. This experience with the Essenes widened the scope of a previously narrow vision and brought forth a loving connection to these divine beings, without needing to be in the cultural box.

As par for the course, I stumbled upon the next phase of life's adventure not long after returning home from Triangle Lake. One day I happened upon a flyer of a teacher arriving from India who offered Kriya initiation. He would be coming in the fall to Breitenbush Hot Springs, in the Willamette National Forest. The event, a weekend-long retreat, included meditation and teachings from Sri M. Many teachers come and go, travelling into town, though with appreciation I don't feel the call to go see them. But then there are those in-the-moment sparks of soul that catch my attention, letting me know, *This way!* This flyer, Sri M, was such a spark.

The first weekend with Sri M was fabulous. One can't help but feel enlivened in the Cascades, held by the mountains, and steeped in the numerous hot springs. Sri M gave new-to-my-ears insightful teachings and offered a meditation technique in preparation for those interested in receiving Kriya.

Sri M also was connected to Babaji Krishna, like Yogananda was, but through another guru lineage. The Kriya initiation seemed to follow similar guidelines, although I couldn't be certain, since I opted out of pursuing it through Ananda. I really couldn't say why Sri M or the Kriya spoke to me at this time. I hadn't felt a call toward Kriya before. I could only assume that then it wasn't time and that now it was.

Returning home after the weekend, I was consistent with my new practice. I was never a highly disciplined practitioner, which I often felt guilty about. I was relatively consistent, meaning that I meditated and/or did my spontaneous posture practice, filled with the presence of Divine Mother, almost daily. However, the timing was not always the same. I tried to amend that as I began in this new direction. Immediately I was able to feel the impact of the new meditation, and it left me intrigued by how much stronger the Kriya was. I questioned if I'd be able to handle it. Initially, I felt ungrounded and spacey, and internally I felt a sense of quickened vibration. This made me feel cautious, but I relied on faith to hold me steady. Once I began to acclimate to the effects of this practice, though, I found that a deeper stabilization grew from it.

The practice left me highly present and in the moment. I could feel an impact on the mind, perhaps even the brain, but more so it was the inner state of quietude, clarity, and presence that was apparent. Witness consciousness was front and center. There was a similarity to the early days with Gurudev in that stories didn't hold much weight and the nonattached truth was easier to discern. I felt calm, loving but detached, and nonreactive.

I had been on a learning curve for the past three years. Each new wave of experience put me through my paces in the mind. There had been ebbs and flows, and with each ebb there was an underlying fear that I was losing touch with the forces teaching me. But karmically, and often comically, the flows often kicked out the resistance and the fear-based stories of ego, which left me feeling humbled as the neophyte that I was. Either aspect of this cycling ebb-and-flow current found me struggling in uncertainty, with only brief times of reprieve. By the gift of grace, eventually I experienced a deeper, more permanent shift. This was never by my own doing.

I always had questions: Was this new state because of the introduction to the pre-Kriya meditation? Was it that my consciousness had expanded to a new way of being? Was I simply becoming familiar with the subtle realms? Had there been sufficient karmic clearing that left me with a clearer, higher vision? Did I feel amply protected from whatever unnamed evil I feared lurked in the shadows? Was I realizing that anything I saw outside of me was truly only within me? Were my stories, ideas, and ego stances dislodged enough from the gross physical layer that an expanded freedom was at hand?

The questions could go on. I'd always been compelled to analyze. I wanted to know, to understand intellectually, what the ambiguity expressed through the experiential. But alas, this path was a complete mystery. I had theories and took to heart the teachings of our world's most respected spiritual teachers, both alive and deceased, and I sought out answers hidden in texts of the major traditions. Sometimes I found information that made sense. Sometimes I found nothing. Sometimes I stumbled upon information that was far beyond my scope of understanding, only to receive an experience that confirmed it later. Sometimes I found my experience to feel more valid and true than another's intellect. Eventually, the seeking dwindled as I realized that what I needed was truly within. As I grew into the right kind of vehicle to receive, I trusted I would continually know more deeply.

37

The time Byron and I were at my mother's created sufficient openness for new energies to be received. When my mother would pop by, or stay at her house every now and then, I imagined her to wonder if Byron and I ever really did anything. His perch was on the couch in the living room; mine was up in our bedroom. I had the few clients I worked with, and Byron had a couple of houses he still cleaned. Eventually, he let go of the houses and worked part time with adults with developmental disabilities. Still, we were home most all the time. We were both very internal, clearing, and spiritually filling. Our life was very much a mystery to those closest to us. We functioned appropriately and normally, yet we were never fully ourselves, particularly at that time, because we were both touched by Spirit's grace ongoing, in our own individual ways.

I feel that one of the things that made us such perfect vehicles at this time for connection was that we were not partaking much in the outside world. This isn't to say we were completely hermitic. We walked up to the movie theater in St. John's and had pizza occasionally. We enjoyed outings to Powell's Books, one of the world's most fabulous bookstores, and to our favorite spiritual bookstore, New Renaissance Books in Northwest Portland. And of course we went to the farmer's market and grocery shopping. I loved to go out to breakfast on the weekends.

Otherwise, we were loners, homebodies, and very much in our own world. The benefit this had to our state of being was relaxation, which supported the body to be open for higher energies. We weren't subject to the unending array of stimulus from traffic, crowds of people, and noise, or the distractions of running here and there. We weren't dissipating our energy in a scattered, unconscious fashion. We didn't watch TV or follow mainstream news. We disconnected from the cultural programming of going and doing as way of life. The excess of that, which is what our modern society encourages, depletes the life force energy and keeps us so highly stimulated and stressed that we disconnect and lose the ability to sense our true subtle essence or the subtle energies trying to commune with us. Byron and I did the best we could, based on what we knew, to keep our vibration high and to remain in states of communing with the divine.

I mastered beingness at this time. Though *it* had mastered *me* in the past, I like to think I remastered it at this time out of choice, rather than out of necessity because of imbalance. Our room looked out over the Willamette River, and we had a view of a beautiful hillside. The St. Johns Bridge, which I had an affinity for because of its essence, which I felt to be graceful and feminine, was also in view with the backdrop of an open large sky. As fall neared, the leaves changed colors across the river, amid the ever-present evergreens of the Pacific Northwest. Portland, having a shorter summer and lengthened seasons of clouds and rain, offered up stunning skies. I was content to lie back on the bed and gaze at them floating by.

Whether it be while be-ing in our room or be-ing in the bath, inspiration would pour into my awareness. The relaxed, nonstimulated, open, and receptive state I was in much of the time allowed me to connect deeply to my human form as vessel and vehicle for the will of the divine. Whether it be for new insights, for inspiration of topics to weave into my sessions, for writing, or for the qualities of divine Love and Compassion to fill this being, each opportunity offered an experiential lesson of embodiment, which supported a deeper knowing to thus guide my life with.

As I'd been feeling more connected to the energy of Mary Magdalene, I felt her teachings beginning to take form in my life. One example was shown to me one afternoon while I was resting in the bathtub. I could hear the sounds of construction work in the neighborhood off in the distance. Relaxing with my eyes closed, I was made more aware, by divine presence, of the thudding sound each time the machinery impacted Mother Earth. The repetitious impact of violence being forced onto the earth sickened me. My body, mind, and heart became receptors to the ways in which humankind rapes our Mother Earth. The many phallic instruments that plunder her surface rob her of her treasured life and discard her into ruin. The pain from the earth reached for and cried out to this one's heart. I could barely stand it as I saw and felt the ongoing assault on her without the batting of an eye by those perpetrating the assault, without the understanding that our earth holds consciousness, that she is alive, that her life offers life-giving nourishment and support. And we take complete advantage of that nourishment and support by attacking her mindlessly.

The sickness and heartache made me aware of *my lack of awareness*, just like the majority of our world population. I finally understood the passionate love and anger of those who hold this awareness, who fight for her preservation and are acting on her behalf. While I'd always been of this ilk philosophically, I was still ignorant of the depth of the damage and pain she experiences. This teaching exposed me to the pain, although limited, that she, the earth, goes through at humanity's ignorant hands. My perception was forever changed. I saw and felt the rape of the earth that occurs daily. For the first time I *knew* her as a living entity that experiences what we humans do to her. A veil had been lifted; my eyes had been blind, and now could see. To this day, it pains me when I witness her plunder for construction, for oil, for mining, for excessive building for "progress," etc. When we are given truths like this, they transform our consciousness. They come from a higher source, conveying knowledge that we are being asked to heed.

My relationship with both Jesus and Magdalene felt very alive and present. Jesus spoke to me at times, and I was blessed on two different occasions with what I can only call a ceremonial ritual. Again, this is a personal and intimate experience that is almost impossible to share. It also challenges many who are traditionally Christian minded. What I can say about the experiences, omitting the details, is that the impact and effect of this soul's devotion to the divine being of Jesus enabled my heart to be tenderized and sensitized to the harshness of our civilization. It also infused me with the deep compassion of Jesus's words, "Please forgive them, for they know not what they do."

It felt that to be able to tune into the higher frequencies of Jesus and Magdalene, my being couldn't be overstimulated by the denseness of the world. If that were the case, my ability to perceive the subtleties would be nil. My experiences with Magdalene tended to be primarily nature centered. On two occasions, I was guided to the outdoors.

One late afternoon after a session, I was just being in our room, watching the rainstorm outside. It was gray and dreary, and the rain was coming down fairly heavily. I began to feel Magdalene's presence, and my attention perked up at what was to follow. Mudras danced through my hands, and a gentle smile overtook my face. There was an impulse to go outside, but I could hardly make sense of that, and I didn't want to go out in the cold rain. And yet the guidance was insistent. In the mind, I was carrying on a one-sided conversation about not wanting to go outdoors, even though the prompt I was experiencing indicated that I was to do so. There was also the reality that I was receiving a blessing, so it didn't seem right to be giving the petty ego's comfort preferences so much control. And I knew that if I missed this, I'd feel guilty and unworthy of the love of Magdalene's presence. It was often hard for me to remember that was just my human projection of judgment, not the reality of the divine presence.

The next obstacle happened to be that my mother was home. Byron knew when I was with presence, and didn't interfere. I had overcome a substantial portion of self-consciousness and embarrassment about being seen in these highly personal and private states by him. My mother was another story. The shame began to rise. Fear of her stopping me to talk, in conjunction with what she would think if I were to go out into the rain like a madwoman, was a whole other issue. The impulse was strong, though. I knew I just needed to put the personality self on the back burner and focus on what was true. The guidance felt strong; it was almost a sense of urgency. As I came through the kitchen, my mom did attempt to converse. I felt odd, but I just moved silently through, with her voice echoing behind me as I exited the house, out into the rain.

She, the presence of Magdalene, took me to the park, which was less than a block away. The rain felt cleansing and healing. Whatever was being moved through brought tears and sobs wailing through me, merging with the wind and rain. I felt the forces of nature mirroring the inner and outer. The energy of Kundalini, Divine Mother, moved the body, and mudras danced the hands as I was brought down onto the wet and muddied earth. Weeps and wails of cries poured forth, connected to a mystery from a distant time and space. Bellows of laughter followed that were almost hysterical and out of control. There were moments of thinking, *Wow! I really do look like a madwoman.* The thought passed as quickly as it entered.

The ego was washed away in the next moment, as I felt complete connection to nature and a reveling in all its elements. At the point of my release from this unified state, I was lowered onto my knees in prayer position, filled with quietude, gratitude, humbleness, and peace. The rain fell, washing away that which I do not know. Grace held ego's embarrassment at bay, even upon my entering the house wet and muddied. I stripped off what I could at the door, and without a word I walked up to the third floor and ran a hot bath. There, in the nourishing waters, an extension of the primal water of the sacred feminine, I continued to receive the bliss-filled state that Magdalene's grace had left upon this soul. I bathed and received her song through my being:

"The Living Word is that flow like water. It moves in, through where the spaces allow; where there is no clinging or mind stuff. As it flows, it expands and forms new life and understanding within. This Living Word brings transformation and transmutation. But only if its ways of knowledge are followed, and the heart and mind remain open."

When gifted with these blessings as they first wafted into my life, I had a hope, a clinging that desired to forever remain in these states of wakefulness and clarity, completely present and unattached to the personality frivolities. The movie *Brother Sun, Sister Moon* tells a story of Saint Francis of Assisi, whereupon his awakening, he disassociates himself from family and community to devote himself to God. There is a scene where he is working devotedly on resurrecting the disheveled church in the country, and he is visited from his friends from town. He is clear, present, and completely unattached to the worldly charade. This is what I ached for.

Deep down, the longing for a complete surrender of his kind had not ceased to be embers burning in my heart since this journey began. With each ecstatic moment of connection comes the return to this mere human state of being. It is the place of integrating what has been shown, taking the actions and focusing the will to come into the divine will through personal effort. Thus far it hasn't been my karma to wake up in a flash of revelation, never to return to the me, the personality that I am. And yet, I still find that hope lingering when Spirit whisks me into the heights: *Maybe this time, I won't need to come back.*

38

Many traditions contain different dietary restrictions, at least at certain times of the year or for specific holy days. Interestingly, as both Byron and I have experienced our own unique process of waking, personal lessons of karmic knots, and ways in which we feel Soul/Spirit communicate with us, food has been a focal point for us both. It's when experience lines up, without personal intention or effort with religious testament, I feel a truth is being revealed. Byron's travels in this vein have been particularly revealing, as it sheds light on how often our personal pain and tribulation, becomes our salvation and purpose.

By the time we moved in at my mother's, Byron had already begun dealing with the reality of food addiction. I appreciated his reflections and that he shared some of his habits and secret behaviors with me. He had no obvious physical signs of over eating. He was a healthy male, nicely built, ate hefty portions, but was in no way over weight. It was the habits, the pre-occupation of mind regarding food, the second and third helpings, free food, and secret binging that weighed on him.

Though he had enough 'taken off his plate' with his new diet restrictions through Food Addicts Anonymous, there was a knowing growing inside of him that he was going to have to become a vegetarian. He didn't say much to me about this. He usually processes things internally and doesn't speak them out loud until he's ready to move in whatever direction he's been contemplating. Therefore when I began to shift my enthusiasm toward raw foods upon his return from visiting his parents, he felt overwhelmed. I did my best to offer support and harness my excitement. He had been a rock for me continually; I wanted to be able to be that for him.

39

Nye Beach on the Oregon coast had become our regular destination since we first started dating. I took Byron there for his birthday in October of 2003, just a few months after we met. We enjoyed the Nye Beach Inn right on the beach and wandering the streets of Newport. In 2005, we went once again for his birthday. This was to be a double celebration trip.

As we were walking along the beach the afternoon of his birthday, the wind blowing as it does all year, and bundled in our hats and coats, out of nowhere Byron introduced the subject of having a dog. I was surprised since he wasn't a pet type of guy.

"You know, I've been thinking that maybe in a few years I could be open to a puppy," he shared.

"Wow. That's great, since I can't imagine my life long term without a dog. But where did that come from?" I giggled.

"I just wanted you to know I'm warming up to the idea. I could maybe enjoy that."

"That's awesome! Of course I promised Urisk that he'll never have to share a house again with dogs, but after he's gone, I'll be ready!" I said with much enthusiasm.

"Well, it's gotta be the right timing," he said with a sense of backpedaling, but I knew it was just my excitement overwhelming him.

"Yeah! I'm so happy you're warming up to a pup ... or two!" I had a puppy clock ticking. Personally, I wasn't called to have children and had no desire to be a mother. And Byron felt the same way about fatherhood. But dogs—that was a whole other matter!

Dogs open my heart, pull me out of myself, bring out the rare childish part of my normally serious and intense personality. Not having children, I felt, kept me from the maturation rituals of parenthood and maybe some expressions of adulthood. Dogs would be a necessity in my life.

Byron had been setting the stage during our walk on the beach. Later that day, he asked me to marry him. There was no hesitation in knowing I wanted this union with him. Sacred union had called to me for years, and I felt that this was something we could share. I loved him in a very different way than I'd loved my previous partners. I loved not his potential but who he was, as he was. There was nothing that I felt needed to be different. His qualities of warmth, grounding, laughter, clarity, sentimentalism, and romanticism; his connection to God; his relationship with his parents; and his strengths and vulnerabilities were beautiful. I witnessed and reflected on these qualities with love and appreciation. Though we are on complete opposite ends of the spectrum in most things, there is an automatic balancing that happens between us. It didn't take us long to recognize the opposites in the other, yet we made room for them respectfully and saw the perfection of them.

I had stopped believing in marriage until Byron. Well, I should say, I wanted marriage in my twenties, but not long after I was sober, I saw how prone I was to a path of constant change. Personal growth, learning life lessons, and moving onto the next transformation only intensified in my thirties, and then the awakening process hit full bloom. I felt that to remain in a long-term relationship would require my partner to be able to embrace the spiritual cycles of death/rebirth in me and for themselves. And this is also what I loved about Byron.

He longed in his own way for awakening, consciousness, and God, and that became our foundation. I felt the longing for sacred union, which now actually had the opportunity to become a reality. There was an excitement in exploring what that really meant, and that exploration felt deep, satisfying, and enriching to us as we moved forward to create a sacred marriage.

Everyone was thrilled with the news. Ideas and planning for the following year became the focal point of many of our conversations to come. We all, being Byron, my mom, and I, discussed the prospect that he and I would remain there at the condo until after the wedding, at which point we'd see what each of our needs were.

From the time of saying yes to marriage, I felt many changes percolating in me. Winter ushered in feelings of vulnerability and the vague return of raw pink skin. I found myself taking refuge in Mary Magdalene. I rarely experienced her presence in the ways I experienced Jesus or Yogananda or Sri Yuktswar, or my gurus for that matter. My experience of her took the form of her revelations *given life within me.* Only a few times did I receive beautiful love-filled words of her wisdom.

Magdalene spoke to me on winter solstice, revealing her golden thread attached to Mother Nature. As she began to speak, I felt her presence on the left side of my head as I sat in meditation.

"You must reveal the truth, not only to yourself, but also in your life. The veils are unraveling. You must be strong and brave enough to look and see."

I felt sadness over the fact that I wasn't strong enough or able to see clearly. Apologies for letting them down leapt forth. I continued to feel like I was letting down the beings, who so lovingly guided me. Projection of my limited perspective or not, it always weighed heavy on my heart.

"We are aware of the labor and its pains. Do not put yourself in the fire unless it is for purification. Continue to see and know that we both reside within."

In quietude, as I sat humbled and in awe, she departed. Her ways were continuing to be made known on the subtle realm.

The remainder of the year was uneventful externally but rich and enlivened inwardly. Planning for the wedding brought a new excitement and more connection with my parents, for which I was grateful. My own deeper healing and seeing was enabling me to see and love them both more fully. We'd had a nice family Christmas holiday celebration, and ringing in the 2006 New Year was done while Byron and I slept. More time was available until mid-January, when clients returned to their routines again and made new resolutions.

I'd begun working for my dad, helping him around his house, cleaning and organizing. This was a time I valued and appreciated. There were some missing years for the two of us, and spending time together in this way allowed us to grow closer. It also gave me an opportunity to spend some time with my younger sister, who lived with my father part time. Her mother and our father were together after my parents separated. For many years, they didn't live in Portland, so whenever I got a moment or two to see her, it was a gift.

Whenever my brother and nephew came to town, they usually stayed at my dad's as well. His home was the gathering place. While none of us were particularly close, as I moved along my path I simply enjoyed whatever connection we all could have, rather than longing for something that wasn't. My nephew was a sweet, shy, quickly growing boy. And my brother was quite funny, with a quirky sense of humor. I experienced moments where my attachments to wanting more from our relationships would fling themselves into the free-spirited enjoyment, but I'd learned not to take this neediness I carried so seriously, and over time I was able to let go of it altogether.

Upon the return of spring in 2006, Magdalene's guidance continued to lead me into the outdoors. We, she and I, found a tree that seemed to be a favorite for us. It was in the park right by the house. After the first two times of being led there to witness the intricacy of veins in the leaves that were bathed in the summer sun, this became my be-ing place.

Awareness would float in and out as I stretched out on a blanket under the canopy of branches. Often I had my journal with me to make notations of clarity or guidance. Many of the knowings that fluttered in were messages from the heart. Some of them were painful; others, full of elation. The emphasis felt to be on transforming, clearing, and opening the heart center.

I began to experience days in which the heart opening had no protection. I recognized the intensity of the world's pain and suffering. It's no wonder we've been given a shield to buffer the intensity of the reality of the suffering of humanity. The awareness of it otherwise would be more than we could handle. This energetic information also helped me to understand how the hardening of the heart takes place. The pain of this world is often insufferable. The unending stream of stimulus and energetic information tumbling around us at any given time felt more palpable and overwhelming, particularly when I was in densely populated areas where I couldn't help but be in the energy fields of others. This ability to protect myself, automatically and unconsciously, from the onslaught of energy was stripped away from me, I felt. I wondered if this vulnerable state was what highly sensitive people or empaths endure through their lives, as I know they are able to feel much more than the average person. This is one reason why this segment of the population has difficulty in crowds, in the company of too many friends at once, in loud environments, or in the company of individuals who have a tendency toward anger or violence.

Most of us, however, have learned to shut this out as we grow up. We block things out and pick and choose what energies we let into our field. This statement is misleading. This process is a subconscious picking and choosing. And the quality of what we pick and choose is subjective in part to karma, which will influence the quality of environment, people, and situations we invite in.

During this period of time, I felt as though all my protection was pulled away from the heart so that I could experience the reality of pain and suffering. This was a personal and collective clearing process. Moments would arise in which the heart was in such pain with no apparent cause to point to. I couldn't stop crying. The heart space felt wide open and exposed and raw. There was an overwhelming sense of grief for all those who lashed out from their personal unhealed horror of what lives inside of them, then inflicted it on others. I felt isolation for the lonely, for those who felt overlooked and unloved. I felt sadness for the walking dead among us who look as if they have it together but have sold their souls in one way or another and became compliant in numbness.

Driving downtown to the farmer's market one Saturday morning, I felt as if the homeless people pulled my heart into their lives, and the pain was excruciating. A deep empathy and compassion for the homeless wasn't new for me, but normally there was a layer of protection that comes naturally when keeping a healthy emotional separation. This guard was no longer present, and it hurt badly. The drive felt chaotic and naked for me. It wasn't at all a comfort zone to have these experiences or meltdowns in front of anyone, even Byron. But there he was. He'd been witnessing these meltdowns more frequently, but this time there was no place for me to hide. And the beautiful man that he is, he simply held space, drove in silence, and waited for it to finish, holding me tenderly as we made our way through the market in the aftermath.

This always left me feeling completely emptied of mind. Silence, humility, and a deeper capacity to hold love was instilled. I could never tell exactly when it was going to begin. And after I was released from the force that opened my heart, it was as if the protective layer had been reestablished, though a new level of sensitivity remained. The feelings, the overpowering emotions, I couldn't excavate to that degree of my own accord, even if I went inside searching for them or had an intention to evoke them. But the knowing left me silent and humble and bearing true compassion.

I've talked with others who have had these expansive experiences, and something that's common and important to say is that these experiences sound personal, but in fact there is a very impersonal element to them. This goes for most of the blessings, which to me is what they are, given via visceral experiences. There is little remaining of the ego/personality at these times. Of course it is present, but the way I feel it, it's sitting in the corner in the back of the room, behaving itself by being quiet. It might make a stir in those moments when the mind wishes to protest based on some pop-up story of the personality. There is a choice at hand in those moments. One may remain centered in the emptiness and remain in a nonreactive state, which allows the thought to fade away so that the state of grace may continue. The other choice is to allow that stir to become a rumble and to focus attention on the voice of ego, at which point, most likely, the divine will let go and allow ego its stage.

When ego/personality is set aside, there is a surrendering that is occurring within, to the presence of the divine. I am no longer me—this personality, daughter, wife, or any other labeled character trait. The I becomes only a vessel for what is being received. There is an emptiness of the personality and only an aspect of consciousness that watches, that witnesses. It's almost impossible for ego to be fully present and allow the divine presence to enter in, because in essence, with each experience there is a death or purification that is happening to ego/personality. Every instance evokes a humbleness because none of this is of the doing of the experiencer.

My dad lived over in the West Hills. My route to his house was over the hills, scenic, and into the country. Nearer to his house, the area was more populated, but not horribly so. The main road was two lanes, and rarely was traffic congested. Driving on that main road, getting closer to his house, one day, I witnessed a guy in a truck two cars ahead of me hit a grown deer. The person in the car in front of me slammed on his brakes, as did I. Then I jumped out of the car. The driver who hit the deer had sped off after the point of impact.

All traffic had come to a halt. Kneeling down next to the deer, my heart was breaking. His eyes were staring, his breathing was uneven, and anger rose in me. I wanted to be praying for this creature as I heard someone calling for help, but instead my mind was filled with rage. I was angry at the person who had hit this deer and then run away. I was angry at "progress" for usurping all the land, forcing animals out into vulnerable and unsafe territory. I was angry at the hard hearts of those who were frustrated that they couldn't get to where they were going because this animal was in the road. The internal tirade was my own toxicity as well, my own ignorance being projected outward.

Magically, in the midst of the tirade, I received a blessing of deer medicine and also the presence of Magdalene. An altered sense of sight was the first thing that caught my attention. Everything around me seemed to become soft. Next, looking into the deer's eyes, seeing the detail of his lashes, my heart emptied of its anger. It was interesting because I could feel ego wanting to hang onto the anger, feeling justified in all the wrongs that were at hand. Yet the emptying prevailed, and softness filled my heart. I felt the message of compassion coming through. The deer wasn't angry; he was saddened by the ignorance. Not for himself, but for us, humanity. We were truly victims of our own blindness. I felt like I was lifted in a bubble of gentleness and forgiveness. I felt the fear and sadness that the person who had hit this beautiful defenseless creature must have felt. I loved. I looked around at the chaos of traffic, this deer in the middle of the road, and myself holding his large head and crying at the dichotomy of horror and grace. We were all contained in the same space, existing simultaneously, yet in very different realities

Finally a police officer was able to make his way through the lines of cars. I could see sadness in his eyes, confusion, as he asked what needed to be done. The deer was fading. There was no way of knowing whether he was in pain or not. The officer said he was going to shoot him. He didn't have a choice. People were gathering.

And I saw in their eyes a sorrow. I said a last prayer. I thanked the deer for its blessing.

I was able to make my way through a circular driveway, sobbing as I left, to witness the man who had hit the deer returning to the scene. As we passed each other, he looked horrified and grievous. I heard the gun sound. I was no longer angry. Compassion welled up in me, as that man would be the one living with this death on his conscience. The bubble carried me to my father's, and I was thankful he wasn't home. I felt the urge to send prayers to all who were there, and I trusted that the deer, this teacher of compassion, would move on elegantly. I put Shimshai into the CD player, and I cried, grieved, and prayed as I cleaned.

Native Americans living closely to nature know the qualities and energies of nature's creatures. They understand the wisdom of their medicines and the ways in which the animals can guide, teach, and, yes, bless those of us who pay attention. The gifts I was given that day, the compassion and forgiveness and unconditional love, are indeed the medicine of deer. Before this event, I had attributed the totems and medicine to dreams, and occasionally to animals crossing my path. But this was an experience of an animal, again I say, literally imparting this knowledge, this blessing.

I say "again" because I feel it's important to realize the world is made up of unending subtle layers. If we fail to realize that our symbols, our archetypes, the forces of nature, and creatures all carry consciousness and the ability to interact with our consciousness, we miss out on the expressions of God, Goddess, Great Spirit. This connection happens beyond physical science, beyond rational mind, and outside of our control. The world and our very beings are vast and expansive mysteries that we have the honor and birthright to encounter.

40

As my and Byron's wedding approached, my connection to Magdalene's energy became more prevalent. My heart chakra continued to expand, accompanied by continued purifications of that center's consciousness. Although my mother and I had been living together with some of our hard patches behind us, there remained a protective layer for me. There were still many areas in which I felt misunderstood or unseen. And while my attachments to having those needs met had lessened, there was a lingering of distance and deep sadness. The little self often had difficulty remaining in the truth of perfection known by the higher self. I missed the old relationship that my mother and I shared before the gap of awakening. As for my father, I felt more clarity and grounding. I felt like I had been able to release much of what I had carried over the years, and I appreciated the new relationship we'd had the opportunity to develop as of late.

Our spending time together while planning the big day, drew us all closer together. There was an armor being stripped away and a new vulnerability being born within me throughout the year of planning my and Byron's wedding. I felt an unconditional love growing more present in me, which also *enabled me to fully receive that my parents did in fact love me.*

In relation to my parents, I began to let them off the hook for all I'd perceived was lacking in the past. There was a new lesson unfolding, and that was one of receptivity. It started to become clear to me that the blotches of smudge on my perception made it challenging to discern clearly what was true in the parental dynamics. More and more, I saw it was an inside job. Granted, my parents may have had shortcomings. What parents don't make mistakes? This is normal. More importantly, though, I was recognizing they had done the best they could. I was grateful to them as parents and I began to feel how much they loved me. Once that was taken to heart, along with the understanding of karmic perfection, I set them free, and I was set free.

My heart opened to their enthusiasm, their happiness for me, and their desire to be helpful and involved in this sacred event. It became more evident to me the specific ways in which I had trouble receiving their love. *Because I couldn't receive it* in the past, I believed in the story that had been created, that the love wasn't present. One of the gifts of our wedding preparations together was that I had ample opportunity to really *see* and *feel* their love. When I was able to take that in, receive it, the relationships were transformed. Though the openings were in stilted stops and starts, thanks to my own feelings of worthiness or guilt, the process of healing had begun.

In the weeks leading up to our wedding day, I was internal and reclusive, held by divine presence in periods of ecstasy. These states made it difficult to participate in the decision-making and planning for the event. During these inward periods, I tended to have a strong sense of detachment from the external life and others. The periods called for doing as little as possible and particularly having minimal interaction with others. In the very early stages of waking up when I first encountered this kind of detachment, it felt like numbness. I felt unloving, unsentimental, and uncaring. This had frightened me then. *As time went on, I recognized it as a taming or temporarily cutting off of the habitual patterns of personality, and experience taught me it would pass.* Usually when I returned, personality and all, I discovered less reactivity and more clarity. Less judgment and more compassion. Fewer uncontrolled stories and a better ability to discern. Less distraction and more presence.

The task at hand for the summer festivities was to monitor my energy and come out to function in ways needed for our sacred day, but also to reserve the inward time. Only Byron really understood this dance, and he did as much as possible to stand in for me if needed.

41

After my first serious romantic relationship, my first love at seventeen years, I'll be the first to say that my choices weren't always the healthiest. My romantic partnerships were reflections of my emotional/mental health. Once I got sober, and then after I began to awaken, I became healthier, and so did the men I attracted into my life. Subconsciously, I had chosen men who were unavailable for the long term: drug addicts, alcoholics like me, or those I knew I couldn't be with long term or vice versa. The last two relationships prior to Byron were wonderful, but still the long term wasn't an option. Jace was much too afraid of change and found my processes drastic and overwhelming. And Caleb, who evolved just as rapidly, had his own direction calling to him.

Then came Byron. His availability and desire for marriage brought me face-to-face with my own fears of commitment. These were fears I wasn't aware of, since I'd always been able to point a finger away from myself when it came to discerning the reason any given relationship had ended. Today, I still stand by those choices. Those relationships weren't truly in the cards, although they were integral to the journey. However, the pattern had never enabled me to see my fears very clearly.

The inner turmoil I found rearing its head as a sacred vow was nearing roared stories of being trapped. *What if we have different wants and I can't do what I need to do to grow? What if we both grow in different directions and we've made this life commitment?* In the past, I was a leaver. My first love left me, and I vowed subconsciously to avoid that feeling of rejection again. I always was clear I could leave at any time. If things got bad, if I was more unhappy than happy, I'd leave. When I'd had enough of the drinking, the drugs, the lies, and the distrust, I knew I could get up and go in order to take care of myself quickly. Even though I'd been married before, we were both in our early twenties, just kids, so it didn't hold the permanence that I faced at this time. The impending marriage made it feel more complicated, and I felt hemmed in.

I felt blessed to be able to process these fears with Byron. Once I had spoken them out loud, I was able to see the humor and irony. I knew I had so much to learn in a marriage—in a marriage to the right person. It was time to learn about long-term commitment, healthy sacrifice and compromise out of love, the growth that blooms from challenges, and creating a bond on the ideals and spiritual beliefs we both shared. Even as commitment fears crept up as the wedding neared, I remained conscious with them and felt them in the same way I worked with all of life. Never did they to any degree threaten my moving forward. It was a simple task of witnessing the dying of the old to bring in the new.

By the time of our wedding, August 20, 2006, we were both ready to step into our future hand in hand. The wedding itself was at my uncle and aunt's, south of the city in the country. My aunt and uncle had extended the generosity of their beautiful home, surrounded by green lawns, outlying green fields, and a gentle creek shaded with lush willow and oak trees. They graciously tended the gardens and the grounds, creating an inviting and peaceful environment for this special day. We had all planned together the details of the day, but my family carried out all the work involved with love. My mother created such lovely displays of beautification. My father made sure all the guests had what was needed, running to the store to ensure no one lacked.

The weather was perfect, warm and sunny. Byron and I created the music for the entire day, setting the tone and mood. Our guests were primarily family and close friends. Some of Byron's college friends made the trip to Portland, as had his family members. On my side of the family, my beloved grandmother and most of my aunts, uncles, and cousins attended. My biological father, Jim, my namesake, and stepmother came from back east. This was to be the first time since I was three years old that my fathers were under the same canopy. There were awkward feelings on my part at times, but ultimately it was wonderful to have them both present for this milestone event.

Tim, the minister at the little church in Southeast Portland, officiated the ceremony. We trusted he would be able to hold the space we intended. By our sides for the ceremony were my sister, Loren; Byron's sister, Emily; my closest friends, Sandra and Caroline; and Byron's best friend, Connor. Caleb played a beautiful song he'd written as we entered the circle of the ceremony. I wanted my brother Sam to be a part of the ceremony and invited him to play his harmonica, but he had opted out. All of the flowers were stunning, prepared by Fiona. And the vibrancy of green life was everywhere, the trees, the grass, the fields. So much life, light, and love that day.

For the year leading up to our wedding day, the colors green and pink were permeating my life. It became another living testament to the actuality of chakra energies. I had appreciated neither green nor pink prior. As a matter of fact, I was rather repelled by both of these colors. Green is most commonly known as the color for the heart chakra, and pink radiates the compassion of the heart. Because of their manifestation and the fondness growing in me toward these colors, and the healing at hand, it was clear that the energy of Divine Mother was purifying this center.

The initial turning point in feeling a resonance with the vibrations of these colors came upon me one day while just being. I'd been drawn spontaneously into a yoga nidra state, and Magdalene's presence was with me. She said, "Shed tears of joy, not of sorrow, for you are being called. Let the tears flow, and allow them to help you see clear. Wash away the world, and bring in new sight. You are not lost but preparing to be found. The beauty you hear through my voice is also in your voice, holding us as one."

It was following these words that my inner vision was flowering with pink. The heart was soft and expansive. Grace was flowing. In the past, pink felt too soft, vulnerable, girly, sissy, feminine. I had repelled the color, just as I'd avoided as best I could those qualities of being. Yet in the year of marriage preparation, accompanied by Magdalene's teachings, the hardness of heart was softening, being filled with compassionate qualities of the divine feminine.

Green was seeping into my life very cleverly. My eyes were overtaken with more moments of the enlivened greens of nature, with Mary Magdalene's guidance to be under the trees. The vibrancy of all the green that would embrace me and Byron called to us when we chose the space for our wedding. Before I knew it, green was the color we chose to accent my wedding dress. I had fallen in love with green! As my heart continued to soften, to open, and to love, pink and green filled my heart.

While the outer wedding day was perfect, a certain amount of intention went into creating what this day was for Byron and me spiritually, in the inner realm of our union. Together, we called in the Christ Consciousness and the Light of Divine Love. In support of this intention, we were honored to have Shimshai and MJ Green

Mountain, whom we were first introduced to by the Essenes, as the musicians for the night. We wanted their music to speak to our guests, to their hearts, so they could feel the presence of the divine.

For us, this wasn't as much of a party as it was a devotional celebration, of our union not only with each other but also with the Divine. We wanted to invite the sacred qualities of peace, love, divine presence, and joy to touch those who shared this day with us. And to our joy, people were touched by the spirit of the sacred. We had many people, friends and family, express how it was 'the most beautiful and peaceful wedding they'd experienced.' They said that they'd 'felt moved at a soul level.' Some, who hadn't really known the direction our lives had taken, were surprised at how spiritual the wedding was, which made it feel even more special. We were so happy that people we loved had been touched by something beyond us, illuminating this force alive in their lives as well. The best testament to the day was that of my thirteen-year-old younger sister, Loren: "I'm so in love with everyone and everything here today!" And that was our sentiment as well, in love, in gratitude, in spirit.

42

Our honeymoon took us to Northern California and Santa Cruz. My dad generously wanted to send us somewhere more exotic, but we really just wanted something simple and relaxing. We drove down the coast and felt completely absorbed by the radiance of Northern California. As soon as we crossed over into the redwoods, we felt surrounded by magic and a vibration that lifted our consciousness.

We were both feeling the need to change our diets, although that would be different for each of us. We were using the honeymoon as a time of enjoying the send-off of old habits by indulging. Splurging on food was high on the list, along with exploring beaches, enjoying some coffee shops and bookstores in Santa Cruz, and loving the places we were temporarily calling home.

The third night, once I was all tucked in for sleep, I became vaguely aware that we were surrounded by those guiding and teaching us. As usual, I wanted to know who was with us and tried to explore the vibrations more consciously. Instead, I simply opened my heart and heard the message: "Remove the mind, and let go of creating division. Allow unity to be present." I drifted off to sleep held like a baby.

Upon our return home to Portland, newly married and wedding planning complete, we were open to what the Universe had in store for us next. There was a sense it was time for some changes. We just weren't clear exactly what those would look like, and neither of us were feeling a pull in any specific direction.

Byron attended an evening lecture at Powell's the second day after settling back into home life. As he walked into the bedroom when he arrived home, it was clear he was in the midst of a clearing.

"Are you okay?" I asked.

"I had to leave early. I've got so much energy moving right now." He collapsed on the floor and allowed the spontaneous movements to flow. They were quick and sharp, with his hands creating many mudras.

"I'm going to give you some privacy, sweetie. I'll be downstairs."

"No. Stay," he insisted.

"Okay."

I sat myself across the room on the bed and entered into meditation, giving him privacy, yet providing the support of my staying present. An hour later, he was still in the throes of Divine Mother. Two hours later, the intensity of the spontaneous kriya movements had calmed. However, he was still clearing. This wasn't his first experience of Divine Mother's insistent presence, but it was his first intense clearing thus far. I felt nervous and did my best not to project my fears onto him and his experience and not to interfere in any way.

In the slowing of the kriyas, he got undressed and climbed into bed. The mudras continued. Through the night he developed a fever, and all the while Divine Mother was holding him in Her grasp. Off and on, he was emitting sounds similar to those of animals. Grunts, snorts, and squeaks could be discerned. In the aftermath he shared that he had been karmically experiencing himself as these animals. Through the night I placed rags under his neck as his body was burning up. By morning when I found a thermometer, his temperature was 102.2°F. I called my mother, who told me where she kept aspirin. Once the aspirin took effect, the sweats began.

For the next twenty-four hours, I changed the sheets numerous times, gave Byron sips of fluid, and made sure his temperature was managed. All the while, he surrendered to the ways of Divine Mother's purifications. Neither of us slept. He was in and out of different states of consciousness, and I was keeping watch and taking care of the basic needs.

Byron surfaced a little more than a week later from the worse phase of the purification. While the intensity had calmed after two days, he had remained bedridden with an off-and-on fever above 100°F. A transformation had occurred, and when he came back to normal consciousness, he was a committed vegan. He'd planned on easing into veganism more gradually. Nope, no taking his time. Straight to veganism. He was given the experience of being a variety of animals, feeling what they feel. For instance, he'd had the experience of being a cow. In this state, he felt the profound gentleness and love of that being. In the presence of Jesus, he was also shown that he had enacted the killing of animals, and felt the intense grief of those acts. He was told that his habits of eating animals and his attachments to his diet were inhibiting his spiritual progress, as well as holding up the work he needed to do in the world. This was both a death for him and a rebirth.

Surrendering to a greater will sometimes requires walking in the fire. The purification he found, abiding by the will of the divine force, brings sacrifice. But truly the sacrifice is that of those things that ego desires to cling to, which often keep us trapped in darkness, separated from our inner light and truth.

This transformation was timely in that I'd been feeling more and more called toward a raw foods diet. Byron's parents had bought me a book for my birthday, just a couple of months earlier, which was inspiring and uplifting me. The author is a renowned teacher, doctor, and elder in the raw food movement, Gabriel Cousens. His book *Spiritual Nutrition: Six Foundations for Spiritual Life and the Awakening of Kundalini* was a treasure trove of learning on many levels.

After I received the gift of Dr. Cousens's book, learning he too was an Essene, I felt a full-bodied charge of *yes!* Exploring his website was sparking inspiration. He founded the Tree of Life Rejuvenation Center in Arizona. As I read about the Tree of Life, a live/raw food healing and wellness center and Essene community, I could feel the heartstrings tug. Dr. Cousens also unified the Essene tradition with the Native American Lakota tradition and had been a disciple of Swami Muktananda for over twenty years. And he was empowered to give Shaktipat initiation. I appreciated so much the honoring of the multiple traditions because I felt I too was learning that the core spiritual truths were held in all traditions.

The day I was enjoying all the research on Dr. Cousens and the Tree of Life, Byron arrived home from work to my overwhelming excitement.

"This is where we should go!" I expressed as soon as he walked in the door.

"That's not going to happen anytime soon." His look said it all. In other words, *Don't even go here.* He was still in the beginning stage of making the transition to veganism.

"But remember all that amazing information we learned at the Essene gathering? The raw diet is powerful. Just check out the website. They have work/Seva programs. They hold a Lakota Sun Dance ceremony, and he does Shaktipat."

"I'm interested in learning more, but not now and not by immersing myself in a community of raw foodists." He was holding his breath. "You're overwhelming me. I don't want to look at that now."

When I felt new awareness that spoke to the soul, it was easy for me to get completely swept away. This often overwhelmed my beloved. It was a two-way street with me learning to temper my flow of energy and respecting his threshold. When I allowed it, he was like a grounding rod for me. Byron, on the other hand, had to learn how to allow my enthusiasm to bring more spontaneity to his energy and let me know when he was at the threshold. Even though I could often see the signs in his breathing and the coloring around his eyes, it was sometimes still challenging for me to rein my energy in.

As we moved forward, we found a nice balance as to how to accommodate each other and take care of ourselves in the diet arena. Once Byron cleansed and became vegan, I addressed the Tree of Life again. However, he still wasn't ready to begin on the raw food path. It was important for me to respect that he was mourning the loss of his relationship with food—its associations, its comforts, and the joy food brought him. It was a whole new ballpark he was playing in, and it took time to adjust.

After his spiritual clearing, Byron's area of study shifted dramatically from the political arena to the daunting issues of veganism. Not just the health ramifications of meat eating, but also the horrors of the meat industry, the cruelty to animals, and the politics of corporations vested in a culture of meat and dairy consumption.

Being a vegetarian, I didn't find it too difficult to make the switch to veganism, although it didn't happen right away. The education that he was gaining, I too wanted to learn about. Yet the statistics and cases of animal cruelty were too harsh for me to hear. With only snippets of eye-opening and heart-wrenching information, though, I too was a vegan within a month or so.

43

Straddling Byron's deeper shifts, I was experiencing new levels of awareness, and teachings were being given to me to continually move me forward. The night after Byron stabilized from his divine purification, my night was filled with intense and visceral dreams.

I was walking home from somewhere, and I looked to see a man climbing a huge water tower. It was odd that the huge tower was trembling with his minute amount of weight, I thought. The trembling soon became a quake, and the monstrous water tower slowly came crashing to the ground. It was a sight that challenged the mind. There were people around, but we all stayed, gathering together.

Just at this moment, there was a group of dogs on a sidewalk, which was quite cold, and snow was carpeting the walkway. The dogs were freezing and dying from the cold, and they were being adopted out for care. A number of us began to move the dogs into a building, where it was warmer.

The next thing I knew, I was standing with a couple of other women, relatively young, and one began talking: "Jesus had come to me and washed me clean, but He had to come a second time."

She was wild-eyed and trembling. She and I looked into each other's eyes intensely, and I felt compelled to make a mark like a star next to her left eye. There was some relief in our connection, relief that we both understood something. Our bodies began trembling and shaking, and we clung to each other, holding on to one another so as not to fall from the shaking.

As we held each other, I felt myself drifting into meditation. Automatically, I felt self-consciousness rush in. I pulled myself awake and away from her, feeling bewildered. All of a sudden, people were running and screaming everywhere.

We looked up into the sky, and there were laser-like lights slashing through the clouds. As the clouds parted, the sky was filled with a shimmery, vibrant, soft, pinkish-melon color. Small clouds of this color were forming and were bunching together, almost like bunches of roses. They were perfect pink roses filling the sky. Everyone was mesmerized.

Then the sky parted again. This time the sky was filled with swarms of angels flying all over above us. Their wings were white and electric-blue. Cherubs, maybe? The sky had captivated the crowd's attention, but then chaos broke out. It was as if there was a war in the skies above us. But the colors were so beautiful and hypnotizing. People started running everywhere. They were covering their eyes, tripping over one another.

The sky continued to show visions. Inside of me a panic was growing. I knew this was it. Fear and heartbreak overtook me. Byron wasn't with me. I wouldn't see my family again. I felt compelled to go look for them, for Byron. I was scared without him. I couldn't look at the sky anymore. The mind couldn't handle it. It was like the mind would break if I looked. I felt the impulse to sit down in prayer and meditation. I was torn: find Byron, or let go within? There was a sense that if I sat down and entered into a meditative state, the mind wouldn't feel the pressure and instead would know the truth that all that was happening on the material plane wasn't real.

I woke up with a start, waking Byron, my heart racing, I was sobbing, and Divine Mother was moving my body in convulsive movements. Something deep was taking place. It was beyond my understanding, but it was playing out through my whole being. I tried to share it with Byron, but I couldn't do the beauty of the skies justice, or the intensity of the messages.

The next dream, that same night, was shorter and less detailed. Byron and I were on vacation somewhere. We were both riding an elevator with four other people from India. We were all heading up to the same place, a room on the fourth floor of a hotel or apartment building.

When we got out of the elevator, I became sidetracked and wandered into the room with the people from India. They had formed a circle with pillows, and someone was in the middle of the circle lighting incense. I pulled up a pillow and knew Byron would be joining any minute. As I was getting situated, I looked out the large picture window, and there was a monstrous almost smooth and very dark wave heading toward us. It was looming and immense, carrying a bus and a boat and a couple of other things in its crest. They were toylike in comparison to the water formation.

As the wave approached the window, smaller waves tapped the window, and a splinter of the glass fell out. No one in the circle was running. We were all calm, peaceful, dropping into meditation. My only lingering thought, again, but calmer, was about Byron.

When I awoke from this second dream, there was little emotion, but the wave and the scene of all of us entering into meditation were both imprinted on my mind. In the second dream, I had a sense of maintaining a higher consciousness and clarity, which the first dream lacked. The need for Byron's presence with me at the end held weight; that much was clear. Dream interpretation has not been a strong suit for me, but many of these types of dreams or visions have a quality that never dilutes in image or in bodily sensations. They don't fade from memory. These were of that ilk.

A gift I received via these tumultuous night states was that following this night, I felt my faith strengthen in God. There had been the presence of something powerful in those dreams. Though I couldn't put my finger on what had created the shift, the shift of faith had deepened, and I was in gratitude. I wasn't attached to any concept of God per se. But I didn't think of Him as a man or person in the sky. I believed He/She/It was multiexpressions, dimensions, and realms of consciousness, light, and energy. And I trusted it implicitly.

In the divine perfection that I reveled in, just two days after these dreams, I received a call from a woman who assisted Sri M in organizing his trips to Portland. She was calling to say he would be in town the next week and would be doing a public talk, as well as offering the complete Kryia initiation to those who had received the preliminary technique the previous year at Breitenbush.

When I felt a connection with a teacher, I always fantasized that they would be the one, the teacher for me. I missed having that special, heart-centered connection that was present with Gurudev, and I continued to long for it. I felt a bit like the Ugly Duckling in search of its mother. It was a continual challenge to accept the blessing and guidance that was showered on me from the many without form. I carried guilt about this and felt unworthy often of their graces because of this issue. I didn't in any way disregard these divine beings. It was that I worried about my sanity still, and about what other people would think. I felt I needed an in-body authority to give me permission to believe what was happening in my life, to be of service, to offer my gifts, especially when these gifts were intertwined with what couldn't be seen. These insecurities amounted to a tremendous roadblock in my path in many ways. It was the karma I had to work with, and it weighed heavy on me often.

During M's first visit, when I had the privilege to have an audience with him, he encouraged me to keep teaching. He assured me that if I was transmitting a spark for awakening, Shaktipat, then it was a responsibility for me to do so. And, he stressed, it also entailed the responsibility of my highest integrity toward my awakening. I felt such a relief after his permission, but soon insecurity crept back in.

On his return, I had more questions for him, if I would have the opportunity for another private meeting, and was eager to move forward with Kriya initiation. I was blessed with both. Two days after receiving Kriya, I had a private meeting. I had stayed consistent with the prerequisite technique and gave myself time to retreat from it when I felt it was too much or the mind was shifting perceptions too quick. I wanted to ask if it was okay to practice Kriya in the same way when I met with M.

One of the issues he addressed was a problem I was experiencing with my stomach. An intense need to eat constantly had been upon me for periods of time, off and on, over the previous year. He affirmed it was part of a permanent opening taking place and said that I was to simply follow the guidance and needs that Divine Mother provided me with.

"I also wanted to share with you," I said, "that I've been in the beautiful presence and guidance of Mary Magdalene more and more often." I felt shy. I had not spoken of this subject out loud to anyone but Byron.

He smiled big, and his eyes shone. "I am pleased. That is a beautiful connection to have. It is good."

"I get concerned that I'm drinking from too many streams, rather than diving into the depths of one. I know that hopping around from one tradition or teacher to another can dilute the energies and the practices, and therefore the teachings don't take hold," I said, explaining my worries.

"Let me ask you this. Do you see a lot of teachers? Do you seek out new teachers like me?" he asked.

"No. But I do follow the impulse when I feel it. For instance, I felt an impulse toward seeing you. But most of the time, it's from inside where the contact originates. And the last direction I expected was to be led to Jesus and Magdalene."

"You need to worry less, question less, and trust more" was his answer.

"Okay." I felt silly and small. "Can I ask about one more thing? "I have maintained the prerequisite practice from last year, but in truth, I did have to take a break every now and again. Sometimes it felt too overwhelming. My mind wasn't working properly. It was getting garbled and confused. I didn't know what day it was, what month I was in. Normal life things just had no foundation anymore." He listened as I continued, "After my first Kriya practice Monday night, after you gave the initiation, I felt like a 'whoosh' of energy. It was overwhelming. I guess I'm wondering if it's okay to take breaks as needed?"

When I completed my thought, M asked me, "Do you really want to take a break? At each new stage, the foundation will shake. It will become unstable. But you must keep moving through it, and it will stabilize at a new plateau. Do not be afraid, because the direction is upward, not downward. The energy is rising to new levels, altering everything down to the cellular structures. You can shorten your meditation times, of course. When you feel unstable, call on the help of Babaji. He will be there. And how badly do you want to reach God? When that desire overpowers everything else, then one lets go completely."

I was grateful for our talk. We had a moment of silent connection through our eyes. I felt love and loved. "I'll keep watch over your progress. Maybe someday you will give initiation."

Our time ended. The questions hung in my mind: "Do you really want to take a break? How badly do you want to reach God?" I knew that I'd only know if I progressed. I did have the quiet rumblings of fear echoing. *How do I know this is safe? How do I know I'm not being led astray?* The old fears still held enough sway to get my attention with these questions. However, experience was now informing me that the fears were empty. I hadn't been led astray once, only closer to my own wholeness, to a deeper faith, and to greater connection to God.

44

I found an internal connection with M once I began my Kriya practice. He was able to assist with technique in the beginning. His direction was to pick the times I would practice and allow me to be disciplined in those times. I did the best I could, but I was certainly not perfect. Ever since the vertigo I was very sensitive with low energy and tiredness. My adrenals never felt completely replenished. For better or for worse, my lifestyle for years allowed me to be in tune with my natural rhythms. If I needed extra sleep in the morning, I slept. If I needed to go to bed at 7:30 in the evening, I did so. If I had extra energy and felt called to get up at 3:30 in the morning to meditate, I did, with the freedom to go back to bed. If I was processing a lot emotionally or mentally and felt tired, I took care of myself.

I scheduled my sessions according to what was going on at the time, but regardless, I was able to have time in the morning, as nothing I was scheduled for began before 10:00. I did my best to assign myself a steady time for meditation and hold myself accountable. I'd give myself a B– if I had to grade myself on discipline during this time.

I did indeed hit new heights vibrationally. Energetically, a sense of lightness became the norm. I often felt ungrounded and spacy. After one particular meditation, with M's presence, he shared with me that I was to receive a blessing from Babaji. Uncertain as to exactly what that meant, or when it would be offered, or if I would even realize it when it manifested, I let go of any attachment, yet I remained open.

Sessions with clients were always changing. As October enveloped us, I was aware that with certain clients, there were distinct changes as to what was being drawn through me. I had clients who were awakened energetically, and we were working together with spontaneous postures and meditation. They received it matter-of-factly but didn't seem to feel a call to go to the depths that the practice could offer them. I recognized that karmically, they were in a different place from a couple of other clients who were embracing and deepening quickly, receiving transformational shifts of consciousness. The latter were fewer. In the beginning of working with people, I had to let go of my expectation of what I thought they were getting out of our time together. I had to allow each individual their own timing and unfolding.

What became clear was that those who seemed to be diving in deeper and opening up to this path called forth a presence through me that wasn't me. I was receiving the experience of being a vessel, a vehicle for the divine to enter into the physical realm.

To be sure, for a while I resisted. This kicked up my fears, just like when the deities were present in the early stages. It wasn't how I had understood channeling that I had great caution about. I stayed completely aware, conscious, and ultimately in control. Divine Mother was always present as I worked with each person, but soon I could feel facial expressions again spreading gently over my face, and the sacred hand gestures danced forth.

My clients weren't usually aware of anything I was doing during a session unless I was supporting them physically in a release. But under normal conditions, once they were acclimated to Divine

Mother's guidance, my duty changed. I was primarily there to hold space. Though love always felt present as these new energies rose to the surface, it took me a while to surrender to them—my familiar pattern.

Once I began allowing them to come through, I became the vehicle through which guidance and affirmations of love would be spoken to my clients. Sometimes melodies and toning sang forth. Oftentimes I felt Jesus or Magdalene with us, filling me with wonderment and amazement as blessings streamed forth for my clients. I felt blessed and in awe of the reality around us at all times, things that the majority of humanity isn't aware of, rejects, or is frightened by. It is the literal presence of God, in the myriad of forms of the One, that is here to assist each and every one of us when we're ready. Wrapping my head around these new insights, I found it took time to integrate them into the mind, but the heart and soul were truly already in alignment.

It was becoming evident that the self-consciousness of my personality, the stories and resistance, was inhibiting what I was sensing was my purpose in this life. I felt my own ignorance too often. I felt sad and guilty when I believed I'd failed to integrate the blessings being offered. Though I tried not to judge myself, I still fell into this trap. I was also feeling fear around being completely transparent about what was coming through me, but I had no idea how to explain it in a way that sounded sane. For me, watching to see that each person was indeed moving into wholeness, in whatever that meant for them—finding deeper peace and clarity, cultivating their heart space, and maintaining normal states of physical health—was a guidepost I employed in assessing their direction. Beyond that, I felt clear that their experience was perfect for them, and for me, for reasons I had no knowing of. Spirituality being the personal journey it is, I encouraged them to listen within for the gurus/teachers, guides, or saints, and the traditions that spoke to them personally, and to follow that call.

In a stupor one day, filled with self-consciousness and judgment, I was journaling, trying to get out from under myself. I was guided to feel my heart. I couldn't tell who the presence was, but I felt the gentle breeze that oftentimes accompanies Jesus and Mary. The guidance being spoken in my mind was also flowing onto the page through my writing:

"The point to remember is that you are given direction. This may seem impossible, but as you once learned to walk, it gets easier. You want to be ready for what is to follow. You need to know that the container being formed is solid and sturdy. You don't need to know what all of this means now. You will come to know. The container will be both internal and external, and both realms need to be prepared for you. Your work and passage will be revealed to you. You are here to serve, and service will become increasingly your motivation. Be solid in your sense of service and devotion, and you will be carried through all you need. Be open to ideas that seem foreign to you. You will follow appropriately, for We are with you. Do not be afraid or worried that you're falling short. You know by now, your growth is in phases. Grow and integrate. You are held each step of the way. Simply follow the instructions, the faith and guidance you feel down deep. The love will always carry you because it is Our love always growing within you. Keep following. Keep feeling. Keep listening. Keep trusting. Keep loving. Keep doing what you're doing. Don't have expectations; simply keep being true."

After receiving this blessing and affirmation, I felt filled with Love for days, not the lowercase emotional love, but the unconditional, Universal Love. This Love was coupled with Joy. Again, it was not merely happiness but was the state of consciousness, of Joy, which is a divine quality. I was drawn into silence, spaciousness, where Love and Joy were experienced. All that mattered was being filled with this energy, with a truth that was always present. *I saw, too, that the Divine, God, Source, needs us, needs our humanity. We are vehicles to do the work here on this planet, to draw down the qualities and energies that vibrate at a higher frequency.* I felt my whole being, soul, call out, "I only want to be a holy vessel for You!"

My entire being was going through more uplifting than I'd ever experienced for any prolonged period of time. And the test was upon me to see how much expansion I could hold, when M's foreshadowing came to fruition. In all the elation that I'd been held in, I had forgotten completely about the blessing to come. He came to me one night while I was going to sleep. My attention was drawn into the third eye, and then it, the attention, was taken down deep into a stillness. Om was vibrating through my whole body and head. I was shown an emptiness that exists underneath and beyond all else. I fell asleep in this emptiness.

The next morning I arose for my regular routine, barely remembering the night prior. When I finished my meditation, I began to feel that familiar pull inward. I had some resistance because I had some things I was hoping to work on. Instead I took my tea up to the bedroom and surrendered to the direction of just being for a while. I barely drank any of my tea before I was pulled inward. I began feeling love and gratitude for M, and then Babaji appeared. Rather, his vibration was present in my awareness and heart.

Over the next three days, I was held inward for long periods of time, interspersed with periods of being outward, but I was never released. The states of Love and Bliss were present almost nonstop. I felt extraordinarily high, barely in the body, and out of the mind. I didn't feel able to speak, nor did I have any desire to. I canceled the one session I had scheduled and avoided Byron at home. I was feeling great love for Babaji, M, Jesus, and Mary Magdalene. I felt love for Yogananda and Gurudev. I saw how my mind separates and divides each of these divine beings, but in essence They are truly all a part of the One Source. Though I would again forget this truth, for these days I knew it with depth and clarity. The experience of this oneness and the union filled my consciousness. My face couldn't stop smiling, but the smiles were as if from a force radiating from within, a reflection of the Bliss.

Every now and then over these three days, I would be released briefly and feel somewhat normal, only to be swooped back up into the arms of Love and Presence and Joy. The last night of Babaji's blessing, I felt him in various parts of my body. *So interesting,* I thought passively. At one point I woke up feeling his presence, him, at my knee. By the forth morning, I felt him fading. Every now and again, I felt like I could glimpse his presence, but it seemed like I was instigating it from the memory of the intense, bliss-filled experience.

I knew I wanted to remember what the truths I'd gleaned were. I wanted to hold them in the core of my being, but alas, by the next day, I'd swung to the opposite side of the pendulum.

45

The dynamic of what goes up must come down, and to the same degree, was the reality that crashed in the afterglow of Babaji's presence. I hit a bottom with agitation and crankiness. It was painful on multiple levels to come back to earth with a thud, after the high vibe of Babaji. There was sadness, but with my natural edge toward hot emotions, it just added to the agitation. It was in these moments when I became acutely aware of how painful it felt for me to be in this body, with this personality, with all the ignorance I carried. The moments of freedom, these divine gifts, seemed to make being here that much more challenging. I have learned this to be a lesson that not only I, but also others, need to navigate.

During the last couple of months of 2006, I felt in the midst of challenges. A heaviness hung within me, and my practices drudged up feelings of hopelessness, helplessness, and stuckness. There were moments when I felt like I was drowning under a thick ice formation. I'd peek out from a crevice, then get sucked back under. There were other moments when I felt like I could take off the heavy garb of identity, just disrobe and let it go. My days plodded along with feelings of confusion and lostness. No matter how much I tried to remind myself, *I am not these feelings. I am not these thoughts. I am not this personality,* I remained attached and identified.

Just before Christmas, I was contacted by one of my closest friends from AA. It'd been years since we'd seen one another, and needless to say, many things had changed in my life. Yet sadly, she was still immobilized in hers. We had a lovely time together, and I was so happy to see her. As we were saying goodbye, we hugged, and as soon as I released our embrace, my right shoulder blade grabbed on with a spasm. The spasm grew and clung during my and Byron's holiday trip to Indiana and was still creating great pain upon our return. How did this happen? Did I make a wrong sudden movement during the hug? Was I clinging, once again, to a friendship that would always be incomplete? Did I take on her energy? I had no idea; I only knew it lodged into a weak point in my body and held on for dear life. Nothing made it better. Massage, chiropractic adjustment, even inviting Divine Mother's gentle movements to bring healing and relief, all seemed to make it worse.

After a couple of months, I felt I could no longer stand the intense pain. I took to desperate prayer. In my heart I called forth the Heavenly Father, Divine Mother, Jesus, Magdalene, and M, to help me. I'd been lingering in emotional darkness and physical pain, for as long as I could bare. Regardless of how this muscle spasm was initiated, what it'd been revealing about myself, in the form of tendencies, attachments, and dense stories, were proving to be hard to shake, dissolve, or dislodge.

I set up a temporary space down by the altar in the studio, committing to remain there for as long as it took to move through the blocks I, ego, was clinging to. I prayed to be stripped of what must be shed. I prayed to surrender to divine will. I prayed for the courage, strength, fortitude, faith, and trust to meet the death of the characteristics of my being that were no longer serving my highest good. I prayed to be a vehicle and channel for divine Love and Light. I prayed to shed this outworn skin, that I may be reborn. I prayed for the grace of the divine to create greater sacred space within this being.

In my sheltered sanctuary, I began the surrender. I remained in solitude as much as possible. During an initial visit to the chiropractor, I learned that I had three ribs out of place. After they were adjusted into position, as I lie in "being," I felt a clear rising and surrendering of fear, self-consciousness, and resistance taking place. I examined how my thoughts, behavior, and energy are easily drawn downward into shadow aspects of the lower centers. I was being taught how much energy and consciousness it takes to remain stable in the higher centers of truth and love. A divinely guided contemplation was transmitted. How to rise from the lower and cultivate the higher?

There was space to examine once again how the right side, the masculine expression, the yang, that which orients outward action into the world, continued to be a challenge for me. It wasn't so much moving into the outside world for me *as it was how I was with that movement.* And more often than not, the energy funneling through, if left solely to my devices, was aggressive, ego based, frustrated, and self-conscious.

In contrast to this, I was aware that when the presence of the divine, in whatever form that took with me, was funneling through me, it was more yin, gentle, harmonious, loving, and nurturing. I felt the qualities of the Mother in Her nurturing aspects. Though I had experienced the fierce qualities of Her force, I wasn't getting the sense that those qualities were what I was to bring forth. I did act in those ways in my lack of conscious awareness, but the contrast was that Her fierceness was purposeful and ultimately loving.

As I lay in reflection, with very little journaling for days since I could barely use the right side of my body, I allowed clearer awareness to enter into me. One afternoon, I was able to hear my mother and Byron in the kitchen above me. I could vaguely hear the neighbors next door, on the other side of the wall. I was drifting into an in-between state of consciousness, with thoughts of Byron and my parents drifting around in my consciousness. Just for a short while I felt myself, my personality self, dissipating. I felt empty of the characteristics that make me the identified "me." I felt grief and loss. I grieved *not* being attached and *felt the fear of not being attached to certain things and characteristics.*

I reflected that these characteristics keep me, as the small self, here, as part of the world on this plane. I saw that without these personality characteristics, my relationships to those I love would be vastly different, and I felt the pain of letting go of the familiar dances we have together, especially I and my mother. The personality dynamics between my mother and me keep me greatly lodged in my personality, more than the dynamics between me and anyone else in this life. There are a myriad of emotions this entails for me: frustration, fear, grief, responsibility, dishonesty, loss. And then I drifted to sleep with a heavy heart.

So this death process I had prayed for was showing itself in a graceful emergence. Ironically, even in times of just being and trusting the organic unfolding from within, an aggressive "I" aspect of ego / the small self still did its best to be in control. My reaction when I realized ego was continuing to push was to judge and chastise this "small self." I noticed, in contrast to the self-diminishment, Divine Mother's gentle whisperings that told me, "Fall back. Step back, and allow that which needs to step forward into the space to do so. Allow the truth to rise to the surface."

I heard. I obeyed. I focused on the breath, only to witness the small self, pleading and begging to be shown what was in the way of my seeing. Again, feelings of self-judgment about the thick habits of ignorance that enveloped my consciousness were hard to shake. I felt under the pressure of ego and its push to be in the mix or else. Ego fears the right thing won't happen. Gently the whisperings came to guide me again:

"Do you not see that it is your begging and pleading that interferes with your receptivity? Be quiet in the mind, but also in the heart. Step back and see it is right there. You spend so much time focusing on wanting that you miss the fact that what you want is present."

Every time I was spoken to, my whole being softened and quieted. Even if just for a moment, in those reprieves I *knew* the truth of the whispering voice. On the final night of my miniretreat, I felt the presence of Jesus, Magdalene, Babaji, and M gathering around me. I immediately apologized for not being more diligent about my meditation practice during this time. M's guidance came through: "You are in the right hands. We will come together again when this work with Divine Mother is done." I felt grateful and relieved to hear him. I felt my love for him. I thought to myself, *How odd that our relationship is as anchored as it feels.* But I also reasoned that I have a limited knowing and understanding of connections in previous lifetimes.

After this exchange with M, I felt Divine Mother enter into my body with gentle waves. She asked me, "So you wish to be a mother?" There was a moment of alarm that went through me. I in no way wanted to be a mother literally. My distracted thinking was refocused on the right shoulder blade as I felt Her massaging motions along the shoulder, the rhomboids, and the back.

The next thing I knew, in a vision, I was being carried high above the earth. She was speaking, but I lost all recollection. As I was raised high above, I felt the earth as a living entity, as Her, the Great Mother. Dropping down into the atmosphere, the clouds, into the mountains, trees, and oceans, I felt Her beauty and the pulse of Her life-beat.

Then I was sailing down into the cities, the buildings, the concrete, the mass and matter, in and among the humans. She told me She has no favorites. I felt connected to those bound in darkness and pain, and I felt Her mourning for their suffering. I felt connected to those walking in normalcy, asleep but contented. I shared Her love for them through their sleep life. I was connected to those who cling to organized religion and experienced Her love for them. Although there is blindness, Her hope was palpable for those awake and awakening, of which I was one. I felt Her joy. But none were favored over the others. I felt each were on their own karmic journey coddled in Her ever-present support. She holds each in Her heart and hands.

All the while her massage was alternately painful, evident by the clinging tension and relief in the tensions' microreleases. Next, in the vision, I was brought face-to-face with each person I had prevalent issues with. As each issue was illustrated via thought and sensation, She massaged different areas in the shoulder, arm, and back. I was shown where and how I hold judgment, impatience, insecurity, and fear and how I withhold love. I felt great pain physically and emotionally. She neither shamed nor consoled me. She laid it all out. I saw pieces of me, the karma I carry in body, mind, and soul.

When I had absorbed that lesson, realized and felt each piece of me, She then introduced into my consciousness the suffering of those in my life. She showed me their pain, their needs. She allowed me to see them through Her eyes, as if I were the Mother. She allowed me a glimpse through Her perception of truth, love, and compassion. Each person in my life whom I judged in some way was brought in a circle around me. I was in the middle. She gave me time to see clearly what each individual needed.

With Her encouragement, compassion, patience, and presence, She told me, "You must pull from your own spring of love, the love of Me in you."

As I met each person in the center of the circle, I was able to feel the shoulder area hold, resist, or release. I was instructed to put into practice what I'd been shown, to see all people as Her children and love them with Her love.

When I'd returned from this journey or vision, when Her presence had vacated, my entire back and shoulder felt like pummeled meat. However, the next morning, after I shared the experience with Byron, it felt almost normal. Again, I couldn't even comprehend the gifts and blessing I'd been given. To know there was this kind of love and attention given to humanity was more than I could hold.

Over the next couple of days it struck me that the tarot cards I had pulled just a day or two before this journey had been cards of both the Earthly Mother and Divine Mother. I felt that one of the lessons revealed drawing the subtle energies of the Divine Mother down to this plane of the Earthly Mother. I felt a task for me was to merge these two worlds within my being and in my life, to find the balance within this physical form and personality, and to infuse them with the highest consciousness, of Truth—, Light, of the Divine. It was clear that one more time, the body as a sacred vehicle and vessel was showing itself in my consciousness.

I recognized the right shoulder as a teacher that pointed me to the shadow aspects of myself that I didn't want to see. Immediately following, I was hypersensitive to the qualities of energy that moved through the right side and right arm. With the presence of excess force, I stepped back from myself and entered a state of nondoing, until I could function from a place of neutrality. When I became aware I was rushing to *do* anything, I slowed down, let go of all I thought I needed to do, and examined the motivation behind it.

My relationships with those challenging individuals became smoother, which means that I let go of the stories I'd created about them and how I perceived I was affected. I had been given the opportunity to see them clearly, with love, and to discover how I could be of service, with the highest degree of consciousness available to me. Some perceptions were permanently shifted. One or two needed constant reminders if I was to remain awake and clear about my triggers. With these shifts I had a greater opportunity to perceive the truth beyond these forms.

For instance, the projections I harbored about my mother's feelings toward me, including that she didn't like me and that she felt I was dramatic and crazy, shifted. I had to be accountable to myself first and practice more self-compassion and self-acceptance. Honoring the crazy was also freeing. By turning awareness to the *projections I put on her*, I had clarity that this was a trip I laid on myself. She may or *may not* have thought any of these things. It didn't matter anymore. I accepted myself, and that allowed my love for her to deepen and expand.

46

In the spring of 2007, Byron and I felt it was time for us to move into our own home again, which worked out well because my mother was in need of her space back. This required both of us to make some choices around employment. Byron had still been caregiving for adults with developmental disabilities. He felt like he no longer wanted to do caregiving. Instead he began driving for NAPA in North Portland and surrounding neighborhoods. He'd often found peace, out on the road, driving.

I had wonderful clients whom I intended to keep working with, the only problem being that only a couple of people paid my rate. The others paid what they could, as they could. For me, the satisfaction was in knowing that people's lives were changing and growing because of the work we did together, but that did little for my pocketbook. I knew that if Byron and I were to move, I needed a more stable income. That led me back in the direction of caregiving. I'd had a break for a while, and the prospect of having dependable income again felt freeing.

Simultaneously, we began our apartment search and my job search. I found a couple of options that looked promising on Craigslist as far as employment, but the housing situation was looking bleak. There were four jobs I was interested in, but none felt completely aligned. Except for one. Felicia was in her nineties. She was paralyzed from the waist down but had a mind as sharp as a tack. The day of my interview, I drove up to her home in the hills, feeling nervous. I didn't feel as pumped up with ego as I used to in the past when I interviewed. For years I was a great sell of all my attributes and skills. I was able to sell myself with outgoing, personable friendliness. Not that any of it was false, at least not too much, but it was a bit overblown. I couldn't sell anymore. I hadn't realized in the past that it is a delegated job of ego to sell oneself in that way that is needed in the world. This is one of the ways ego serves us. I'd lost the touch.

When I walked into Felicia's home up in the west hills, I was met with the breathtaking view of the city below. Her son Joe was there. He was very friendly, genuine, and courteous. Felicia drove her wheelchair into the living room and smiled politely. As soon as I saw her, I was in love. My heart burst, and I had no understanding as to why. We all talked. Her speech was somewhat impaired, as the paralysis had originally included her throat. She was sharp and eyed me like a hawk. She gave very little away as to where I was falling on her acceptance meter. I left feeling oddly unsure.

I could safely say I had rarely if ever, been turned down for a job I interviewed for. I usually always felt in control and secure. I couldn't remember ever walking away with this uncertainty. Not long after I returned home, Joe called to let me know they'd gone with another caregiver. I was shocked and disappointed. I loved Felicia, and the love affair was over before it even began. This forced me to look again at the other options.

Meanwhile, Byron and I searched for a new home. This was becoming a dead end. He and I were continuously at odds regarding money, preferences, location, and cleanliness. We decided we needed to take a break from looking for a time. I had flashes of some of the lessons in the not so distant past concerning my clinging and forcing things, versus trusting and following what felt aligned with the will of the Universe.

The Universe, it seemed, kept throwing up mini-roadblocks, including interfering with my interviews for the other positions. I took that as guidance. I gained clarity, too, that my fear of financial insecurity was inhibiting my faith that the right job would reveal itself. That awareness enabled me to let go of the other positions, knowing they were not where I wanted to be, regardless of the roadblocks.

The next day was Sunday. Byron and I went to go view a couple of apartments that looked promising, but in reality they weren't. We both were unattached, since we recognized that attachment wasn't serving us. We ran some errands and had a lovely afternoon in spite of the housing situation. Not long after we got home, I received a phone call from Joe, asking if I was still available. He said that Felicia would be happy if I would come to work with her.

I was floored and thrilled. The person they'd hired was a no-show, no-call for her starting shift. When they reached her, she said she'd taken something else. I was going to get to work with this woman who'd lodged in my heart after all. It just took letting go and allowing larger forces to orchestrate the appropriate lessons and provide the outcomes of what was meant to be.

Feeling fully open to the flow and grace of the Universe, I told Byron I was going to jump on Craigslist one more time to see if there were any new listings. The first listing I came upon had just placed under the North Portland rentals. It was a beautiful, large, two-bedroom basement apartment. The pictures revealed the classy remodel that had been done, and the spaciousness of the unit was really appealing.

"Hurry, honey! Come look at this!" I yelled to Byron downstairs.

"Wow! That's awesome! I love it." He was as excited as I was.

I scrolled down and started laughing. "Look! It's just up the road. Let's go now!" I said.

"But it says here that they're only showing until five, and it's five 'til. I think we've missed it," he replied.

"No way," I told him, picking up the phone to dial.

"Hello?" a woman's voice said on the other end.

"Hi! My husband and I just saw your post on Craigslist. I know you're done seeing people today, but we live just a couple of blocks away. Is there any chance we could stop by and see the unit now?"

"Sure. That's fine. We still have one more couple coming as well." She gave me the address. Byron and I jumped in the car and drove up the hill.

On that Sunday, we received affirmatives from the Universe—our new home and the job I had felt aligned with—as well as lessons in the forefront regarding trusting the divine timing and flow; letting go of attachments, because they constrict the flow; and the knowledge that we always will get what's perfect if we trust in that which is greater.

47

Our new abode was beautiful. The owners, Will and Candice, who lived above us, had created an amazing apartment. We had two bedrooms, one of them being my studio and meditation room. The kitchen was huge, which was perfect for Byron since he was the cook of our little family, and opened up with a bar into the living room. The bathroom was beautiful and elegant. There was new carpet throughout, a spacious utility room with a brand-new washer and dryer, and a large enough entryway to be a third room.

Again, Urisk was to be an indoor kitty. Being the shy guy that he was, he wasn't attached to going outside. He was indoors at my mom's and would be again here. He made no dashes to the door, no milling or restless pacing. He found contentment quite easily.

The first morning I arrived at my new job, as Felicia and I sat eating breakfast and getting to know one another, I felt an overwhelming urge to express my love for her. It felt inappropriate, unprofessional, and out of place, but the sentiment leapt out of my mouth, accompanied by tears and laughter. She simply looked at me with her eagle eyes. She was silent for a moment, and then said, "That's good you say what's on your mind."

My caregiving shift was seventy-two hours, live-in. I did miss not having more time at our new place, but overall I felt grateful and happy with how things were turning out. At Felicia's, we caregivers had the downstairs area as our home away from home. Felicia appreciated routine and structure, as did I. We had great talks over meals. She usually had specific tasks she needed help with, and she enjoyed her alone time as well. I had time to continue my practice at Felicia's in the evenings.

At home, I continued to see the small handful of clients on my days off. It took no time at all for me to find my spot outside under a fruit tree, in the empty lot next to our house. On my days off, in the mornings, I pulled out the pile of things including my blanket, my pillow, whatever books I was studying at the time, and my journal. I carried them in two trips out to my sacred tree space. I enjoyed daily rituals, and it didn't take long to recalibrate my flow accordingly. After I pulled my pile out under the tree and set up house for the day, I'd do yoga and meditation. Breakfast was next. Then I'd come back out to my new perch with my little pot of green tea and commence with my morning.

I saw clients in the afternoons, and I had one evening client. I made dinner and had it waiting for Byron when he arrived home. Usually he found me still out under the tree, at which point I'd gather my pile and deliver it to its holding place 'til next time.

For the most part, life had become quite fluid. I was in the flow and at peace. Without being completely conscious of how I was creating my life, I had managed to do so in ways that supported balance, quietude, and inner attention. Stress created from outside, from chaos, adrenaline, or overt dysfunction, had been eliminated along the way. For most of my life I'd been a stress-monger without knowing it. It wasn't until sobriety in my mid-twenties, that I was able to recognize I was addicted to stress and adrenaline. For most of my life leading up to sobriety, and really for the first five years, I thrived on chaos, emotional turmoil, anger, and love seeking.

My present life brought a sweet simplicity. Although I had dreams and goals, financial abundance had never been a pressing need for me. I lived under the poverty level almost always yet never experienced poverty mentality. I rarely felt I was ever going without, and there wasn't much I wanted. Time was what I valued most: time to study, to dance, and to work with those things I was passionate about. And now, I valued time to go farther along the spiritual path that I was being led down. On those days sitting under that tree, listening to the birds, flowing with my personal rhythms, I had an appreciation for the embrace of peace I was resting in.

It was the time with Felicia that brought up any discontentment, restlessness, or questioning of life's perfection. The difficulty was not in any way related to Felicia. She was a jewel, and I never lost sight of my love for her. I also hadn't lost sight of the belief I had that I was with her for a reason. The intense love I felt for her was like none that I'd had before with a client. I was in love with Babalicious, as I called her, the first woman I cared for. I was with her for three years, and she always remained in my heart. But this felt different. The fact that I hadn't been Felicia's first choice also made my presence there interesting to me. As she explained on our first day together, discussing why I wasn't hired initially, she was worried about my size. I'm petite, for sure, and though Felicia was about my size, she still needed lifting and some transferring. Whether there were any other reasons she passed me by, I'd never know, but there I was.

Within our second week together, even with her reserve, our relationship was developing into one of sweet affection. My favorite time was at night, when it was time to get her into bed. Once she was transferred to her bed and in her nightgown, I could take off her leg braces. The braces allowed her weight to be supported during any transfers. She continued to hope that one day she would walk again. Once she was ready for bed, I'd scoop her up and swing her into a reclining position. Pillow adjusted. Blankets placed how she liked them. And last I covered her with her "binky." This was like her security blanket. I'd pull it up and tuck it under her chin, at which time her arms would fly up to give me a hug. I'd bend down and put my arms around her, and we would exchange a good-night smooch. In the bedtime moments, I lost track of who we were in present time. I felt like this was a daughter I never had, from some other place and time, and it felt like the feeling was returned by her. Unknown karma is a curious thing, and in this case it spurred my intrigue of past connection.

The discontentment that existed in me had been born out of the inability to integrate caregiving into *my* idea of my life purpose. Once I began actually providing private sessions and experiencing otherworldly support, as well as witnessing the awakenings of clients taking place, I felt that to be my purpose. Caregiving, just as cleaning, had been a means to get to my true work.

My ideas and my agenda were in conflict with reality. It was beginning to cause inner friction and create new stories of suffering. The time with Felicia became an experiment with consciousness. I was committed to be her legs, her independence, and her freedom and to support her quality of life. I witnessed a pattern unfold in which I saw my ability to stay present, awake, and conscious dwindle over the seventy-two-hour shift.

Usually, the first day of my shift was smooth and fresh. I'd had time to rebalance my energy with a focus on what I needed to care for myself. I arrived on Thursday mornings, ready to be of service. I rarely slept well at any overnight job. Caregivers learn to sleep, if they have such a luxury, with one ear open at all times, just like new mothers I presume. I also had a lot of fear issues when it came to being home alone. Granted, I wasn't alone, but I was the one responsible, and I was the only one who would be serving up any protection needed if something bad were to happen. What this really meant was in case anyone broke in to cause harm.

In the late 1990s, when I worked with Babalicious, she lived out on an acre of land in the country, south of Portland. I also worked a seventy-two-hour shift with her. Having no immediate neighbors, in a large two-story house, I was infused with fear every night. I had established a night time ritual and feared that if I missed the ritual that would be the night danger would occur. I'd start downstairs, which wasn't in use anymore, and check all the doors, rooms, and closets. I would double-check the main floor doors and leave a light on in the kitchen and living room. There were sliding doors separating the kitchen and living room, and another door in the living room from the hallway and bedrooms. I closed the two sliding doors, which someone would have to walk through in order to get to the bedroom. The sliding doors were loud and my last means of protection. They served as the alarm system, so to speak. Why all the fear? I wouldn't understand this until years later.

At Felicia's, it wasn't as difficult for me. There were neighbors less than a stone's throw away on either side of the house. After she went to bed, I'd sneak my pillow and blanket up from the bedroom in the basement, locking the door to the downstairs behind me, and make up my bed on the couch in the living room. I felt embarrassed about this. I don't think she ever knew I slept upstairs with her. But this didn't mean I slept peacefully.

By the afternoon of the second day, my attentiveness would begin to wane. I could sense my energy levels drop, which would open the door for my mind to start running its stories of woes. After two nights of little sleep, I found that the third day brought about frustration for anything I deemed unnecessary. Felicia never asked for anything that would be unreasonable to anyone. Yet, when tired, my selfishness would rise to the surface and I'd feel put out, even though rationally I knew this was my job.

One of her favorite things to do was to rearrange things in the living room. It was so clear to see the difference in who I was when I was refreshed and present versus tired and cranky. Felicia's home was something to be proud of, and she was indeed proud of it. She wanted things clean, orderly, and attractive. When I had energy, I loved helping her beautify her environment. I understood the importance of this for her. Her creative side was looking for an outlet, and I was her body to carry out what she couldn't do for herself. I loved being able to be a part of this with her. On the contrary, when I was tired, the me who showed up never outwardly, but energetically, was contracted and snarky. The thoughts that had their way ran the gamut from *We just did this last weekend. Why do we need to do this again?* to *It's only us here. What difference does this make?* Complaining inwardly, I'd feel judgmental of the situation and of myself. I felt sad and guilty because I knew better, but the other part of me that felt drained also felt like I wasn't living up to my full potential of being a caregiver and giving genuine care.

In those moments, love was squelched. Clear seeing was blinded. Selflessness was eroded. When my energy dropped, everything felt dragged down, and it was difficult for me to see that nothing had changed except my perception and attitude.

Phase one of this experiment required awareness of how I was affected by low energy. Next came the practice of engaging my will to hold my energy in the heart, to stay open, loving, compassionate, and of service.

My intention was to let go of my preferences when with Felicia, to let go of my needs and my perceptions or judgments of right or wrong and to respect her perceptions. The living practice, so to speak, was to stay connected to my desire for her happiness and her needs, to remain mindful that while I was there with her, my time and energy was about her and not about me.

It was a process that had moments of success and moments of tripping over myself. However, I knew I was on the right track. The practices of the inner realm were being translated into the outer world. Purification of ego was happening at every step of the way. Strengthening the upward flow of energy into the higher centers was being cultivated. Remaining awake was proving to be a full-time job!

48

Consistency of my Kriya practice was growing. There continued to be challenging short phases of instability of the mind, acute awareness of changing perception, inability to gauge time, day, or date, and fluctuations in my energy levels. I felt as though I had gained sufficient experience to hold all the changes without fear or reactivity. There was enough familiarity with what I was feeling to adjust accordingly, acclimate to the new, and continue onward.

Curiously, during this time, there was a diminishment in the audible guidance I'd been receiving over the previous couple of years. Occasionally, I would get the feeling or sense of Magdalene's presence or Babaji's. I missed having that guidance available. It brought me security as well as a closeness to these divine beings. There was also the sense that perhaps it was time for me to grow up and not be as reliant on their tangible presence, and instead to have faith that what I needed was inside of me. I was always being cared for, which was a constant reminder I received from all of them. In this I needed to trust.

In all the routine being established during this summer, Byron and I were never completely out of the loop of transformation. I had undertaken the reading of a text that jumped out at me at the New Renaissance Bookstore. It was a beautiful white leather-bound text from the third century called the *Pistis Sophia* with the translation/ interpretation by J. J. Hurtak. Mary Magdalene is a prime figure in the text, and her wisdom is highlighted. This ancient Gnostic text was a dense thick read, of which I only accomplished about one-third, and much of it went over my head. This was my area of study on my days off, sitting under the tree and feeling nourished.

In the meantime, Byron was enjoying learning to make new vegan dishes, and I was enjoying eating them. His interest was slowly extending into research of raw food nutrition. There were two raw food festivals in just a couple of months that we were looking forward to attending. One was at Mount Shasta in California, and the other in Oregon at Camp Adams.

I couldn't get enough of the *Pistis* it seemed. Although I couldn't intellectually comprehend much of the text, comprehension was happening on a deeper level, energetically.

"Remember when I told you about that first recognition I had that everything was energy?" I asked Byron as we were driving down to California on our way to Raw Spirit.

He nodded to indicate that he did.

"And of course we've felt that we're getting some kind of energy transmission with the music we love, like Shimshai, Rusted Root, and our chanting music." I was winding to my point.

He nodded again. "Yeah. Exactly. That's the goodness we're feeding ourselves!"

"Well, I've been reading the *Pistis* now for a few weeks, and I don't get much of it intellectually, but I've been feeling strange lately. It's like I'm seeing visualizations of what I'm reading about at random times, sometimes when I'm drifting off to sleep or when I'm sitting in meditation."

"That seems normal. When you're really into something, it occupies inner space," he commented.

"True. That's what I thought at first, and that may still be the case. But what I'm noticing is that when I see the visualizations, I feel them too. I wanna say in the body ... and I think that would be accurate." I was looking for a way to put words to the experience. "I guess I feel like one would see a blueprint of something, but it's going through ... me, or my subtle bodies. I feel it when I'm reading too. As if there are reverberations through my body and mind."

"It's like you're downloading it," he pointed out with some excitement.

"Yeah. I think so. That's what I started out saying. It's the first time I've felt the vibration, the actual life force, in this way, the consciousness, that I'm taking in the living energy of this writing, yet I have little idea what I'm taking in. I'm not sure how I feel about it. I almost stopped reading it last week, but it feels familiar and right."

"Why would you stop reading it?" Byron asked.

"It was feeling like a lot of something ... I don't have words for. I was actually feeling kind of dizzy here and there. Not vertigo-like dizziness, more of perceptions spinning in my head. Feeling confused. But then it evened out. I don't' know. I suppose it could be the kriya too," I explained.

"You know how sensitive you are, and your fears always jump up first. But it always stabilizes."

"I know. You're right. But I don't think there's anything wrong with a little caution," I added.

We arrived at Mount Shasta in the afternoon, where we checked into our motel and then moseyed around town. The event didn't start until the next day, so we had time to get acquainted with the town.

The next morning we awoke nice and early, gathered our belongings for the day, and headed out to the festival site. The food was clean and cool in the heat, and very nourishing. The lectures, just as we'd experienced at the Essene gathering, vastly expanded our views on health and spiritual awakening. A couple of the speakers we had heard at the gathering last summer, but a few of them were new to us.

Later in the afternoon I found a tree to go sit under, since the sun's rays were everywhere with little shade to go around. I felt like I wanted to meditate, or I could say meditation felt like it wanted to take place, but I wanted to hear the couple of speakers from the Tree of Life first.

The two who spoke were sharing about Gabriel Cousens's work at the Tree with healing diabetes through a live/raw food diet. They also shared about some of the programs that the Tree offered, including the Essene priest/priestess training. My heart started pounding, louder than the pitter-patter that always got my attention. Emotion rose up, and my mind was racing. There was definite resonance with what I was hearing.

After their talk, not able to see Byron anywhere, I went back to our blanket under our little tree and felt like I needed to calm myself. It was important to hear soul's call regarding what had just been spoken about. Feeling aligned with the Tree wasn't coming out of nowhere, but I wanted to be balanced in how I received whatever message was being given. I dropped into my breath and simply stayed connected with its flow until the mind calmed. There were random thoughts here and there floating through, intermingling with the awareness of festival activity all around me.

My thought then drifted to how few trees there were in this event field. I felt how happy I was to be under a tree again, just as I loved the tree at home, and then I felt, *Yes! The Tree!* I saw that the ministry call had been in me for some time. When I feared I wanted to be a nun, it had frightened me. It was a call to ministry. But the reality was that I didn't know how that could manifest for me. But, *Yes! A ... priestess.* I felt all discombobulated inside. With the thought of that title, a dizziness skewed my orientation. I felt perception moving in and out of present time. There was great resistance. It felt similar to my inability to say *God* way back when. This felt even more awkward. The word felt pretentious. I felt resistant and agitated. Yet, I felt a resounding *yes!* There was no doubt about that.

As soon as I finished with my meditation, which ended abruptly with inner chaos triggered by the term *priestess* being used in the program description, Byron sauntered up. He took one look and knew something was up.

"What's going on?" he asked cautiously.

I went through the whole story of how I'd felt listening to the couple from the Tree of Life talk, how the trees I'd found to sit under came into my mind, and then how the Tree of Life was felt as a yes.

"So, I want to go to school at the Tree to be an Essene minister!" I found a way to bridge the gap of my resistance, at least temporarily, by using *minister* in the place of *priestess*.

"Wow." And that was all he said.

"Well, what do you think? I'm not a nun, but it's probably the only place I'll find the same kind of fit. I mean, we both have been quite aligned with the Essenes. It feels right." I was talking excitedly but trying not to overwhelm him.

He sat quietly. I did my best to stay quiet and give him the chance to take in what all this might entail. Our dynamic was one of polar opposites. I could be spontaneous, quick, and ungrounded, whereas Byron was slow, steady, and pragmatic in almost all things. Over the years we'd learned to work quite elegantly with one another, more often than not.

It took him a few minutes to process the news. I thought I should give him some space and use the time go the bathroom. Upon my return he was ready to talk.

"So what exactly does this training entail?" he asked.

"I don't know," I answered.

Next question: "Will you have to go to the Tree?"

"I'm not sure, but I think so. It sounds like they have certain workshop and class requirements there."

"And how do you get started?"

"I don't know. But as soon as we get home, I'll find out all the info. I just know it's the right thing. I feel it!" I said.

"I believe you. The Tree's been sitting on a back burner for some reason. Okay! We'll see what's next."

The day had been quite hot, but the evening brought cooler temperatures, awesome music, and the light of the July full moon. I took time out for myself to wander at the far end of the field, away from the crowds, but within just enough earshot to be uplifted by the music.

Sitting in the field, bathing myself in the iridescence of the moon's light, I fell into a sweet meditation. I'd been full of excitement since the decision to move toward the Essene *ministry* ordination. "Why did I have such a hard time saying *priestess*? The word made me feel all a-tremble just thinking about it, let alone uttering it aloud. My thoughts were floating around the awareness.

Meditation began to quiet my whole being. I felt a sense of grounding. I felt open to what the journey had in store. When I rose to head back into the party, I decided to walk the long way around the edge of the field. I wanted to remain completely absorbed in the moon rays. While I was in appreciation of the solitude and beauty of the night, I became aware that walking with me were Jesus, Magdalene, Yogananda, Babaji, and M, my teacher, and for the first time, I experienced the presence of Mother Mary. I was taken aback. She had never been on my radar. I hadn't ever felt drawn to or connected to her, yet there she was. I felt them all affirming the direction I was moving in, and they were also conveying the unification of all religions and divine paths.

Regardless of how they all appear different in the world, in ritual, and in ceremony, and regardless of to whom or how worship or reverence is conducted, there is a common thread, the thread weaving each of us into our highest self, in Love, Compassion, and Truth. I felt blessed and vowed to do my best to remember the truth of unification and not get caught up in the mire of division.

Ironically, the next morning was ushered in with an abrupt darkness. I had been dreaming, and in the dream I was having a sensual encounter with someone whom I didn't recognize. While it started out benign enough, it escalated into my being brought to orgasm and being violently violated. I woke up with my heart racing, frightened, crying, and with a sharp pain in my womb.

Byron awoke in response to the urgency coming from me. I was doubled over from the cramping in the area of the left ovary in particular, when he gently shook me to get my attention.

"What happened?! Are you okay? Honey … what's wrong? Say something!"

Crying and tongue-tied, I had no way to explain what had happened because I didn't really know. Finally, with his comfort and patience, I recounted what I could remember of the dream.

"But then, it just all started feeling wrong. And then the pain, like someone was thrusting into me. I tried to wake up, and for a minute I thought I was awake, and it just kept happening. Finally, I just forced myself to sit up and felt this cramping!" I began crying again.

We were both silent for a while, both disturbed with no logical explanation of what had taken place. I was also perplexed that the night prior, I had felt so held and protected, but then now I felt as if I'd been attacked and violated. This wasn't boding well for my sense of safety or my sanity.

"There's something I haven't mentioned to you that may be connected to this. I'm not sure, because I don't really know what 'this' is or was." I wanted to fill him in on some other subtle things I'd been noticing lately.

"What's been happening? You usually tell me when things change."

"I can't say exactly for how long I've noticed this or when it started for sure. I thought my eyes were playing tricks on me …"

Byron hurried me along, asking, "What's been happening, honey?"

"I have been feeling like I've been seeing things out of the corner of my eye. Like little movements that catch my attention, but of course there's nothing there. It happens randomly, and it's been so quick and invisible that I felt like it was just my eyes playing tricks," I shared.

"What do you think it is?" Byron asked.

"I have no idea. But there have been a couple of instances at Felicia's, at night, when I'm just barely drifting off to sleep." I continued, "I've been awakened feeling like something is walking on me. It's similar to one time back in Southeast Portland when I woke up thinking Urisk was walking over me, to then realize he was right next to me, sound asleep."

"Why haven't you told me? How long have you been feeling that at work?"

"I'm not sure. I mean, it's all been so ... like it's just my imagination playing tricks. At night, I usually relax and do some gentle breath work, and after a while, I roll onto my side. You know I can't lie on my back, or I'd never actually sleep at night. So when I roll onto my side, I no longer feel like anything is around me."

I thought for a minute, trying to make some sense of the material and subtle planes of existence that I had learned are always crossing over. In most cases, for most people, our sense perceptions are limited, or the subtle senses haven't been activated to feel this.

"I absolutely love the *Pistis Sophia*, but I think I need to take a break from it. I feel like I haven't been right since I started reading it," I said decisively.

"I know you mentioned that. I thought you just needed time to adjust energetically." He was now feeling some caution.

"Well, maybe so. But it's a big, long text. I've known I'm affected by its energy, which could go on for a long time while I make my way through it. Also, though, it deals with entities in the lower, denser realms. It just makes me wonder. All this is new territory."

I was not certain that this ancient text was introducing unwanted energies into my life; however, I felt like discontinuing study was a necessary direction for me. Obviously, I wasn't strong enough or equipped with the tools to deal with this. With the book put back on the shelf upon my return home, it wasn't quite the end of the invisible tricksters or the recurring pain in my left ovary, however.

49

Upon our return home from Mount Shasta, the first task at hand was to find out all I could about the Essene ordination. I sent away for an application, which was in depth and lengthy. Once that was completed, I mailed it to the Tree of Life. There was nothing left to do but to wait for the phone interview and the processing of my application and essay. I was excited and nervous. Many feelings of being exposed and seen, and the shame and self-consciousness that came with sharing about myself, loomed and intertwined with the excitement.

"Do you remember my telling you about my friend Lenora?" asked my good friend Sandra. She had come to stay with me when Caleb had to go to work in the beginning of the Kundalini awakening, during that major crisis point. Her background for years had been Buddhism, which I was intrigued with when we first met at Naka Ima. I was sharing with her what I'd been experiencing with the invisible gremlins, as I was calling them.

"Vaguely. What exactly? She was the gal you met who had gone through a pretty intense awakening, right?" I asked.

"Yeah! For a period of time, she was able to see the entities that are everywhere in the subtle realm. She could see them connected to people and hanging out in certain environments. It had her really freaked out for a long time," Sandra explained to me.

"Was she ever attacked?" I wondered.

"I don't know. I can ask her though. Or maybe you two should meet. As far as I know, it was a phase, and then it passed. She believes these energy forms are always around, but she can't see them anymore."

"Maybe we could meet. I guess it's like the third eye, which can perceive more subtle realms and can get really opened up. The Kundalini when it's circulating in that center can illuminate both dark energies and light." I was pondering out loud.

Sandra told another story that felt helpful: "I remember talking with a friend who'd gone to see a visiting Tibetan Lama share a talk. He invited those who wished to receive a blessing to form a line. When it came to her turn, he tapped her third eye. She said that all of sudden she saw these horrible events flash before her eyes. She was so upset. From then on she had the gift of sight, but so much of what she saw was scary events, which she saw either while they happened or just before."

"Man! That would be so hard. What does that say about one's karma, about one's natural inclination of thoughts and perceptions? Just like I have to ask why I have attracted this kind of activity. What's my karma? I guess too, that is the risk of opening the third eye before the heart center is purified. Do you know what happened to your friend?"

"Not really. She harbored a lot of anger about that blessing, which felt more like a curse to her," Sandra said.

More pondering, theorizing out loud: "I imagine that to have that kind of gift—I suppose the word could be used lightly—you'd have to learn *how* to work with it, how to become conscious with it and try to use it for the highest good," I said.

"Yeah. I think so. And to learn what her lesson was regarding that kind of manifestation of sight. But as far as I know, it embittered her, and she felt victimized by the whole thing," Sandra said somberly.

"It certainly gives me food for thought."

I was now more highly attuned to the things I saw out of the corner of my eye. It didn't happen all the time, but it was happening. Normally, within a couple of feet away, I would catch an invisible glimpse of energy ripple, maybe around a corner or jumping behind furniture.

On my return to Felicia's, the first night I was feeling anxious when it was time to go to sleep. I decided not to even spend the time on my back relaxing. Instead I rolled onto my side and began to drift off. As I was drifting, I again felt something crawling on me, and I jumped up and threw the covers off. I sat there feeling helpless and was almost in tears. When I lay back down, I pulled the blanket over my head and prayed for protection and help. The rest of the night I slept undisturbed.

The second night brought a minor taunt up around my head, mussing with my hair, it felt like. Any allusion to sexual feelings in my dreams that night awoke me immediately, at which point I'd tuck the blankets around my body and ask for protection. The third night, as I was almost asleep, I felt something pull my breath out of my mouth. I awoke with a start and felt fear, but now anger was rising.

I began whispering loudly so as not to wake Felicia down the hall: "*That's enough! You are not welcome here! Leave now! I've had it. No more games. Back off!*" Fear was diminishing, and I was now officially pissed off.

A resolve came over me, reminding me of a rape attempt I experienced when I was twelve years old. During the attack, I had my wits about me, which continues to surprise me to this day. In the midst of conversing and doing my best to stall and talk my way out of the danger I was in, I asked the question, "Does this have to do with sex?" I added, "If it does, I don't do that kind of thing."

The perpetrator then said, "You have to learn sometime, and now's the time."

My ire rose instantly to anyone trying to control me, and I stated loudly, adamantly, and clearly, "I will learn when I'm good and ready. You can't tell me I have to learn this now!" In the end, I did get away without incurring physical damage. I did incur emotional damage, though.

I was ready to take on this stance now with the gremlins. I was done dealing with it. In the anger and self-preservation, I continued, "You are cast out by the Light and Love of the Lord Jesus Christ. All the Beings of Light are now called on for protection, and you are to go!"

I really didn't know if this was going to work. It sounded like it should. As I lay down to sleep, I called out and asked for continued protection for both myself and Felicia, and to cast out whatever was in the house. My warrior staff was out and ready, and I slept soundly.

On the worldlier end of things, over the next couple of weeks I waited patiently—patiently for me, that is—for some response from the Tree. I was anxious for the interview and praying to be accepted. I heard some other good news, which gave me another area of focus: M would be returning to town. I was able to schedule a private meeting and made my list of questions. I had a week before his arrival.

I'd been rereading some of *Spiritual Nutrition*, which was helping give me some perspective on leaks in one's energy field. I connected the dots of blood sugar issues and illness, which can deplete the protective energy field and create openings for undesirable entities. I hadn't been ill, but I had been dealing with a recurrence of hypoglycemia. I also had been wondering if these gremlins had been attached to me for a long time and I just hadn't been able to perceive them until now. Although I hadn't been harassed for a while, I was still concerned and felt I should have an understanding as to how I'd created an opening for this in my reality.

50

Patience was a heavy lesson on the table of my learning. The desired direction of movement was in sight, yet the time requirement necessary for all pieces to fall into place was testing all areas of my patience and my ideas of control. There were rumblings and tremors of foundational shifting, which were exciting and anxiety producing because so much was unknown. There were only glimmers of possibilities, or sensory impulses nabbing my awareness, but nothing with any kind of solidity, which was always challenging for me. I was living in the gray zone; ambiguity was trying to befriend me.

By the middle of September 2007, I had yet to have my phone interview with the Tree. Schedules weren't aligning. There were a couple of instances when a phone interview was set with Sally, the assistant, though the call never came. My expectations, black-and-white thinking, and judgment of dependability and follow-through were all on my chopping block. I was vying for control in a plethora of internal ways, only to become more twisted up in self-imposed knots.

I had heard back initially from Sally with congratulations on the acceptance. I was in, but I still needed to have the phone interview, which would inform me of other needed details and would allow the Tree to gather some final information from me. I was thrilled about the acceptance and had already begun shopping for the long list of books that I'd be studying. Some books I found at Powell's; others I had to order online. In my mind something more significant needed to take place via the phone interview before I could completely believe this new chapter was indeed going to happen.

Byron and I had looked over the options of how often I'd need to fly to Arizona for the workshops, how many workshops I could do back-to-back per visit, and what the additional cost would be for the travel. I knew I wouldn't be going down to do any of the on-site classes while I was still with Felicia. Some of them were two weeks at a time, and she just didn't have enough caregivers to cover those absences. However, I was ready to begin the at-home study aspect as soon as I could.

There were also some personal challenges when it came time to explain to family what my plan was and why. Making it more complicated was the fact that my reasoning didn't make sense to the more critical thinkers in my family. My father and some extended family wanted to know exactly who and what the Essenes were and how I would minister from that tradition. Others wanted to know why I wanted to do this. And if I tried to integrate the terminology of *priest/priestess* into the mix, that seemed to confuse them more, since those titles implied more of a Catholicism slant.

Because I functioned intuitively, I didn't have all the answers yet. And some things I wouldn't really know until I was already committed to the adventure. There is an irony that I really do function from intuition for most things in my life, and yet I'm also known as a control freak by those who know me well. These two forces within me can sometimes feel like dueling banjos.

In the midst of our calculations, Byron and I realized it was going to be almost impossible for me to travel back and forth given our income.

"I think we should just move there," I said after one of our talks.

"You want to just pick up and move there?" asked Byron, as he took a deep breath.

"I know they have job openings at the Tree all the time. Maybe we just go and live there."

"In community? Right. Neither of us do community very well. You said that you will have to be at least 90 percent raw for the training, and once you're ordained as a priestess …" He was reasoning when I cut him off midstream.

"Please don't use that term. I'm preparing to be a minister. I've tried using the other word, and it just doesn't feel right. It's *minister*. I'm preparing for the Essene minister ordination," I stated firmly.

"Okay. Whatever. My point is, I'm not in the same mode you are. I'm not ready to be a raw foodist. I'm not interested in living in a spiritual community. That might change down the road, but not now," he said.

"Listen, I'm not ready to go anywhere until Felicia passes. She's doing great. That could be years. If it's that long, I may reconsider, but right now, I'm here for the long haul with her, despite my own struggles with caregiving. I'll have plenty home study to keep me busy for quite a while as well. I'm just throwing out options, ideas— brainstorming. Nothing is written in stone."

We were still learning how to communicate with each of our extremes. I often threw out ideas as if they were real. I relate somatically. I get a sense of how a situation might feel in my body by pretending as if. Outside-the-box thinking opened up other possibilities that might otherwise be missed. Byron was still learning not to take every idea I had literally.

"Maybe we'll just move to the town where the Tree is located. Who knows?" We ended the conversation on this note.

More things were up in the air. Timing unknown. Path unknown. Destination unknown. The question of patience rubbed me in all sorts of opposing directions. One afternoon with Felicia, I was having a minor tantrum about people following through with appointments, or the lack thereof, and she just held me steady in her gaze until I was done. She looked right through me and called me out on my lack of trust and faith. She told me I wasn't the one in control, no matter how much I wanted to be, and said I was only making myself miserable.

"Think about it," she said as she wheeled herself out of the kitchen to go brush out her wigs.

She was right. I needed to just let go and trust in divine timing. "How many times do I need to learn this lesson?" I asked myself, feeling like a deflated balloon. I was acting like the spoiled child my spiritual grandfather had scolded me about.

I let go. After Felicia set me straight, with her eagle-eye sight on me, I was able to see myself more clearly, and I knew I needed to trust. That Sunday, after arriving home from my shift with her, I got the call from Sally. To my surprise, the call was short and sweet. It was limited to another welcome. She made sure I had all the information of scheduled classes and the booklist. She asked if I had any other questions. That was it. All of my fretting for a fifteen-minute conversation of confirmations.

Two weeks after the phone interview with Sally, Felicia died. It was Saturday evening. Dinner was finished, and we were getting ready for dessert and our Saturday night ritual of watching *The Lawrence Welk Show*. We both loved the dancing. Though we had gotten her to the hospital, later that night she died from a stroke.

When her son called me on Sunday morning to let me know she'd passed, I wasn't surprised, but the heartbreak rushed forth. I'd tried to learn from the deaths of other elders I'd cared for. I did my best not to have regrets. When Babalicious died, not only was she the first death of someone close to me whom I was deeply connected to and whom I loved tremendously, but also much of my pain was tied to my regret.

My last night with Babalicious, I'd been impatient with her. I hadn't slept for the two previous nights. One of the reasons was that my fear issues were rearing their heads. In conjunction with this was the fact that every time she woke up, I had to get through all my internal chaos in order to get back to sleep.

She too had been experiencing her own anxiety in the night, waking up frightened, anxious, fearful, and needing the commode. Once she relieved herself, we'd climb back into bed. I'd snuggle her up, and we'd talk and say some prayers. Sometimes I'd read something soothing to her. We'd talk about why she was scared or anxious. She didn't know for sure, but soon enough we figured out she wasn't prepared for death, and there were signs indicating that she was nearing that event. Our last night together, after her numerous anxiety attacks, prayers, and going to the bathroom, I was exhausted. I told her she just needed to go to sleep. I cuddled her, but it was a cold cuddle. I could tell, and no doubt she could. I told her we'd already been through all of this, everything was fine, and tomorrow would be here soon enough. Any sensitivity I'd had, had flown the coop in my seventy-two-hour exhaustion. She was asleep when the next care shift started, and my last memories of our time together were of my callousness to her needs, feelings, and vulnerabilities. I was devastated.

The evening of her funeral, as I sat doing a ritual of goodbyes and apologies, and loving her deeply, I began to sense her presence in the corner of the room. I knew she was with me. She understood and was loving me in return. This was when my perception of death really changed for me.

I'd done pretty well with the two other clients who'd died in between Babalicious and Felicia. I had done my best to keep my focus on being of service and staying connected to Felicia's needs. The day she died, there was a baseball game on that she was pretty excited about. Not a sports fan in the least, I declined her request to join her for the game. She understood, also knowing that Saturday was my chore day, since my shift ended on Sunday morning. I checked in on her here and there to see if she was enjoying herself, which she was. Before dinner she'd been in her room straightening her dresser and her wigs. I called to her a couple of times that food was ready. As she rolled out, she asked me while laughing, "You know what I like about you?"

"What?" I asked back.

"That you remind me of me," she said, laughing.

"I hope that's a good thing. Is this because I've been calling you? Let me guess, it's the impatience, control, and high expectations we share, which also has a tendency to make us a little cranky." I was also laughing. I knew we shared some qualities, and she was taking the proper opportunity to share her wisdom with me.

"That's right!"

I was flattered by her compliment, even though I knew the qualities she appreciated swung into both categories of attributes and deficits. I appreciated our humor together and the affection that was saved for the good-night hug. And I deeply regretted not watching the baseball game with her. That was the one time I felt I'd failed to rise to the occasion of doing what was the right thing, and it happened to be on the day she died, September 29.

51

Felicia's death changed everything for Byron and me. I couldn't help but wonder if this was an expression of the Universe's timing. I felt in some ways like she'd helped me along my way. Many people believe that things just happen, that there doesn't always have to be some underlying reason or spiritual meaning behind everything. I believe that can be true. But I also believe there are many connections like an invisible web between us, circumstance, time, and karma.

All of this coincided with the timing of our six-month lease ending. We had no ties. Granted, I had family in Portland, and it was definitely my home. But maybe it was time to move on. The most sensible choice, not that we were that sensible, was to move down by the Tree. Byron didn't feel any need to stay in Portland. He had moved to Portland in 2002, just after finishing grad school in St. Louis. At that time his restlessness and the percolations of awakening called him out west. Portland drew him then, but he didn't have deep roots there.

Byron and I didn't need to discuss this move long, not once we got past the idea of living in the community at the Tree. That was a *no*. We set our sights on the next logical place, Tucson, Arizona. It was only a couple of hours away, and with it being a college town, we had no doubt we would find what we needed to sustain ourselves. Now the question was, when?

For our wedding, our gift request, if people were so inclined, was to make a financial offering to our future. At the time, we didn't have our own home, and I had most anything needed for nesting. We didn't really know where we were going to be led next, and we had always lived simple and light and intended to continue that way. It was through the generosity of others that our gift money, which had been put into savings, was now going to assist our move and getting settled in Tucson.

This decision was made just a few days after Felicia's passing. By the end of the week, we received a call from her son, Joe, asking us if we would do him the favor of moving into her home while they settled the estate. We were taken aback, and I told him we were intending to make this move in the next few months. He said a few months would be perfect. They didn't want the house sitting empty, and they trusted me to care for things as she would have liked. I was honored, and of course I was happy to help. It was all falling into place very quickly, in ways we couldn't have even anticipated.

With wheels in motion, the packing began, along with weeding out wasn't absolutely necessary for us to have when we moved. The intention was to fit all of our belongings, Urisk, and ourselves into our little Dodge Neon. The first weeding process would take place during our move to Felicia's. Byron was keeping his job at NAPA, and I would move sessions to the downstairs when we moved. Thankfully, this was fine with Joe. If I trusted those who came into the home, so would he. Our time of departure from Portland was slated for the end of December 2007.

Our families took it all in stride. They were learning that they didn't know what to expect from us and to leave their doubts at the door when we announced crazy ideas.

The move into Felicia's was much more painful for me than I'd anticipated. Joe and Carol had cleared some things out of her room, and the upstairs bathroom, where we'd be staying. Space was cleared in various cupboards and drawers, in the kitchen, bedroom, and bathroom to make room for our minimal belongings.

The first day I was there alone was deeply sorrowful. I found myself sitting in the living room, apologizing for not watching the game with Felicia, for being impatient when she wanted to rearrange the living room, and for not being more enthusiastic when she wanted to teach me to cook. Although I knew I was a good caregiver to her and that we had a lovely rapport, and although she knew I loved her, I still felt I'd let us both down. That's one of the teachings of death, I've learned over the years. It is those gifts that we don't even realize at the time one is alive to be gifts that are vital—gifts of ourselves, time, and selflessness, gifts of the heart.

When I looked out the window, I remembered her happily greeting that view every morning. It was her ritual to wheel out into the living room, look out the large windows, and greet the morning sun and expansive view with gratitude. As I put my and Byron's clothes away in her room, I could still see her organizing with care what she could in her room. Walking down the hallway, I imagined her whipping past me. She was a speed demon in her wheelchair, even in the house. I missed her greatly.

The first night as Byron and I were falling asleep in her room, I saw the night as she did. The green glowing numbers from the clock. The trickle of sheen from the neighbors' outdoor light. The outline of her closet doors and dresser. And I imagined our good-night hug. The basement door was closed and locked just as I'd always done. Urisk was upstairs with us, so he could settle in once again to the smaller space upstairs, not hiding away in some unknown crevice downstairs.

At 7:00 a.m., we were awakened to Felicia's closet doors gently banging. Not too loud, not too soft. I didn't move and quietly asked Byron, "Did you hear that?"

"Yeah. It woke me up. What is it?"

"It's the closet doors," I whispered.

"It's probably Urisk," Byron said.

"Nope. He's right here next to me. It's stopped, but I bet if you look at the clock, you'll see it reads 7:00." I was feeling a rush of excitement. This was her wake-up time every day.

"Huh. You're right, it's seven," he responded.

I was smiling and softly greeted, "Good morning, Felicia!" Still as on time as ever.

This morning wake-up continued for a week or so. There were mixed emotions for me. I wanted to help her move on and was not sure how. And I missed her and loved knowing she was still somewhat with us.

Since I was only focusing on the private sessions, I thought this was a good opportunity to deepen my own practices. It made sense to give myself extra attentiveness to my time with Divine Mother and Her spontaneous movement. I'd been fairly steady in my meditation practice, and at the last visit with M, he said that when I felt ready, I could extend my meditation and increase the Kriya technique. As a part of the new beginnings, it felt appropriate to dive in deeper.

52

One morning while sitting in meditation before my client arrived for her session, I felt the pull of Divine Mother walking me through the house into Felicia's room. As I entered, I was confused as I was left standing in the doorway without further inner direction. Just about that time, the doorbell rang. It was Fiona arriving, so I put my attention on our session.

Over the next couple of days, this guidance appeared a couple of times. It seemed I'd be led to a place in the house, to be left hanging without the guidance continuing. Then as I was making dinner one evening, I felt the presence of Divine Mother rise in me. This time Her hold guided me to completion. I was moved into specific areas of the house. Once I was in the right place, I felt wafts of emotions of loss, grief, deep regret move through me, releasing through my being. My arms and hands were guided into movements, which I could only assume were to clear the energy in the space. I could feel emotions rising to the surface. I could sense they weren't my emotions but Felicia's that were lodged in these spaces in her home.

I remembered Felicia sitting and looking out the corner window of the living room. I had assumed she was enjoying the view and the quiet. But what I experienced through the inner guidance in the space by the window was not simple daydreaming. There was grief. I was now the vehicle for its release. There were a handful of places that I was guided to that held deep sadness, some more than others. I was led finally to a closet that I'd never before opened. There was a deep well of sorrow held in a closet that wailed through me when I was guided to open it. When I opened the closet, I saw, felt, and witnessed something so intimate, I knew her in a way words would never have been able to speak. There in the closet were the remnants of a life Felicia had said goodbye to because of the paralysis. The closet held a loss she'd never speak of. This clearing was beautiful. It was so personal and so intimate, and her pain was honored as it moved through me.

After an hour, I came to, a little quivery, tired, and once again, in very strange territory that escaped all reason to me. I felt incredibly humbled and an indescribable love for this woman. I prayed that I had done right by her, that I had aided her in releasing what had been stuck in this material plane. She had already stopped banging the doors in the morning, to my dismay, I realized selfishly. But after this I prayed for her final exit and blessing for the next part of her journey.

Byron came home to a dinner still in the making. While we were finishing up, I shared with him what had happened. I withheld a few of the details. They felt too intimate, and I would never want to betray her trust, or whatever this trust was, that was given to me.

"I can't help but wonder if this wasn't always a part of the plan. What is our karma?" I asked through tears.

"I don't know, honey." Byron held me.

"When I reflect back on not getting the job and then getting it even though I wasn't the first choice, I feel it's like I was supposed to be here. Then, I fell in love with Felicia immediately, and our night time tuck-ins for bed felt so much like she was my little girl. And now, she died and we were asked to move in here. If I hadn't been here, would her energy have been able to move forward? Would it have been stuck? And how did I happen to be the one who could assist with this process? With everything else this path has to bring, is helping people pass on to the next realm part of my purpose?" More tears of loss and wonderment.

"Sweetie, I really don't know. It's all pretty amazing, that's for sure. Maybe a bath would feel good?" he asked, knowing exactly how much I needed that soothing time just then.

Being at Felicia's temporarily allowed not only deepening of my practice to take place but also time to integrate what had been taking place in Felicia's home. Death became a primary contemplation. I felt intrigued after the clearing experience, and oddly I felt silent and aged—aged from something my mind wasn't wrapping around. But the deepening was understood by the heart and soul. I wondered how all of this connected with the move that lay just ahead. I became more aware of the term *priestess*, my avoidance of it, and the uneasiness inside me when it was spoken. Why would I be so adverse? And what was its connection to all the work I'd been doing, which now included this door opening to death? Or was there even a connection?

In between the small handful of clients I had, I became absorbed in two other books, one from my lovely friend Caroline, called *The Unknown She*, and the other about modern-day shamanism. Both were speaking to me, guiding me abstractly, yet offering familiarity.

On the days when my focus wasn't so internalized, the Tucson Craigslist was the go-to for apartments and jobs. Byron had two good friends from college who lived in Arizona. They both had come to our wedding. Emily lived in Phoenix. As soon as we decided to embark on this new adventure, Byron contacted her, and she warmly extended the offer of her home to us while we got settled. Connor had been a best friend and roommate in St. Louis. He lived in Tucson with his family. We were welcome to stay there as needed, but we chose to remain in Phoenix most of the time.

Scanning the want ads and rentals gave me an idea of what would be available for us when we arrived. During a search for vegetarian or vegan restaurants in Tucson, I found only two, one of each, which was disappointing. However, the main one caught my eye, intention, and determination as a potential place of employment. The website was very bohemian/hippy-like. Though we weren't hippies, we fit more into that vein than into the mainstream. The Middle Eastern vibe called out to me, and there was ecstatic delight when I saw the connections the Caravan had.

Not only was the Caravan a physical restaurant in Tucson, but also they had a crew that traveled the festival circuit and hosted some of our favorite musicians, including Shimshai, who'd played at our wedding. The pictures on the site were images of festival shows inside the large Bedouin tents and pictures from the restaurant. The décor was bright yet earthy colors, floor cushions with low tables, beautifully carved wood furniture from Afghanistan. The foods were vegetarian and vegan, stews, salads, flatbreads, and amazing desserts. I spent hours on the website looking at the photo gallery and some of the videos, getting a feel for our next chapter.

I had not done any serious restaurant work that really counted, except possibly the café at the Alano Club, where I got sober. At twenty years old I'd been a hostess. I did a quick stint as a waitress in a French café, and was a cocktail waitress at twenty-one in somewhat of a rough-and-tumble bar during one of my trips back to Tulsa, Oklahoma, which was where I had spent all of my teenage years in the late 1970s through the mid-1980s.

This limited experience wasn't about to stop me, however. For most of my life, I had the ability to get what I went after. It wasn't so much as I forced myself into situations I wanted; it was more that I intuited that A, B, or C, was going to be, and it just so happened it was what I wanted.

For instance, when Caleb and I were looking for our own home after living in community, we searched and searched for the right home. As we pulled up to the bungalow in Northeast Portland, I knew it was the one. I loved it.

"This is it!" I squealed.

"We haven't even gone inside yet," Caleb said in response.

"It doesn't matter. I know it. I love it. Let's go in!" I was talking the whole time that I was getting out of the car and walking up the sidewalk.

"Oh my God! I love it. See, I told you! It's the one!" I continued to say as we wandered around the eight-hundred-square-foot Craftsman with its huge backyard and beautiful bright sunroom.

There were two other applicants ahead of us once we turned in the paperwork. I wanted it so bad. The initial excitement quickly turned into worried attachment and fear that we wouldn't get it. I was clinging. All the while Caleb reminded me that if it was meant to be, it would be. On the one hand I knew it was ours. I felt it in my bones. On the other hand, I lacked the trust and confidence that the feeling I had was aligned with the Universe. In the end, we were the recipients of the adorable little abode that we called home for a couple of years.

That was how I felt about the Caravan. I knew it was where I was to be. Just as in the past, I felt it in my bones. Byron was just as excited about it not only because of the food, but also because of its history of hosting musicians we believed to be conscious and spiritually evolving the world with their gifts.

Visiting with my parents the next time, I wanted to show them the website. One could say I held them captive in the process for longer than they needed, but they were gracious enough to indulge me.

"How do you know you really want to work there if you've never visited? Things aren't always as they appear online, you know," my dad said with his practical sensibility.

"I know that what you're saying holds weight, and well, I could be disappointed when I get there. That's just how it goes sometimes. But for now, this is where I'm setting my intention," I replied.

"There's no guarantee they're going to be hiring when the time comes for you to move down there," said my mom.

"Maybe, maybe not. I've already sent the owner a letter and résumé. I gave her our estimated time of arrival, and hopefully I'll hear something back from her, just to touch base ahead of time."

"Don't get your hopes up is all I'm saying," cautioned my dad. "You'll want to check it out before you commit to anything."

"The thing is, I *already know* this is where I'll be." We all left it alone at that point. Our philosophies in life were at a point of divergence. I appreciated their input and knew they had valid points. However, I operated in a very different way. I often called it *the path of the body* or *the path of the heart*, which really meant I lived with a strong reliance on intuition. Applying the intellect had its place, but it was usually a secondary application. My energy was already there.

53

The second month of housesitting for Felicia's family found Byron and me finalizing our move time. We figured we'd leave around the eighteenth of December and shoot for being in Phoenix for Christmas. My parents were sad we wouldn't be there for the holiday. And we had plans to go back to Indiana for a couple of days for Thanksgiving, at which point my friend Fiona would come watch Urisk and the house. Excitement was building, while on a soul level I had some unresolved percolations.

The unresolved and discombobulating feelings revolved around the potential ordination when I finished school. I was also feeling challenged by people closest to me to accept the term *priestess* into my vocabulary.

"Why does it make such a difference to you all?" I asked Sandra, Caleb, and Byron one evening.

"It doesn't make a difference to us. But it seems to make a *big* difference to you." I could tell Caleb was going to attempt to put a crack in my wall.

"You talked about how the book *The Unknown She*, focusing on the sacred feminine, is creating anxiety in you." Sandra was reflecting our conversation back to me. "You were sharing how you start to feel shaky and quivery inside. Remember?"

"Of course I remember." I was feeling exasperated and vulnerable with three pairs of eyes staring at me. "Listen, I don't have a problem with the sacred feminine. Have I not been working with and allowing myself to be filled with this sacred presence of the Divine Mother for these past couple of years? Hasn't my life and reality been encompassed with *Her*? So why must I have a problem simply because of a term that I'm just not partial to?" I said in self-defense and denial.

"Honey," said Byron, "you know what it means when you start to feel quivery, anxious, restless, and shaky, like you need to explode. Right?"

I stared blankly.

He continued, "You know you've got a meltdown with new awareness trying to break through. When this is happening these days, it seems like it's connected to your resistance to look directly at what a priestess *means to you*." He was helping me find focus in the conversation.

"Do you remember when you were invited to that Goddess party a few years ago?" Caleb asked.

There it was. My whole body felt squirrely and I began to squirm in my seat. "There! That's it!" Caleb exclaimed. "That was the expression of resistance. That's what the issue is, right there. It drove you crazy when you heard the term *goddess*, just like the term *priestess.*"

"You're right! I don't like those terms. I do have resistance to them. They sound pretentious and kind of woo-woo to me," I affirmed.

All three of them laughed. Sandra commented with a grin, "Sweetie, you have to admit, your judgments on woo-woo don't hold much weight. Of all people!"

"How many judgments have you had, labeling things as woo-woo and not wanting anything to do with them?" Caleb was recapping his years of knowing me. "Let's see. Channeling. Energy work. The reality of chakras. I guess we see what time has done to those blockages of resistance!" He was laughing at the situation and at me, and I had to admit, I had fallen prey to *some* of those things that I couldn't explain or felt were too out there.

"Now," Sandra added, "it's the resistance to whatever your perceptions are about priestesses and goddesses. Just remember, as you've often said to me, 'Whatever we resist persists.'"

"This isn't new for you." Caleb grew serious again. "This is an area you have always been struggling with. The feminine, the yin, softening. I'm not saying the Goddess or priestesses are all warm and fuzzy, but your resistance has been deep, and it seems like it wants to show itself. Whatever that means, we don't know."

I wanted to be thoughtful and vulnerable in my response. These were the three people who knew me the best, in all of my glory and then not so glorious. They had watched me struggle through some harrowing, mind-expanding times, and they each have also witnessed the walls I had built up for self-protection and secrecy, guarded at the gates with control and judgment. I wanted their assistance in getting clear, and yet I resisted truly being seen. That combination was a conundrum.

"Here's what I want to say. I know these terms have some charge for me. On the surface I can easily identify things that repel me. There's a side of me that is a purist. For instance, just because I do yoga, I'm not a yogi, even though I could say that the yoga I've been blessed to experience feels to me to be more pure as a spiritual path of yoga, rather than the commercialization of yoga we have grown accustomed to. However, for me, it's a title that holds weight and experience and wisdom that I can't claim. So, no, I won't use this term. *Priestess* and *Goddess*, yes, I'm triggered. I feel like I have no true knowledge of their meaning. I feel like all these terms hold keys to sacred knowledge. They are titles of mystery, and they're thrown around in common everyday usage. Does it have to make a difference? Maybe not. But that's not how I hold it, whatever it is. I know it's bigger than me. Are you all following me?"

They're an attentive audience, and I appreciated that. "Continuing on then. On a deeper level, yes, I do struggle with the feminine energies and the qualities of softness, surrender, and vulnerability. And I do have a yangness, more masculine energies or hardness, in me, trying to maintain control. I know I'm out of balance. For instance, this book that's triggering all of this right now makes me feel anxious and overwhelmed. When I read this account, it sounds as if this woman has turned over all control to a very disruptive force. It feels very chaotic to me. There are interviews with women who are leading lives surrendered to the brink of what I perceive as chaos." I saw a smirk or two on their faces. "I know. I'm the pot calling the kettle black. But it's all relative. I don't want to live without some control!"

I could feel myself getting emotional and shaky. I witnessed them all taking witness of my reactivity. "Does it feel like some of the guidance that comes through me, such as the mudras, has a ritualistic or initiatory expression? Yes. Does it feel like it holds sacred keys of priestess or Goddess knowledge? Okay, sure. Yes. But do I understand the knowledge? No. Can I claim it without understanding? I don't feel like I can."

"Okay. Points taken," said Caleb. "But you are going away to study to be ordained as an Essene priestess. You say minister, but the program is priest/priestess, correct? So how do you feel about that?"

"At this point, I feel just as I explained. Now, if this learning sheds more light for me about those mysteries, which is what I'm hoping, and if I feel like I can stand in whatever shoes those are, then I will accept the title with honor. Ya know, I'm hoping that my studies will help me to understand the mystical life that moves through me. I want to understand and embody what I'm given. But I'm not going to call myself something that I haven't embodied in a pure sense," I said.

"And how are you going to deal with your feelings about it in the interim?" asked Sandra.

"She'll break down at some point," Byron said quietly and knowingly. "Babe, you know your deepest desire is to surrender, and it just has to fight through all of these other layers that ego clings onto."

"He's absolutely right!" Caleb said laughingly. "We've all seen it! We know how it works. Resistance to shambles, to opening, to the next stage! Better you than me!"

"Thanks. I think." I finally softened. I was blessed to have all of them, even though I didn't realize it or show it most of the time.

54

Who's to answer for sure "Which came first, the chicken or the egg?" The next series of events held that type of rhyme and riddle. I was still grieving Felicia, even though it felt like she had moved on. I couldn't imagine the pain that a spouse goes through after the death of their loved one, while still living in the home. I knew Felicia for only a matter of months, at least in this lifetime, and yet looking around, I saw her everywhere.

I allowed the grief to come as it needed. In the meantime, I was becoming aware of Urisk wanting to spend an unusual amount of time right next to me, or even sleeping on me, for long stretches at a time. His abnormal behavior piqued my curiosity, which demanded I watch him more closely. He was barely eating, and within a short period of time, he had stopped altogether. It was time for a visit to the vet.

The diagnosis concerned his thyroid. They gave me medication for him that helped, and before too long, his appetite increased again. However, he was still a little sluggish. When I knew we were out of danger was when he no longer was my lap baby. This was a relief, but I missed having cuddles with him. My and Byron's move date was nearing, and we hoped Urisk would be healthy enough to travel. I was slowly beginning to realize how empathic he was and how much my, our, energy impacted him.

In the meantime, my psyche was working with an interior crack, threatening to break loose. One Sunday, I had my weekly date with my little sis through Big Brothers Big Sisters. We were trying to get extra time in together with the move coming up. This transition was going to be hard for her too.

Driving out to the outlying east side of the city, I was rocking out to Rusted Root, my favorite album of theirs, *Remember*. This whole album was a powerful catalyst for me often. It is one of the most accurate musical renditions of the awakening process I have ever heard. The music and lyrics illuminated what I knew but didn't own and failed to have words for, and served as a reflection that I wasn't alone on this path. I often felt isolated in my experiences. I was grateful to have people in my life who got it or were traveling in their own way, but the truth was that I didn't have anyone front and center going through the same extent of experiences that I was. When I listened to Rusted Root, I felt instantly connected and understood.

I had the music turned up fairly loud and was lost in one of my favorite songs. I could feel that the divine presence was alive and well through me. I felt the energy building inside and a state of ecstasy enveloping me, so I pulled the car over. I sat there and completely surrendered to the bliss and electricity streaming through my being. The mind was being filled with things that I would not remember in the aftermath. This day, though, my whole chest was feeling like it was going to explode. The currents felt strong at the heart center. Love filled me, but there was also a pressure building that was in excess of what I could handle or move through efficiently. I turned off the music, intentionally brought myself back into my personality self, took a deeper breath, and allowed myself to acclimate to the normal state of being. When I felt settled, I started the car and proceeded to pick up Jackie for our lunch date.

That evening I returned home to some wonderful-looking dinner Byron had made. We chatted a little about the day. He'd had alone time while I was out and enjoyed that peace and quietude. I checked in about Urisk as we began eating. I received a positive report. He'd eaten a couple of nibbles and taken his medication with a little struggle, Byron said. The next thing I knew, all of my energy suddenly emptied out. I was exhausted. I could hardly keep my head up or my eyes open. Lifting the fork made my heart rate race, and chewing just exhausted me.

"Babe, I'm so sorry. This looks so good, but I think I've got to go to bed," I said groggily.

"It's only six o'clock. Are you okay?" He looked concerned.

"My body must have not done well with that green tea I had at lunch. I guess it's just caught up with me. Maybe I just need a little downtime." I pushed myself away from the table and went in to bed.

After I'd rested for an hour or so, I felt better. Upon getting up, I was hungry and wanted to see how Byron was doing. I warmed up some food and joined him in the living room. I ate, and we chatted for about ten minutes before I began to feel exhausted again. I noticed my heartbeat felt rapid and sluggish. An odd combination. Once again, I excused myself, kissed him good night, and went in to bed. Sleep was what I needed.

For the next two days my body would cycle in extremes. I would feel rested once I lay down, but then exhaustion would follow quickly behind once I moved around after any given nap. On the second day, I lay in bed for the third nap of the day, and it was only around eleven o'clock in the morning. I was staring up at the ceiling. Thank goodness for my practice and patience of just being. I found comfort in lying and staring. The heart rate evened out. I needed to attempt to track exactly what had taken place and assess whether or not I needed to go to the doctor. For better or for worse, I no longer felt the need to rush to the doctor as I had in the past. Because of that, coupled with all the odd things that my body goes through, it often just took some reflection and time before the body would come back into balance. I hoped this time would be the same.

I backtracked to the driving on Sunday with Rusted Root ecstasy. I knew that was a lot of energy coming through. I also reflected back to the increase in my Kriya meditation. The breath work had felt challenging, and I could tell the rhythm of my breathing was trying to adjust. Then, of course, there was the grief I was still carrying for Felicia and my worry over Urisk's health. Not to mention other eruptions on subtler levels. I suppose I had my plate full energetically. I drifted off.

In a half-asleep state, I felt the presence of Jesus and Magdalene. *Am I dreaming?* I asked myself. It had been a while since I'd received them. I felt Jesus speaking to me from *above*. Above where? I wasn't sure, just *above*.

"You must let go of your confusion and stories about why you are here at this place and time, in this house, and about the role you are being called to."

Then from *below*, at the base of the sternum, I heard Magdalene: "Little bird, you are flying, falling, flying, falling. The falls are not failures. They are your lessons. By believing in the failure, you miss the moments of flight."

Jesus from *above*: "You must rise to meet Us. We are always in your presence, and you are always in Ours. But you must rise upward. That is part of your lesson. We will not come down as We did before."

Magdalene, from *below*, at the heart: "You are being filled with Love. Love will show you the truth and the desire to move outward and give, to teach, to be compassionate. But this isn't a personal love that fills you. You will hear the call of soul, and it is Love that will guide you to meet the call."

Again, I heard and felt Jesus from *above*: "You cannot let go completely, no matter how much you may wish. It isn't your time. But you will continue to let go, and the desire of release will grow within you. You are too attached to the physical body. Do not be so frightened as the vibration of your heart transforms.

"You do not get to grieve the passing of that soul in the way you know. It is to be released and helped to move onward, which is a part of your work here. To grieve on the personal level is not a luxury for you, as it lowers your consciousness away from truth. To lower your vibration and consciousness is to attach to the physical form. This soul may still have some remnants of energy remaining, but it must be set free."

Attention shifted to the heart, *below*: "There is a loss for you through this transformation. You are undergoing a kind of death of lower consciousness by aiding here. You now begin to see the death process in a new way. The mourning for you is the loss of a younger, naive version of you. The old you is dying away."

Jesus from *above*: "You will cause more distress in your being by wanting to grieve, by not letting go of the confusion of this world. It won't transmute in the way needed if you hold on to the desire for the grief. You don't need to talk about it. You don't need to write about it. Your task is to remain in a state of raised consciousness."

Although I was in a soft state of mind, I knew I was awake. I recognized that I was being guided into functioning from a higher level of consciousness, that I was being required to raise my energy to the higher centers, which was where I would find the higher truths, whether for the purpose of connecting with these divine energies or to be able to perceive the truths beyond our mundane world and consciousness.

Receiving this guidance also enabled me to see that there were deep changes taking place, not only in the physical heart but also in the energetic heart and the consciousness held therein. It was also clear, once again, that what happens on one plane of existence affects the other planes.

Around one o'clock that afternoon, I felt strong enough to get out of bed. I had a bite to eat and even felt able to tidy up around the house, but as soon as I began to sweep, the action of moving my arms made my heart begin to race. I started coughing, and my heartbeat became the paradox again of sluggish and rapid. Sitting staring out at the expansive view from the living room picture windows, I felt sadness wanting to creep in. *No,* I thought. *I need to keep the energy lifted.* I sent prayers of love to the soul of Felicia. I whispered, "It's okay. You're free to go from this plane. This is a new beginning." My whisperings were really to remind myself of what was true. If there were particles of her remaining, I didn't think they were her anymore. More pressing, I knew I needed to go to the doctor.

The natural health clinic had a Chinese medicine office just down the hill in Northwest Portland. It wasn't terribly cold out, and Byron wouldn't be home until after five o'clock that evening. I left him a note letting him know where I was and asking him please to pick me up down there when he got home. I was the only one with a cell phone, as we're late bloomers in the tech world.

I put on a sweater and a hat. I tried to carry my purse, but the weight of it made my heart palpitate and race. Instead, I put my credit card, ID, and phone into my sweater pocket and began the descent down the hill. It was harder than I'd anticipated. Walking a few yards required me to sit and rest for a period of time. I tried to call my mother, Fiona, and another friend or two, but no one answered. I didn't bother leaving messages. I couldn't go back up the hill. The incline would put me over the edge. I needed to finish this journey I'd begun. *How fitting,* I thought, since there was no going back from the Kundalini process. Just like this, I had to travel as carefully and consciously as possible. Walk and rest. Walk and rest.

A couple of hours later, I arrived at the doctor's. I had no appointment, which gave me time to recuperate. The heart rate was all over the place; palpitations were skipping to and fro. It seemed that when the heart felt sluggish, almost like mud trying to move through the valves, was when I'd cough. I did my best to pay attention to how each shift in sensation connected to other systems' functioning. The sluggishness made me cough. The palpitations made my breath shallow. The increased heart rate made my chest tight. And when everything was calming down with stillness, my breath would release and deepen, or I'd yawn.

The doctor was shocked that I'd come down the hill as I had when she began her intake process. I liked her a lot. She wanted to run some tests. She drew blood and took my pulse and said she would have results back in a day or two. I tried to explain how quickly this had come on and what had preceded it. I could tell it wasn't clicking, that the dots weren't connecting, so I let it go. I'd learned not to try to discuss the energetics of Kundalini, even with doctors who have a high degree of awareness, but I thought for sure this time it would be clear.

When I received my test results, they said I was severely anemic. My iron count was frighteningly low to the doctor. I, of course, was curious as to how it could have had such a dramatic effect rather than a gradual one. I wasn't getting an answer. I was prescribed eggs and yogurt, as our compromise, since I wouldn't eat meat. She also gave me some heavy-duty iron supplements and suggested I begin using magnesium. I had an EKG scheduled for the following week to check my heart.

55

The same heart patterns and exhaustion I'd been experiencing continued for a few days after I began the regimen prescribed, and then they lessened over time. Needless to say, a Thanksgiving trip to Indiana was out of the question. Byron would need to go without me. Use of my hands and arms, and sometimes even lifting the utensils to eat, made my heart rate increase with an uneven rhythm. I couldn't lie on my left side without the sluggish feeling in the valves, so I found myself on my back with a small pillow positioned along the spine. This alleviated tightening of the chest and contraction of the breath. Life-transforming moments appear when death is seemingly close at hand.

There were many moments during this period when my heart was racing so fast or the sluggishness was making me so weak that I almost wondered if I was dying. Lying in stillness, watching my breath and listening to my heart pounding in my ears, so loud and fast, I saw fears rising up and vanishing. The fears all had to do with control and fear of dying. In those moments, I surrendered. If this was my time, so be it. I let go. I drifted off in the racing of the heart, which eventually slowed. I let go into the pounding with no need to control it. I became one with the sensations, as I'd learned during the long clearing I'd had in the early days, guided by Gurudev. Nothing more to fight. I put my trust in God. The gift I was receiving was that by embracing my own death, fear released me from its clutches, at least while I was succumbing to it in stillness. I drifted off in peace.

Strength was being regained slowly but surely. I wasn't needing to go to bed every other hour during the day, but my energy level was very low. I would become exhausted easily. Therefore, I did what I could, I did it slowly, and I let go of what couldn't get accomplished. The tests on control and fears, however, weren't over.

Urisk was still having issues. The medication, though supporting his thyroid, made him unable to eat or drink. There were constant adjustments made to the dosage. I felt like I was living in the presence of death all around me. The lesson I'd received from Jesus and Magdalene regarding the personalizing of love and looking at death from the lower centers of consciousness was feeling challenged. My baby, Urisk, was slowly withering in front of my eyes. I had to wonder what else he was mirroring. It just so happened that Byron also had some thyroid issues at this time. Was Urisk's disposition a reflection of us, energetically?

He was trying to communicate with me, and I was doing my best to hear him. He would literally come to me and lead me to his food and water bowls. I had given him very shallow bowls because it seemed as though lifting his head over the bowl's edge was too challenging for him. We'd sit at the bowls, and he'd just stare at them. If I intimated in any way that I was leaving him, he'd move toward me until I sat back down on the floor with him. Sometimes if I put my fingers in the water. He'd try to drink or lick it off my fingers. Occasionally, he'd nibble at his food.

My heart was breaking even more. The emotions would erupt in palpitations and anxiety, or the beats missed would create a sluggishness, which would make me start to cough. Confusion was abounding. Urisk was in no condition to travel, nor was I at this rate.

We had only one month left to stabilize if we were going to move forward as planned. My thoughts were all over the place, trying to find a handle on some degree of certainty.

Should I leave him with my mother and fly him down to Tucson? I couldn't put him through that. *Should we just change our plans and stay?* No. I knew all of this was a part of the transformation into the next phase, which required our leaving Portland.

Is Urisk dying? Is he fighting to live and looking for assistance to eat so he will live? Will he continue to suffer like this by taking this medication? Is he trying to die but I'm selfishly forcing him to stay?

I was witnessing his vulnerability, his anxiousness, and his instability, as well as my own. However, it was my responsibility to lift myself up so I could be there for him. Regardless of what choices were made, he needed to be by my side. I wanted him with me, and he needed me. I prayed to heed what he needed on this physical plane, while being mindful of what was called for on the soul plane. I believed Urisk was indeed trying to live. We just needed to figure out the right dosage and experiment with food, and if he needed me to help him eat and drink, I was dedicated to that.

I was feeling better every day and was always surprised at how much farther I still needed to go. I went in for the stress test and EKG. They detected one blip during the test. It just so happened, they reported in the end, that I had a congenital heart defect. One of the valves doesn't always work properly, so they told me this was one of the reasons I felt the sluggishness when the blood wasn't pumping properly. They didn't detect anything else related to the palpitations when I was experiencing anxiety. Again, I asked questions about changes in breathing rhythms, about the grief, and about the anemia, and how all of this had come about so suddenly. "Stress. Refrain from stressful situations" was the only answer I was given.

When Byron returned from Indiana, we began discussing our plans more thoroughly one evening. To be more precise, Byron was discussing, and I was attempting to pin down the specifics, code word for *control*.

"So, babe, have you found out from Connor what time lines we'll be able to stay at his place when we get to Tucson?" I asked as we sat down for dinner.

"No. Not yet. I figure I'll call him when we get to Emily's" he replied simply.

"Wouldn't it be nice if we knew ahead of time which weekends are best for them for us to make the trip from Phoenix? They may want to know ahead so they can make their own plans." I could feel my chest beginning to tighten.

"I don't think it's going to matter to them. We'll be in the guest house. I really would like to spend time with them, but it isn't a necessity that they be there. I know we'll have time together once we get settled. However, it works out will be fine." He continued chewing his food nonchalantly, going with the flow.

"Clearly we have two different ways of going about this. Since we're going to be more or less homeless for a while, I feel like it'd be helpful to know when to expect to be in the temporary home-away-from-home spots. If you want to wait 'til we get to Emily's, that's fine. But then will you schedule in the dates that will work for them, so we know ahead of time how to plan things" I was feeling a rise in anxiety. I got up from the table, went into the kitchen, and took a couple of drops of the passionflower tincture, along with a dose of Calm (magnesium powder), adding it to a glass of water. I drank it down in one gulp.

I gave myself and Byron a little break from the conversation. "I've been looking at the routes we can drive. It'd be nice to take some smaller scenic roads when possible," Byron said, going to get his maps.

"Oh my God. Are you kidding me?" My voice rose with anxiety, and I could hardly catch my breath. He looked up at me, startled. "We just need to get there. The sooner, the better. The most direct route. The safest and most populated route."

"I thought more of a scenic drive would be more relaxing," he said innocently.

"Honey, listen. I appreciate that. But we have a sick and nervous cat who's barely hanging on. I feel like I'm barely hanging on. We need to have a solid plan. There is no way I want to risk any of my other crazy fear issues jumping to the surface by taking empty rural routes. I can't do it. I need to travel by daylight. I need to know we have motels available to stop before dark. I need to know there are plenty of gas stations." I was almost yelling now, coughing, and feeling exhausted.

"I'm sorry. I just thought it'd be fun," he said, looking like all the air had been let out of his balloon.

"I know. I get it. But it won't be fun. It'll be stressful. I wish I could go along with you and have a fun time. Maybe at some other time. Please, not now." I was calming slowly, but the tension was remaining steady because I felt guilty for putting him through all of this. He was working so hard and just wanted to have some enjoyment on the start of the new adventure.

"Okay. I need to look at the passes. If we leave in the next couple of weeks, I think we'll be fine." He changed the topic.

"We should probably get chains, don't you think?" I asked.

"Hmm. I don't think we'll need them ..." He didn't have a chance to finish.

"We need to have chains! It's better to be safe. We don't want to be stuck. Okay?" I insisted.

"Okay. I'll get chains."

"Thank you."

Silence ensued. My need for control was clinging tightly. My fears bubbled up uncontrollably. I'd ruined his dinner. I knew he hated getting into intense conversations while eating. Not to mention, it's very unhealthy. I had to wonder if he regretted his choice of a partner. I'd tried to warn him in the beginning, but there are no ways to predict a path like this. Taking leave of the dining room, I stopped to bend down and give him a kiss. I took another dose or two of the tincture, did the dishes, and went to lie down to read and rest.

56

The plan was set in motion. We were leaving on December 18. All of us. The limbo-land we were hanging in was too stressful for me. This chapter needed to close. During our family Christmas, which was obviously celebrated early, it became all the more apparent that it was time.

Before the early Christmas shindig, my mom and I were talking, getting things ready for my dad and sister's arrival. Sam and my nephew, Evan, were still trying to wake up from a late night upstairs, and Byron was in the living room reading.

"So, dearie, how are you feeling? Better?" she asked.

"I am feeling better. It's changed a little. Sometimes it feels more like my lungs are having a hard time breathing, but everything they prescribed seems to be working. I'll keep doing the eggs and yogurt, at least until we get settled and I start my studies. I'll need to make big changes at that point. But the iron supplements are great," I explained.

"Are you going to the doctor again before you leave? It'd probably be a good idea. What do you mean about the feeling in your lungs and the breathing issue? Is it shortness of breath?" She looked concerned.

"Yeah. More or less. Don't worry though. I'm feeling better. It's just a phase," I said calmly.

"I don't think you should be so laissez-faire about all of this. Especially if it's developing into something new." She was feeling the natural concern of a mother.

"I know, Mom. I'm paying attention. There's a lot more going on than meets the eye. It's only showing up in the body," I started to explain what was happening on the subtle levels, but thought better of it.

"Honey, all of this is not a game. You're not a doctor, so there's no way you know whether it's a phase or a symptom that needs attention." I could feel her love and fear, but I knew we were coming up against the wall of limited understanding.

"Mom, listen, we can't have this conversation. We're both going to get stressed out, and we both just want to enjoy the day. I know you worry. I'm on top of it. But this goes back to the coffee date we had over five years ago, before I went to see Gurudev for the first time." She was busying herself with the food and seemed distracted, but I knew she was listening.

I continued, "I told you then that my biggest fear was losing our relationship, that a gap would form. That is what has happened. I've been unfair to expect you and Dad to understand all of this. It's been selfish of me to force it on you in the past. If there's a time that you really want to sit down and talk with me about this process, I'd be elated to share with you what I think I know. Until then, and probably after then as well, you're just going to have to trust that I'm on top of it. I'm paying attention. I'm taking appropriate measures, okay?"

She looked at me quickly. I could see the vulnerability in her eyes, which always unnerved me. She pulled me to her with a big hug, and with perfect timing my brother and nephew bounded down the stairs.

When the awakening process is under way, the Kundalini must purify the physical body. The ways this comes to be are not easily understood, predictable, or without very real challenges. This is truly difficult not only to explain, but also to expect those uninitiated to grasp intellectually. It is experiential on gross and subtle levels. The road must be traveled directly to even touch the nuances that occur physically, mentally, emotionally, and spiritually.

The measures taken and the time it takes for rebalancing and integration require a deep faith and trust in this very real process. This doesn't take place overnight for most of us, but it is a necessity to cultivate for the highest levels of ease and grace as possible during challenging times.

I felt the lesson regarding impersonal Love expanding. I saw how I especially had been attached in varying shades of gray to my parents' love, approval, and acceptance, hoping to feel seen, heard, and understood. This is just part of being alive on this planet, being a child, and being a parent. This isn't unusual in the least but is all too common.

It was clear I'd been functioning from the little self, that aspect of ego, wanting all the qualities of personality to be seen and validated. I'd been holding my parents and others hostage with my need to be made whole. Every time new awareness arrives, I believe I've seen the light, but there always seems to be another tendril to hook me back in.

Reflecting on the recent guidance, I knew I needed to allow Love, with a capital *L*, to lift up my consciousness, to look at my parents through a soul-to-soul prism, rather than the ego/personality centers. Just as I was told, I needed to stop the stories and the confusion of the energy of this level of consciousness. All of those traits I was desiring from them, I needed to give *to* them. I needed to know they already existed, that wholeness, mine and theirs, was already present. The teaching was similar to the process Divine Mother took me through, with the same blockages lodging in the shoulder blade.

It was time to allow for distance, the distance I'd hoped would allow me space and time to mature and perhaps create a new way of relating to those I loved the most. Time would tell. But this chapter was coming to a close.

There was a quickening upon us. Byron had already given his two-week notice, and our possessions were being separated into categories of Tucson and Mom's house and letting go. I worked slowly and rested as needed. Heavy work, and not so heavy work, was left to Byron. Urisk was eating better with another experimental dosage of his medication. We had some calming tincture for him, and I prayed he'd feel safe and relaxed enough to continue his eating with consistency. My body was all sorts of crazy, which I monitored. I stayed with my prescribed regimen and focused on staying calm.

I hadn't returned to either of my practices, one being the Shakti practice of surrendering to the flow of Divine Mother, and the other being meditation. Both stimulated strong energy activity that was centered primarily at the heart. During the daily rests in the automatic yoga nidra states, I felt Divine Mother massaging, swirling, and pulsing the physical heart and the energy center of the chest. I had complete faith that she was taking care of me in ways no doctor could. She is in essence all each of us is made of, booted up to the next level in the awakened intelligence, which knows exactly how to bring healing.

The Unknown She, which I was intending on completing before we left, had given me much food for thought on how I deal with the feminine energy. The conversation with Caleb, Byron, and Sandra had also been helpful. There was no mistaking this was a rich area for me. As I moved through the book one day, I came to a chapter on a woman who resonates and lives in the flow of the Dark Goddess, which really refers to the inner goddess archetypal energies.

Only a page into the chapter, and an introduction into this woman's chaotic, out-of-control environment and life, my body and mind were thrown into rumbles and quakes. I could feel my chest tightening and resistance attempting to protect me from a final crumble. I felt like I was being swept up into mysterious swirling waters of chaos, the unknown, and death. I felt that I had no control over my strongholds of safety, security, rootedness, or comfort and that I was being forced to let go even more in just a few days. This was also the energy of this particular chapter's interview.

I felt as though I was being shown, without any room for denial that I needed to reconcile this place in me. The important and imperative growth for me was through surrendering into disorientation, the allowance of being stripped layer by layer of identity and attachment. It was the destructive aspect of the dark feminine that was tapping on my door, demanding I flow with whatever life brought.

The dark feminine representations are held by the archetypes of goddesses and deities that protect the processes of life and death, cycles of the earth, and fertility. Some of their well-known names include the Hindu goddesses Para Shakti, Kali, and Durga, and the Sumerian goddess Ereshkigal, ruler of the underworld, the depths of the subconscious.

The more I read, the more panic arose. I kept breathing while witnessing the flashes of how I'd already been traveling a path being described in these pages. I was sensing ancient parts of me that *knew* the territory, that had lived this sacred path before that was unknown to me in this present. And there was one of the repelling words, *Goddess*. My whole being wanted to cringe and escape Her hold. The only problem was, I knew I was seeing a truth for me, for my life, and most likely a peek into past me's before my present time. It all made my head spin.

As I dosed with the tincture, I allowed myself to sink into the inner chaos whirlpooling within me. I surrendered. I reflected on situations that seemed like I was creating suffering for myself, making decisions that would cause stress, anxiety, or fear in my life. One such event came rushing forward that had been a very challenging and vulnerable decision I had made, in order to explore the erotic dance scene. There was a deep past life need to seek resolution in the present. I didn't understand it, I simply felt compelled to follow the soul propulsion.

In the back of my mind, I heard my mother asking, "I don't understand why you do this to yourself." She'd often asked this in a variety of ways. Why I'd chosen such a hard path escaped her.

"Don't you think if I could control this, I would? Do you think I enjoy this constant onslaught of stress and change and chaos? Well, I don't!" would be my response in heated moments.

"Then I don't understand why you choose to do these things. I just worry about you, and if it's scary and uncomfortable, you can always just walk away." She attempted to console me. She loved me and hated to see me in pain.

"I can't just walk away. This is how I learn and grow. This is how I live my life. I don't even feel like I'm the one choosing it half the time."

"I don't know what to say. I'm sorry. I'm sorry this is so hard for you, and I guess I'm sorry that you feel like you have to do it anyway," she said.

"If I could explain it any better, I would, but I can't." And the conversation would end.

With everything that had happened and the directions my life has taken from way back when, I was now looking at it all through a different lens. Had I always been in the throes of these feminine forces? Was the propelling and compelling nature of soul that I experienced actually Her presence guiding me? Was the chaotic way of my life Her way of transforming my being? Were these simply parts of myself from some other time and space calling me to remember something I'd long forgotten? The lens of the dark feminine, the Dark Goddess—was I in Her hands? Is She also the loving, gentle Divine Mother? The inner chaos had calmed. Was I numb or at peace? The resistance had seeped out with the tears, and the denial had been shaken loose at the beams of the mind. I wasn't any clearer really. How to integrate it? What was integrating? Though so much was unknown to me, my personhood, at the level of soul, knew I was coming back home and into wholeness.

A space of expanding love was being created when goodbyes were exchanged at our family's faux Christmas gathering. I was already missing them, along with feeling the realization that absence makes the heart grow fonder. Hugs and love were exchanged with friends; gratitude was shared with clients; and Portland, my home and stomping grounds of twenty years, was releasing me to new horizons.

The car was packed to its brim, with Urisk snuggled in his kitty carrier in the floor of the front seat. I stood in Felicia's kitchen imagining her sitting at her kitchen table, laughing and gesturing joyfully as she did. Her son, Joe, had gifted me her favorite blanket, her binky, which she'd requested I tucked her in with every night. I said my farewell to her home, sent my love and prayers for her continued journey, and thanked her for all she had brought to my life. Although my heart felt sorrow for all that was fading away, enthusiasm was present regarding what lay ahead. All is transitory, and transition was taking place. This chapter was closing.

PART III

57

How refreshing and revitalizing to arrive into the sunny land of
Arizona. Phoenix greeted us with warmth, a place to call home
temporarily at Emily's, and a reprieve from the road. Urisk sailed
through the drive with an array of flying colors. He took to his mini-
mobile-home carrier when he felt anxious. Otherwise he rested in my
lap, sometimes wandering around the piles of boxes in the backseat,
and he utilized his kitty litter accordingly.

I, on the other hand, had not traveled quite so well. Control
and fear were front and center passengers and backseat drivers. Even
with tinctures in hand, I found that the anxiety and panic refused
to be subdued. It was as if veils were continuously thrown over
my eyes and consciousness was dragged down into doom, harm,
and death. The mind ran rampant, triggering heart palpitations,
difficult shallow breathing, coughs, and zinging and quivery rushes
of cortisol, I suspected through the whole body.

My poor husband could do little right. "You're driving too fast!
Please slow down." Read: the speed limit was too fast. "We need
to get to my cousin Jen's by dark. We're never going to make it."
Read: by dusk, so you need to go faster. The mountains and curves

increased the panic. In the long stretches of smooth desert road, I saw only desolation and danger if the car were to break down.

There was beautiful scenery everywhere, from the sunrises to the full moon over the desert. However, I couldn't see the beauty surrounding me. My sight was filled with chaotic thoughts of potential threats: being stranded in the middle of nowhere; Urisk not being able to go to the bathroom; driving off a cliff; no cell phone reception in case of emergency; cold, wide-open spaces at night.

I was clear that I was completely irrational. I saw this to be true, particularly in those moments when there was no focus or imagined circumstance accompanying my fear. It was simply floating freely, throwing its webbing over my eyes, casting its spell.

The living practice was upon me, as I was beginning to call these moments of hyperconsciousness. Trapped in the darkness of my own mind of fears erupting to the surface from who knew where, with the effects of it jolting through my body, I needed to get close to the fear and control. I needed to surrender to its chaos. Driving on our last night, to my cousin's, I knew, just as in times past, there needed to be a drawing of my energy up from these swirling vortexes. My intention was to get clear.

First, I needed to connect to my breath just as it was. "Don't insist it be any different than it is," I said to myself. "I feel the breath is shallow. I feel the heart is racing." I surrendered to the discomfort. I felt fear and surrendered to the fear. I felt I was drowning in fear. I let myself drown, all the while watching the breath. I could feel a calm seeping in. I felt the breath go a tad deeper.

"What's the fear of ... pain?" I witnessed and spoke to myself, allowing fear of pain to be present. In the next instant: "And there's control." I let the breath expand and deepen as it witnessed control. "Ah. Control wants to keep me safe from pain," I saw. My chest softened slightly. "Yes, it's irrational," I said to myself gently. "Don't judge. Be soft." I could feel stabilization. The heart felt rhythmic, the breath was opening, the cough was passing. And there was the amazing luminous moon hovering above us. Beauty.

"That is so beautiful over the desert," I said to Byron, feeling spaciousness settling in ... for that moment. "We must be close to my cousin's, don't you think?" I asked.

"I'm not sure," he replied.

The blanket of webbing! It was thrown back over my head. My vision went black, chaos and fear swirling around my mind returned. Images of dangerous, dark, vacant roads. Fear of dangerous people with ill intent. Disorientation. Fog. Panic. Can't breathe. Heart's racing. And the practice begins again.

It requires energy and focus to lift our consciousness into higher centers of clarity and truth. Thankfully I had the tools and awareness to understand what actions needed to be taken. What seemed dark and looming outside of me was simply the consciousness within me. There was a constant grasping for control. This is how we all live our lives, whether we're grasping for control in small invisible ways or the obvious, gross ways. It's when life offers us the opportunities to transform our consciousness from control to surrender that we are walking in fires of purification.

In the moments when I broke free of the blindness, I could sense the presence of the Divine. But it was only when I could expand enough to feel the subtleties that I then developed the trust that She was there, even when I felt trapped in the dark.

Arizona, the sun, the heat, the fire. That last day, driving through the desert on the way to Phoenix, I felt the wildness of the desolate land. In my inner vision, repeatedly, I saw an image of a naked rotund woman, perhaps in the crone phase, but I couldn't be certain. Her hair was matted and wild. She danced around with vehemence and chaos. There was a sense of intrigue. Where did she come from? What was she showing me? Whoever she was, she welcomed me over the threshold. What was the threshold to? Once again, into the unknown I was journeying, and she was my escort into this next stage.

58

Emily was very excited to have us with her, to be generously hosting us for as long as we needed, and especially to get to spend time with her buddy Byron. Through the Christmas holiday we did our best to ground ourselves. Urisk was first introduced to our room, then slowly he made his way, roaming the house. The final test was meeting Emily's cat Kasey. It was touch-and-go at first, but Kasey, being primarily an outdoor cat, was only around in the evening. Urisk was a trouper. He'd had much experience at relocating, but I was happily impressed with the return of his health and spunk even after this large transition.

Within the first week of 2008, Byron and I set our sights on exploring Tucson. It was a two-hour drive. We left early one morning to miss rush hour. The desert had an appeal, but it was yet to be determined exactly how much it would grow on me. Our mission for the day was to meet the city, get a feel for the areas we might want to live in, and look at a couple of apartments I'd noted from Craigslist. But the highlight was visiting the Caravan for lunch. I had never heard back from the owner. I'd sent an additional email following up on the original one but had gotten no response. I wasn't feeling deterred.

There were a couple of apartments we had addresses for, so we did a drive-by and quickly decided against them. It was going to take a while to acclimate to the southwestern style and the desert altogether. Aesthetically, we were so accustomed to the lush greens, rich woods, flowers, water, and yes, rainy gray skies. In Portland the neighborhoods felt vibrant and inviting. The architecture of Craftsman homes, for me, was warm and comforting. The streets, for the most part, were attractive, and even the commercial landscape had charm.

Tucson was another animal completely. There were no lawns. There was sand and dirt ground with cacti, which one may or may not consider attractive. There were some flowers—on cacti and bougainvillea, which seemed to flourish everywhere, thankfully, for that was the addition of color needed. The southwestern adobe-style architecture was going to take some getting used to, just like the unattractive strip malls lining all the main streets.

The apartments didn't appeal to us, and some of the neighborhoods felt sketchy. However, we weren't the best judges of that yet. Byron had looked at the map and knew just where the Caravan was. As we turned onto Fourth Avenue, we began to feel some relief. It had the same feel as Southeast Hawthorne had, before the commercialism of it began just recently. However, Fourth Avenue in Tucson was much smaller. Instantly we knew this was the alternative, hippy, progressive part of town, as well as being close to the University of Arizona. It was young and hip.

The Caravan was nothing short of what I expected. We were the first ones there upon opening. Most of the restaurant was open air, with heavy canvases over the top to shade from the sun. Inside there was a large bar that was a beautifully carved from dark wood, where they served coffee and teas. The furniture was amazing amid the garden-like setting with the stone floor. The place was colorful, Middle Eastern, with many plants, cushions, pillows, couches, and cushy chairs. Some tables were low to the ground for floor sitting, and others were normal height. There were statues of Buddha and goddesses throughout and a stone fountain off to the side. It felt perfect in all its style and funk.

Byron and I were both full of grins, ear to ear. We sat down and ordered a pot of ginger tea while we perused the menu.

"Everything looks so good!" I said.

"And look, sweetie, they even have some raw items for you." Byron pointed out the items.

"So much to choose from. What are you thinking about?" I asked.

"I'm not sure. I might ask what the server would recommend," he said, pondering the wide assortment of options.

"I think I'm going for this stew. It looks really good," I said, putting the menu away. I wanted to take all this in, and I was scoping out where the owner might be and hoping she would be there.

The server recommended a few things, from which Byron chose the shepherd's pie.

I asked if Marion, the owner, was in. The server said she wasn't there yet but should be anytime.

We thoroughly enjoyed our food, and the ginger tea had some serious zip to it, just how I liked it. While eating, I saw a short woman walk through the restaurant, having entered through the back door. She was wearing a long skirt and tie-dyed blouse. I knew this was her.

"That's her!" I told Byron, once she walked past us. "I wanna talk to her before we leave."

I was feeling giddy and nervous, and the creeping in of attachment. I wanted to work here. When Byron was looking at the check, I wandered into the small area with the bar. I'd seen Marion go in there from the kitchen a couple of times. I was eyeballing the generous helpings of scrumptious cakes, including vegan cakes, when she came out of the kitchen again.

"Hi!" I greeted her. "I've sent you a couple of emails. We're just moving here from Portland, and I was wondering if you might have any job openings?"

"You have no idea how many people want to work here!" she said, throwing up her hands. "I usually have a waiting list of people looking for jobs."

"Do you think you'll be having anything in the future? I could leave you my name and phone number."

"Yeah. That's fine. I don't know. I never know what's coming around the bend next," she said, somewhat dismissive.

I took a piece of paper from my purse and wrote my information, including my email address, and handed it to her. "Do you mind if I check back in with you periodically? You have such a great place here."

Again, without much attentiveness to our conversation, she said, "That's fine. Check back with me."

"Okay, great! I will. I appreciate your taking a few minutes to talk with me." I was feeling slightly defeated.

When I got back to the table, Byron was ready to leave. "Well! How'd it go?"

"Let's go out to the car," I told him. I didn't want to repeat the conversation while we were still there.

Once at the car, I told him it hadn't gone great. I expressed that I really wanted to work there, but it didn't look like it was going to happen anytime soon. He tried to cheer me up and reminded me that what was meant to be would be. Just let go. We both were reminding me.

We had a couple of more apartments to look at. I needed to just stay focused. While we were looking at the second-to-last apartment on our list, my phone rang. We were just finishing up with the manager of one rental. I excused myself. Byron got an application and finished the conversation.

"Hello?" I answered.

"Hi. This is Marion," said the voice. "You were just in asking about a job."

"Yes! Hi!" My excitement peaked. As it peaked, I felt my heart palpitate and flutter. "Yes! I remember!" I said, trying to keep my cool.

"Well, I just had my server and cook walk out today. Do you still want the job?" she said.

"Oh yes. Most definitely!" I exclaimed, no longer cool.

"Great. Do you know anyone who cooks? I need a cook too."

"Sure. I mean, my husband cooks, or can cook, I think! I'll check with him! Should we come in and fill out anything?" I was overflowing with awe and excitement with the turn of events.

"Why don't you come by? I'll be here for another couple of hours," she said.

"We'll be right there in about fifteen minutes or so. Is that okay?"

"Yeah. That's fine." And she hung up.

Byron was walking to the car as I hung up. I was beaming.

"What's going on?" He looked amused and curious.

"Oh my God! That was Marion."

"From the Caravan?"

"From the Caravan! We both have jobs. Well, I think. No, I'm pretty sure! We have to go back there now!" I was rushing him into the car as I talked.

"Wait a minute. What do you mean, we both have jobs? I have a job? Doing what?" he asked.

"Cooking! Can you believe how perfect this is? Her server and cook both walked out this afternoon! She wants to hire us both, I think. C'mon. We need to go." I was feeling excited and stressed because Byron wasn't quite as excited as I was, and he wasn't moving fast enough for my excitement.

"I'm not a cook. I've never worked in a kitchen. Do I want to cook? I don't know if I do." He was thinking out loud.

"Listen, let's just go back there and see what the deal is. You can learn to cook. You cook all the time, and you're a great cook!" I encouraged.

"Cooking in a professional kitchen is totally different. I've never done this. They're gonna want experience," he explained.

"Let's just go. Now. You don't have to decide until you hear what she has to say. But I get the job! It came through! Just like I felt it would." Once he was driving, I was able to relax and track what had just occurred. "I was wondering if my intuition was off after I met with her. I was willing to be patient, but I just felt like it was what was supposed to be. Then I just let go—and bam!"

We both talked briefly with Marion, and it was decided that Byron and I would both start, daytime shifts, the day after next. We'd be trained for the opening breakfast and lunch routine. We filled out minimal paperwork. She wasn't interested in past references. She only wanted the basic information for tax purposes. We were excited to begin, regardless of the two-hour drive to and from Phoenix. The red flags were already flying, but we had blissful blindfolds on tight.

There was one more task for the day: the last apartment for our viewing. The picture on Craigslist looked pretty cute, but I'd learned the images could be misleading. I tried not to get overexcited until we saw the unit in real life. I could tell as we were nearing the unit that it was the one. Just as in the past, I loved it instantly. The adobe wall designating its small yard had colorful tiles embedded into it. The yard, though coarse, dry, and sandy, had some shrubbery and a small mesquite tree just outside the front door. It was well taken care of and had a pool in the back.

When the owner arrived, she was nice and did everything by the book. I felt so grateful that Byron and I both had just found employment, as I'm not sure she would have been open to renting it to us otherwise. We were sold. The one-bedroom, six-hundred-square-foot triplex was perfect for us at this stage. We couldn't move in until the middle of the month, which was fine, and provided all our information checked out, which it would, the place was ours. We drove back to Phoenix with the sunset showering us with the dazzling skies over the desert's vastness. Our new life was rapidly unfolding before our eyes.

59

While I knew that the Caravan was the perfect place for me to be, little did I realize just what perfection meant for this phase of my growth. Life had been teaching me to let go of my control issues, judgments, and fears of ambiguity with gusto. It seemed like once I decided to come to the Tree, the Universe ramped up its focus on these tendencies of mine. Or the soul was seeking a quickening pace of shedding what wasn't true. Either way one looked at it, there were forces at work, beyond my understanding.

I'd recently begun to feel an impatience growing in me regarding my opinions of timeliness and communication. I was seeing and feeling how rigidly I held very set ideas of how I thought people should behave in specific situations. My judgments and projections were searing toward others. Were my attachments and desire to control growing stronger, or was I just feeling them more acutely? All the drama and trauma while at Felicia's had shown me more about the unknown, death, chaos, and of course, control. Ironically, the majority of my life has been made up of these qualities. These things are what led me to try to control things and are also what drew these qualities to me. Yet now it was time for a deeper understanding of my relationship to them.

The Caravan turned out to be painfully perfect. I saw how soul had led me into the perfect storm. From the get-go, the challenges were on. During our first week, the employees responsible for training us never showed up on time, and one day we ended up opening two hours late. For them, a population of hippies, being in the flow came easy. Things happened in their own time. Nothing was regulated by any structure. To the point, there weren't even managers, other than Marion, at the restaurant. There was a philosophy that a hierarchal structure impeded creativity and equality. The management style of Marion was often to let things go with the flow until they reached a crisis point, and then she became an eruptive volcano. I understood all of this intellectually and envied the flow, as much as it terrified me. But experientially, to one who doesn't flow easily, I had walked into a continuous chaos soup.

Byron functioned fine. He did what was in front of him. He let go of needing things to be different. He cooked the food, and he wrote poetry, which he began channeling right after his powerful cleansing just after we were married. Poetry was still flowing through him effortlessly. Wherever a window appeared during work, he wrote. He chose great music for the restaurant. And he had a sense of humor about the daily chaotic situations.

I wasn't as cool. If our doors weren't ready to be opened when people were standing outside, I felt responsible for that. If the nighttime crew neglected to clean the dishes—or anything else, for that matter—I felt responsible for that too, considering we needed clean dishes for the day. The stress would mount, in conjunction with a heated anger. If my shift ended at 2:30, I wanted to leave no later than 2:45. But when the next server wandered in an hour later or not at all, I wanted responsibility to be taken. I wanted others to be held accountable for their behavior, consideration for others, cordial conduct, integrity, cleanliness, and order. This was the structure that made sense to me, and the lack of such structure presented me with ongoing daily challenges.

For the first couple of weeks, while we were still at Emily's, Byron and I spent our entire drive home first with my ranting about whatever my opinions were for that day, followed by hysterical laughter at the whole situation. Emily awaited the nightly report of the day's antics, as literally they were daily. Maybe it was the tables that hadn't been cleared or dishes done from the night before. Maybe it was an employee refusing to make smoothies for the day because they didn't feel like it. Maybe it was one of the employees getting into loud arguments with customers, often because the customer wanted service, but the server was ignoring them. At first, I'd take up the slack. I thought it was important to have happy customers. Quite frankly, the Caravan had a niche in many ways, and no matter how bad the service was, or whether we opened on time, or whether a customer got what they ordered, it was all irrelevant. Most people always came back.

I rode an ongoing roller coaster of clinging, judgment, frustration, and indignation, followed eventually by a forced letting go. I dosed on my passionflower tincture often throughout the day. The stress of the experience, whether by my own creation or by trying to function in an orderly fashion in an extremely disorderly environment, was incredibly overwhelming. Truth be told, this wasn't necessarily an ordinary bustling place that was creating stress. It was the constant unpredictability and *under*whelming attention to detail or completion of tasks that led to surprises encountered around every corner.

I had ego involved, of course. I wanted to do a good job. After I'd become sober, integrity and self-responsibility were character traits I cultivated, aside from control issues. I believed there was the way things should be done. I had a black-and-white perception of good business and service. These aspects were challenged every step of the way. Others may have also felt these things to be important, but going the extra mile, in order to see it through, was an exception rather than the rule.

I held consciousness around the pattern as I watched it develop. I felt deeply that some of my issues that were being whittled away were painful and necessary; therefore, I continued to surrender to the chaos. I knew that at some point I'd be ready to move on, and I trusted I'd know when that was.

In the midst of judgments, I found that there were some really awesome people there. When I could remove them from having any effect on me and vice versa, I saw how much I appreciated them. We never came together in the sense that we'd become close friends, but everyone was genuine.

Byron and I moved into our apartment, from Emily's, just a week before the Tucson Gem Show started. We no longer had to drive from Phoenix to Tucson, and I had a hope that this would help smooth out the workplace edges. As soon as we got hired, the Gem Show was all we heard about. The Gem Show was an event that drew collectors and sellers of gems, crystals, and stones from all over the world. From what we heard, it put the Caravan on the map because it was *the* happening place. They scheduled a great lineup of music, extended the hours, and prepared for wall-to-wall business day and night. I was happy we wouldn't be driving back and forth since our hours would be a little longer during this period and because we had been hired in time to get some training under our belts. I was also looking forward to making some extra money and extra excited for some of our favorite musicians to come to town.

60

Emily wished us well on our final move to our new humble home. Setting up was easy. We went to a small local futon shop for our bed. We'd worry about a frame at a later time. Goodwill sold us our love seat, desk, small bookcases, and TV. We had brought our DVD player with us, some pictures, and a few bath, bedding, and kitchen necessities, with the exception of plates, bowls, and glasses. We bought two of each, and ta-da, we were home. Urisk settled in quick. Our place was small, so there weren't any places for him to hide or get overwhelmed. My vision was that once the Gem Show was over, I'd start on my schooling and create my new routine.

We'd started working three weeks before the tidal wave of the Gem Show hit. I felt good about the balance I was gaining concerning how much to take on. I was learning not to take everything so seriously and yet do the best job that I could. There were some people coming to town who worked this event every year as reinforcements. I felt confident and prepared.

If I could offer an image to describe how I felt internally during the entire event, it would be of the Tasmanian Devil. One difference being that my devil wouldn't be creating the damage but would be in response to the intense whirl of ungrounded chaos.

The first day set the tone. We now had keys to the Caravan, thankfully, so Byron and I arrived early enough to make sure everything was in place for the start of this two-week event. I wasn't sure who the second server was or when he or she would be arriving, but I wasn't too concerned and felt proud that I was in the flow. There were already a couple of people arriving when I opened the front gate. I sat them, brought waters, and proceeded normally. Byron wasn't sure who was going to be backing him up either, but like usual, he was doing what was in front of him, cool and calm.

More people began filtering in. It was manageable, but I was beginning to get overwhelmed. No Marion, no dishwasher, no backup for either front or back of the house, no one at the coffee bar, and no cashier had arrived an hour or so into the day. Before I knew it, the crowd of tables was growing in the dining room, in the coffee bar area, and out along the alley sidewalk. It was just Byron and me.

I was in a whirl of orders, preparing tea and coffee drinks, and tallying checks when eventually I saw some relief arrive. I assumed that Ariel would automatically come to the aid of customers who were now forming a line out the door, but my naivete was glaring, as such was not the case. Going into the kitchen to ask for her help, I noticed Jackson and Marcy and Ariel standing around laughing and talking. I called for some assistance and was waved at nonchalantly, indicating that they'd be there soon.

I returned to the dining room with all the expectant faces staring at me. People were waiting to sit, a line of customers needed to pay, people were asking about their food orders, and others were wanting to order tea and coffee. I was at my wits' end some twenty or thirty minutes later, when Jackson, Marcy, and Ariel were still to be found back in the prep area, hanging out, doing absolutely nothing, with both Byron and me slammed. I could no longer hold it together.

"If I don't get some fucking help out here, I'm walking right this minute! This is bullshit!" I screamed like a red-faced banshee.

This got everyone's attention. Though this behavior was in no way unheard of in the Caravan, they seemed to be taken aback that it was coming from me. Each of them scrambled to action as if to soothe the savage beast I'd become. Not to mention, if I walked, they'd be stuck holding down the scene that was bursting at the seams just on the other side of the wall.

The last couple of hours went smoother with help; however, the assistants weren't inclined to take initiative without some form of delegation. Being so overwhelmed with the sheer constant wave of customers, I had little energy to get angry. I was surviving just to get through to the end of the shift with my sanity. And this was my introduction to the Gem Show in Caravan fashion.

Because the first day was as out of control as it was, the days to follow didn't carry quite the wallop. This in no way means that it was smooth. Nor does it mean we had enough help or that the help who were expected to work did so in a predictable or functional manner. I was grateful that although the night shift actually had more staff on duty, the days, or so it sounded, were easier going. The difference was, each day I let go more and more. I'd get wrung tight like a washcloth and then be done with any expectation for myself or anyone else.

The weeks of the Gem Show flew by in all their glory and shenanigans. There were beautiful displays of gemstones and crystals that adorned some of the tables to be viewed. The diversity of language offered amusement in navigating the menu. The population of traveling homeless anarchists and hippies found the Caravan to be a desired gathering place when they were in need of free water, the toilet, or any leftovers. Some were even willing to do work for food. All-night parties left drunken strangers crashed out on the back couches when Byron and I arrived in the mornings, often with much cleanup. And then there was the big rain that flooded areas of the dining room, pouring through the patchwork of canvases that were the only protection from the elements. The show rolled on as usual; not a beat was missed.

There was one day when a young woman brought in a little elderly woman for lunch. They didn't fit the norm of patrons. As I waited on them before the crowd gushed forth, I fantasized that perhaps I should just return to caregiving. I helped this little woman to the bathroom and appreciated her demeanor and humor. After I gave them the check, they paid and headed down the alley sidewalk. On the spur of the moment I rushed out and asked the caregiver if I could give her my phone number that I'd written on a card to pass onto the family, just in case. She took it gladly, and off they went.

By the end of the Gem Show, I was exhausted and caught a nasty cold. The goals had been to find a home, to find a job, and then to begin my studies. I was almost there. After two weeks with the cold, I'd also cut back on my server shifts and was ready to get down to school business, the whole reason we were in Arizona. There was serious contemplation about leaving the Caravan. The stress level remained high, and I was continuing to utilize the tincture. This place had a wild rebellious energy, which I appreciated for what it was, but I was also fully aware that for me to succumb to its current wasn't going to happen anytime soon. It was tortuous on my nervous system, which really was an indication that I was still grappling with control, which wouldn't find resolve in this establishment. I saw that if I couldn't stand the heat, then I'd best exit the kitchen. The question was a matter of timing. It hadn't spit me out quite yet; therefore, I was willing to wait to see what the Universe had in store.

The other aspect that rounded out life was the joy I found in the Tucson weather. I couldn't believe I'd lived twenty years sheltered by the gray heavy cloud covering of Portland, nine months out of the year. Yes, Tucson was brown and dusty, and most all of the plant life seemed to have a sharp edge or point to it, but I was intrigued by the wildness and harshness, even as it simultaneously amplified the Ayurvedic *pitta dosha* fire in both my personality and physical body. My intensity was about to grow into its fullness in this desert.

The softening effect of the cactus blooms didn't fail to escape my eye, even in the harshness. Nature was doing its best to bring balance to all things. The colors were vibrant in their yellows, reds, oranges, and pinks. The saguaros were tall and statuesque, often donning soft pink or white blooms. The prickly pears with their red fruit were a popular harvest, and walls of bougainvillea were in constant show, in pinks, purples, and reds. There wasn't a lack of beauty; it was simply a matter of embracing the full spectrum of the desert.

What spoke to me immediately was the song of the doves. In Portland, there were crows everywhere. Their caw was the dominant call. They felt brash and aggressive in the beauty of their darkest blackness. I noticed how the Pacific Northwest, with its green, soft lushness, was home to the intensity of the crows. However, in balance, the harshness of the desert was sprinkled with the soft, feminine gentleness of the doves. Their cooing was heard all day. Melting into their soothing presence came easily for me. Our new home was beginning to wrap itself around me with its needles, its prehistoric-sized bugs, the cooing doves, the wide-open skies, and the soon to come wild monsoons.

61

Before we left Portland, I had bought all the books I needed for school, all thirty of them. I wasn't sure where I'd begin at that time, but as it was time to crack the first book, I chose *Reclaiming the Dead Sea Scrolls* by Lawrence Schiffman. I resumed my meditation practice but refrained from doing Kriya. I didn't feel ready. I did, however, begin to integrate the morning and evening Essene Communions.

The Communions were poetic, life-affirming and drew attention and awareness to many of the subtle qualities in all the gifts of life's powers. For example, since Sabbath or Shabbat begins at sundown on Friday evening, the communion invoked the Heavenly Father with the prayer, "The Heavenly Father and I are one." The contemplation of this communion is intended to bring union with the highest frequencies of all planets, as cosmic consciousness is awakened in individuals, uniting us with the Supreme Power.

On Saturday mornings the meditation or communion would bring consciousness to our relationship with the Earthly Mother. The communion reads: "The Earthly Mother and I are one. She gives the food of life to my whole body." The contemplation for this communion concerns all the edible fruits, grains, and plants, feeling their currents of Earthly Mother flowing within, directing the body's metabolism.

The remainder of the days and evenings of the week, it is the angels of the life-giving elemental qualities who are called forth, such as the Angel of Earth, or the Angels of Water, Sun, and Air, in the mornings. And the highest consciousness is of the Angels of Eternal Life, Creative Work, Peace, Power, Love and Wisdom.

Each of these communions brought recurring deepened and heightened awareness and connected me to the natural world as well as to higher thought processes. I felt a living resonance and offering in each, and over time, these glimpses of knowing danced within me. I felt like this practice would set a tone and serve as the foundation for the path of my education at the Tree of Life. Along with the new practice, my studies began, and I was registered for the first on-site class in August.

A rhythm was developing. It often took me a while to fall into rituals and routines. Ritual and routine was stabilizing for my constitution/temperament/dosha. I found the necessary grounding needed to sustain an equilibrium. The routine kept me chilled out in the tendency toward anxiousness I'd been exhibiting. Fortunately my heart was normalizing. The panic attacks had diminished. Mild anxiety still had a hold, but as we settled into our new life, it softened and eventually released.

As we entered into summer, I received a phone call one day.

"Hello," greeted a woman. "I'm calling regarding your interest in a caregiving job."

"Hi! Yes, I sent my number with your caregiver a couple of months ago."

"Hi. My name is Selma. I was wondering if you were still interested in a job?" she said, introducing herself.

"Absolutely. I'd love to talk with you about it." I was picturing that little woman at the restaurant.

"Can you come over to meet me and the family, and our aunt, the day after tomorrow?"

"Sure. I'd love to!"

We agreed on the time, and she gave me the address. I felt pretty good about it. The timing was perfect. I wanted out of the Caravan. It was still tolerable enough in that I hadn't yet felt pushed to invest time in job hunting, but I trusted the Universe was nudging me to the next step in my learning.

I took the leap of faith, trusting that this was where I was being guided, and gave notice that day. I was able to get my shifts covered at the restaurant, just in case the family wanted me to start immediately. I felt confident about moving forward as soon as they requested. I didn't feel the normal obligation of two-week notice, which may be the case in a normal work environment, since this was anything but. Given that we were a one-car family, the hours worked perfect with Byron's schedule, and my new job was only blocks away from the Caravan.

I began the new position with Abby the following week, Monday, Wednesday, and Friday. Abby was a delightful eighty-nine year old, just under my five feet in height. She had beautiful white hair, had a brilliant smile, was affectionate and pleasant, and was in the beginning stages of dementia. She lived in the sweetest little back house of her family's home, which was a sanctuary of beautiful gardens, walkways, and trees, which Selma had put much time and love into. The family was wonderful. They agreed to and understood I'd need time off periodically to go to the Tree for workshops. I was more blessed than I realized at the time.

Everything had fallen perfectly into place. The studies were stimulating and challenging. The new diet of primarily salads and fruits felt refreshing and cooling in the Tucson heat. I felt I had everything in its place and under control. Under control, though it felt right, didn't bode well for me. It was when the settling had occurred in the outer realm that the unsettling was to begin in the inner realm.

62

Nature ebbs and flows. This was one of the lessons taught while I was going through the initial cleanse with Gurudev. I gained wisdom of the contractions and expansions that make up the heartbeat of Life. This plane, the material world, functions within opposites of polarity. I'd learned this, and then I forgot it.

Since arriving in Tucson, I had shifted gears into this new life of doing. For years prior, I'd been very internally focused, reclusive, inwardly pulled with gifts of guidance from some of our most revered spiritual beings. I somehow had felt that it was a phase of internal learning, which I'd next be integrating with intellectual learning. In these short months, I'd lost track of the resistances I'd been experiencing back in Portland regarding the feminine archetypes. I continued to catch the presence on occasion of the wild-haired, rotund crone who'd greeted me upon our entrance into the desert, as she'd dance with abandon at the inner eye. I'd settled in and found stability. And honestly, I liked it.

Much to my dismay, under the fabulous darkening skies and flash flooding of monsoon season, my routine was to undergo upset. My days of study were, for me, days of intense focus and commitment to Essene ministry. Soul had a different agenda for me. It was time to return to the inner world, and at first I had intense resistance. It was greatly inconvenient to my agenda. There came the point however, where I knew surrendering was the only way to get to the other side.

No matter how much I desired or was determined to study, the mind would no longer focus on thinking. I couldn't concentrate or retain what I was studying. My energy was sucked into a center of void within, and the body was directed to lie down. Into the bedroom I was led, where I reclined in Savasana. I'd be taken deep into a state of yoga nidra spontaneously, in which I disappeared and consciousness remained. As if a clock struck the magic one-hour mark, I'd be released and awaken. The first couple of days of this surrender, I thought to myself, *Okay. That's not bad. Now I can get back to work.* As it turned out, I was only given an opening of an hour or so before I was taken inside myself again. This was the new routine Divine Mother, the Universe, Spirit set for me, and past experience had taught me the importance of complying.

On the days I spent with Abby, the inward pull was present but not strong enough to force my hand. It was as if Divine Mother knew it wasn't an appropriate time, but She was also letting me know She wasn't going away. Every now and then, if Abby napped, I would surrender to the meditative state, which would lessen the intensity of Her pull.

When I was at home on my days off, the periods of inward time were becoming greater than the hoped for functioning time. It was as if I couldn't stay awake. I couldn't stay in the world. There was a heaviness growing inside me. At first it seemed as if it was just depression and disappointment, because I really wanted to be disciplined and study. Then the heaviness felt darker and more ominous. It was hard for me to converse with anyone, even Byron. I felt I was carrying some mysterious weight.

I had been under this spell for about two weeks when a new teaching was introduced. I was inward for up to three hours at a time. Awareness was growing of the consciousness of me coming and going, bobbing to the surface and submerging back into the depths. Emptiness was soon infringed upon by a new heightened awareness of beings surrounding me.

In bobbing to the surface, they could be felt. There were three of them in a circle around me. Though my eyes were closed and I was still in a deeply meditative state, I saw them with an inner vision. They were Native American grandmothers. As they encircled this one's body, I felt and saw them performing healings in my energy bodies. I could feel the ever so subtle ripples through the layers that surrounded my physical form. There was a soothing sensation, and I felt protected, cared for. In the ego layer of the mind, there was a belief that this couldn't be real. "It's okay," I murmured to ego. "We know by now that there's so much more than we can know or understand."

A jolt of pain then shot through the left ovary. Even though on the surface there was no reaction to the surprise, the energy layers responded. I could see one of the grandmothers sitting next to me, and it was as if she was probing the ovary. I let go of the fear stories as soon as they arose, surrendered to the sensation, and allowed the contraction of the probing feeling to release in expansion, in its right time. Before I knew it, I had fallen back into the yogic sleep state. I could no longer sense anything or anyone. When I woke up, there was only a subtle tinge of sensation in the area of the ovary. But my emotional state felt very solemn.

Over the following couple of weeks, the grandmothers came to teach me. At the time I wasn't grasping the journeys they were escorting me on. What I did understand was that I was being taken through death initiations.

One of the first death experiences took place on a morning when I felt energized and awake enough to sit in meditation. How foolish was I! As soon as I settled in, I was pulled onto my back and dropped into emptiness. In the vision, I was sitting at the base of a large pole. A vulture sat atop of the pole. Then more vultures appeared. They were tearing at the body, the skin, which was an image of me. There was no response from the reflection of me. When the feasting was done, other Native Americans appeared and began to cover the bones that remained with dirt. Once buried—I couldn't remember how—I seemed to be rebirthed.

This theme continued for a few days. I wasn't visited daily, but there was a consistency. In one of the last visions, a grandmother flew me, in the form of a raven, to a high mountaintop. I could tell she was attempting to teach me something of importance, and I felt shame in the aftermath that I hadn't been able to see her lesson.

Once again, I felt death to be walking me down an unknown path. The heaviness was doubled when, after close to a month of being inward, an old friend and boyfriend called. Jack and I had been connected since we were twenty-four years old. We met at an AA meeting, soon becoming enmeshed in relationship for a couple of years. We were two crippled children trying to form one whole adult. Together we played the relapse and recovery game, until I finally got the message and got sober. All these years later, he continued to struggle with it.

When we first got together, he'd talked about his experiences with ESP when he was a little boy and how it had frightened him. He shared about the myriad tests his mother had him take at the hands of mental health professionals. He carried much fear and anger about these abilities, without any coping skills to mediate them. Jack felt that this gift was a curse, and he learned at a very young age to medicate this sensitivity with drugs and alcohol in order to block out the noise and sights he'd never wanted to begin with.

I got a call one Saturday from him. This came from out of the blue, as we hadn't been in contact for a couple of years. He relayed the most recent events of just being released from jail. While he was there, coming down from whatever he'd been using, he had experienced a bout of ESP that scared him and all the guards at the jail. It seemed he'd been coming down from a major high and started sharing private information, information that he would have no knowledge of, about the guards, with the guards. But what he was calling for was to inform me of something he had seen about me.

"Boog." This was an affectionate nickname he'd never stopped using for me. "I'm sorry to call you with something like this. I've gone back and forth with whether or not to tell you what I saw when I had this bout."

"What's up, Jack? It's okay. You can tell me," I encouraged.

"I don't know. I shouldn't have called you! It's not good." He was stammering.

"It's okay. You can tell me. You're making me more nervous by hemming and hawing about it. Just tell me. Please," I pleaded.

"They say you shouldn't tell people certain things. But I felt you should know."

"Just tell me. I'm getting freaked out and irritated. I can handle it, really. I appreciate this is uncomfortable, but here we are, so please just tell me."

"Okay. Fine." Silence. "Okay. Do you know you have a congenital heart defect?" he asked.

My heart skipped a couple of beats. "Yeah. I know. I just found that out recently. What about it?" There was a feeling of dread quietly seeping in through my pores.

"Well, it's the defect thing. I saw that you're not going to make it past forty-seven." Now we were both silent. It hung and clung to the air. There. He'd said it, and I knew he was frightened for having done so. I was, well, numb.

"It's okay, Jack. I'm glad you told me. It's not as shocking as you might have thought it would be." I wanted to reassure him that he didn't have to feel responsible for this news.

"I'm so sorry. I just didn't know what to do with it." He sounded deflated. "You know, not everything comes to pass, but I just thought you should know."

"It's good. Thank you. I'm really grateful you told me. It lets me know what I need to pay attention to. It makes more sense than you realize. And there are so many kinds of death, I'm learning. So we'll just watch and see. Thank you so much. I should go now though. Ya know, it's a little disconcerting."

"I know, Boog. I love ya."

"I love you too. I'll be in touch," I said before hanging up.

The seeping through the pores felt like quicksand making its way, drowning me from the inside. My heart was no longer racing, but I felt very, very tired. I told Byron I was going to go lie down. I gave him a kiss, curled up on the bed, staring out at the birds gathered on the mesquite tree, and fell fast asleep.

I had little desire to speak for days. I told Byron about Jack's call. He was visibly disturbed but not open to letting the news be an assumption of destiny. I was forty-five. I felt like I had two years in which to take care of any heart center / fourth chakra imbalances. I needed to address unhealed griefs and angers and attend to loving myself. The heaviness didn't feel as much like fear as like a soul-filled aging hit. I felt very old all of a sudden. I was no longer afraid of death like I had been most of my life. I felt like death was truly just a part of the soul's journey from this realm, this phase, and this stage of being to another, and eventually we would all reach the other side. The question for me was, how many more times did I want to return here?

The visions faded after my conversation with Jack. However, the presence of the grandmothers could be seen and felt, doing their work on me, from time to time. I knew I was being assisted. In what and for what was still a mystery. I took a growing comfort in the fact that none of us travel this world alone. That filled me with peace, and it held me in a nurturing cradle as I walked through the next two years.

I said my goodbyes while I was living, through doing my best not to create regrets with loved ones. I felt it was important to be more present in my love for them and allow everyone to be who they were, to love them for who they were. I knew I needed to release any stories, my agenda, or any needs that inhibited the flow of love.

I had begun to form a couple of sweet friendships in town. Though I was still carrying a heaviness within, after a few months it was lifting, and slowly I was returning to myself again. While enjoying tea one hot afternoon with Daphne, I told her about my conversation with Jack and the news it brought. Speaking about it out loud for the first time since I'd told Byron, I noticed I felt vulnerable and rattled. Daphne was one of a kind. She was a traveling mystic who lived in her car most of the time, unless she happened upon a good house-sit situation, which she often did. She lived with a complete trust in the flow of the Universe. Her question to me was impactful and gave me food for thought: "How badly do you want to live?"

The *natural* answer *should* be, "Of course I want to live! Are you crazy?" The answer wasn't that verbose for me. In some ways, I had recognized that I didn't have much attachment to this life anymore. What was obvious for me were the people I loved and those who loved me. It was their pain and suffering that would hurt my heart if I were to leave this plane. I loved Byron, I loved my family, and I had friends I loved dearly, but when my time came, would my death be devastating for me personally? I didn't think so. I felt like my biggest challenge was indeed choosing to stay here. Daphne could see this in me and gave me an opportunity to reflect on that consciously.

In the years before I began waking up, I felt there was so much I wanted to do and achieve and be a part of. That wasn't so much the case anymore. As ego continued to slowly go through the purifications, I didn't have much to prove anymore. I knew I wanted to deepen my spiritual roots with God and complete my awakening, whatever that meant, and to be of service and help others wake up and find whatever God meant to them. Other than that, I wanted to be with my beloved husband. And I longed for a puppy. It seemed simple. And in the bigger picture it was those two simple things that gave me the desire to remain living. Those were my priorities. As the days moved forward, death was continuing to be a living contemplation for me.

63

In late summer of 2008 it was time for my first visit to the Tree of Life. Byron drove me down for my first workshop. I was so excited, nervous, and honored, and felt like a child going to meet some grand character in a story she had loved. I managed to get only one paper completed and mailed in before this visit. I was disappointed in myself. I also felt I was failing to integrate the powerful transformations taking place on a spiritual level, which was most important for my journey.

Always feeling awkward in groups of new people, I found that my self-consciousness was building as we pulled into the driveway. Once I checked in, I was given directions to the *casitas*, the rooms. We drove up the steep hill to the top by the café and simple bungalows. The view was beautiful. The colors of the hills were muted and lovely under the spaciousness of the summer sky. Byron and I went to my room, where I immediately nested, as I'd be there for a week. We walked over to the café before we said our goodbyes, and he drove back down the hill on his return two-hour drive to Tucson.

My first visit and the classes with Gabriel Cousens sent me over the moon. I couldn't get enough of his talks. His intensity had me completely enthralled, and his straightforwardness made me quake. Like times in the past, I was a sponge soaking up all that was offered.

Shabbat, a weekly time of rest, devotion, community, and family, was a wonderfully new experience for me. We celebrated down the hill in one of the gathering rooms. There was tasty raw challah bread and juice; the lighting of candles; calling in the Shekinah, which is the feminine presence of God; prayers; and dance. To end Shabbat on Saturday evening, we all met at the temple, which was up on the hill. The ending is called Havdalah. It marks the entrance back into the world of responsibility and activity.

I was introduced to a grand experience of what a raw/live foods diet could be. Byron and I had been keeping our food very basic. He ate some of his meals at the Caravan, but when we were at home, our salads were monstrous, filled to the brim with all sorts of goodness. At the Tree, however, their recipes included soups, entrées like lasagna made with zucchini, and raw pizza, as well as beautiful salads.

Gabriel's spiritual dietary philosophy was low to no sugar, not even too many fruits, especially when juicing. They stayed away from garlic and onions, which according to Ayurveda are stimulating to the mind. When entering into the conditions of meditation and healing, we were seeking the sattvic state of calm and a peaceful mind. The food was overwhelmingly scrumptious and, for me, incredibly rich and filling.

This first workshop was on Essene healing. It introduced a new mantra and also words of power to practice. I was excited to integrate them with the Essene Communions in the mornings and evenings. We received Shaktipat from Gabriel and an overview of the mystical teachings of Kabbalah. I could feel my path expanding and becoming inclusive, with a deeper connection and more love blossoming forth.

By the end of the first week, Byron found me as he would from then on upon pickup, really energized, frequency raised, highly charged with stories and fascinating information. The highlight of my week, however, was a brief conversation with Gabriel regarding the Native American grandmothers. He reassured me that they were there to assist me, and he told me to think of them as angels. He supported doing my best to learn and integrate what they were teaching, but cautioned me against getting sidetracked from the Supreme Source, from God, by desiring more experiences than were being offered. I knew this to be true from past advice as well. For me it had less to do with getting caught up; I simply wanted validation that my intuition of safety was correct.

It was great to be at the Tree, but it was also great to be home. My body wanted the simplicity of the salads that I loved, my grain breakfast, which kept my bowls moving, and my cherished teatime ritual. I missed both Byron and Urisk when I was away and was ready to begin on my next paper.

What I had been gathering as I perused my schoolbooks, and now that I had made my first visit to the Tree, was, to my surprise, that I was learning primarily about Judaism. I was captivated by what I was learning. The historical background of Judaism and early Christianity was richer than I had ever imagined. What I started to realize was missing, was the presence of Jesus and Magdalene, which had drawn me to the Essenes to begin with. It didn't take long to learn that there were many branches of Essenes, the strictly Judaic to the early Christians. While the studies covered all of this, in differing points of view, some scholarly, some more mystical, the Essenes with whom I had committed to study with were Judaic. My studies were to be of Judaism. Even though Gabriel integrated and taught the universal truths of all the paths he'd walked, his primary focus was on the Judaic tradition.

I was open and trusting of the journey. This wasn't the first time I was met with confusion, wondering, *How in the world is this going to fit in my plan?* Humorously, I was also still under the illusion that this was my plan. Fresh in my memory was the night of this decision, having all of the guides who had been with me, banding together in unity, affirming this direction—including, and not the least, Mother Mary, the one and only time I had felt her presence. I was indeed curious to see how it all turned out.

64

The red rocks of Sedona greeted us the end of September for three days at the Raw Spirit Festival. Sedona was magical. That desert called us to fantasize about a move there. The festival was on the beautiful grounds of a resort hotel. We were surrounded on all sides by the rocks reaching upward to heaven in the always changing colors, depending on the play of sun and shadow. And when the full moon rose behind the silhouetted rocks—speechless.

This was our first Raw Spirit event of this magnitude. There were top-quality speakers, doctors, nutritionists, and music galore. There was no end to the food, to the creativity in preparing fabulous raw food dishes, and of course to the raw chocolate. We set up our campsite and for three days ate, experiencing education by day, dancing and laughing by night. The educational aspect was phenomenal.

Many of the speakers present, including Gabriel, infused Byron with a readiness to move in the raw direction. He was most excited learning about superfoods, which are nutritionally dense, usually high in vitamins and minerals, with a wide range of beneficial effects on the body, most commonly immune system boosting. On our return home, many of these foods became staples in our diet.

Music played 'til all hours in the morning. We had been turned on to a couple of new musicians during Tucson Gem Show who were playing Raw Spirit along with our favorite, Shimshai. On the list of new favorites were Jah Levi and Singing Bear. Our spirits were most certainly high for this festival, our vibration elevated. We felt healthy, nourished, invigorated, and inspired. Just as it had felt coming home from the Tree, it felt good to be home, but there was a definite change in vibration once we entered the city. There was a denseness that couldn't be missed, but what goes up, does at least come down a bit.

We had a giggle at Urisk's expense when we arrived home from the festival. Without realizing its effect, our energy was so expansive, and our frequency was high when we walked in the door. We came in calling to him as we always did when we arrived home from somewhere. As we walked through the doorway, the little guy was so overwhelmed energetically, he could hardly brace himself and was plastered against the wall with our entrance. It took a moment for him to get back on his feet before I could come and scoop him up in our favorite cuddle, which we'd been doing for twelve years. The cuddle was short and sweet, but it was ours.

My and Byron's diets shifted dramatically after that weekend. Byron began feeling inspired to study raw food nutrition and superfoods, along with veganism. He too had finally reached his limit at the Caravan and found a new job as soon as we returned home. There was only one completely vegan restaurant in town, as the Caravan was vegetarian. His new place of employment was Lovin' Spoonful's. It was like the difference between night and day from the Caravan. It was orderly, tightly run, and clean, and food was consistently good and timely.

65

Things changed rapidly over the next month. It had been decided by my employers that they were going to move back east where they were from. Abby had slowly been declining, and they felt it was best to admit her to a facility back home. The decision came quickly. Their house was on the market, and they had asked if I'd fly with Abby back. Her nephew would follow right behind.

Of course, I said I would. I wanted to help, and they had their hands full with tying up loose ends. They had made the plans, and even though there were a couple of things I was uneasy about, I felt determined to overcome them. The main issue was that our plane would arrive in the evening, in the dark, and I'd need to get a rental car and drive Abby and myself about an hour into town. My fear issues were kicking and screaming at me. *What if the car breaks down? What if we're attacked? What if . . . ?* But I'd said yes. The tickets were purchased. I was committed.

These irrational fears that I carried weren't new. They seemed to have surfaced after I entered sobriety. When they were present, they took me over. The irrationality, the fantasies, and the images that coursed through the mind and body terrified me. Over the past couple of years, I'd been able to understand that I was dealing with deep karmic energies and that one day I'd be able and willing to face them head-on. Maybe now was that time. I didn't feel like a warrioress, but maybe one becomes the warrioress by coming face-to-face with the battle.

Three days before the scheduled departure from Tucson with Abby, I'd noticed Urisk hadn't been eating or drinking and was very weak again. I took him to the vet, and Byron and I began to take measures to hydrate him and support his thyroid. Nothing that we did over the next forty-eight hours seemed to work.

He refused to eat or drink. He didn't want me too close to him. I'd read that animals go off to die on their own in the wild. They don't carry the death experience like humans, even those animals that are domesticated. Most often they don't want to be touched because it keeps them tethered to the body, which they need to vacate. I realized that I had to be selfless and give Urisk his space. I needed to do what was right for him, not cater to my needs. The vet didn't think he was in any pain. Her belief was that he was almost thirteen, so he was old and getting ready to die.

The timing was what struck me over and over. It felt as if in order for me not to fly back east with Abby, Urisk was willing to sacrifice himself. Could this be true? During the days of my not so good parenting, I'd made a promise to him, that he would be my number one priority from then onward. I'd always be there to take care of him. If he wasn't going to get better, I wasn't going to leave him. We were in a twenty-four-hour waiting period.

The day before takeoff, I was torn and confused, even in the midst of having made my decision. I had to tell Selma, and it went horribly. She was understandably angry, to say the least. They were between a rock and a hard place. All the pieces had been in place, except now for me. I felt horrible. But I couldn't leave Urisk. And I also felt he was protecting me from something. I had to stay home. Letting others down was always difficult for me in the past. I felt my integrity was in question, and from her perspective, I could see it was. In the end, I didn't go. The next day was Saturday, October 17, Urisk's death and Byron's birthday.

Before Byron left for work that day, he went into the bathroom, where Urisk was choosing to be, to give him some love. They had a moment as I lay on the bed watching them. I'd been watching Urisk for any changes. His food and water were awaiting his partaking. But he gave it no attention. Byron came out and told me that Urisk needed me to let him go and not to hover over him. Byron had predicted he'd be gone in twenty-four hours if I left him alone.

Byron left for work. I moved into the living room to give Urisk his space. The plane I was supposed to be on was taking off. Not long after I'd let him be, Urisk, with his body shrunken to the bone, made a little skip-hop run with his last bit of energy into a cubby I'd made for him by the couch. He curled up there, and when I checked on him thirty minutes later, he'd died. My baby was gone. I sat by him and sobbed, all of my past guilt pouring forth. I thanked him for being my baby, for being such a trouper, and, for whatever reason I'd never know, for keeping me in Tucson. He'd hung on until there was no chance of my leaving. I knew Selma felt my decision was an overreaction and a random coincidence, but I don't believe things of this level of importance happen without powerful reasons. Invisible reasons, perhaps, but not coincidence.

I didn't want Urisk disturbed for at least two days, so I covered him, sat with him, sang to him, and encouraged him along his way that day. I scheduled for the pet crematorium service to pick him up later the next day. Three days following that, his ashes were returned to me in a box with his name on it.

Though his physical form was no longer with us, Urisk made his presence known. His first appearance came two nights after his death. He came in a dream carrying a half-eaten chicken, the neck meat chewed away. At first it was startling, but then I recognized he was free to express his animal nature. He felt really happy and free. For the next few weeks, I'd feel him rub up against me while I was sitting in meditation. These moments filled me with joy. I'd just allow his presence to shower me with reminders that he was still hanging around. Sometimes in the twilight stage of waking sleep, we had our favorite moments. He'd come in his invisibility and snuggle up with me in full abandon, rolling around, giving me his belly. I, or rather a subtle body of me, would partake and pet him, spoon-cuddling him into my belly, and he'd receive fully.

I began to look forward to these visits, but after a period of time, I saw I was relying on him to stay around, with me, in this way. The right thing for him was to let him know he could move on. These moments may have been for him too, a full bonding he'd never really given himself permission to share while he was alive. Either way, it was important to thank him, love him, and tell him that when he was ready, he could depart. He didn't leave right away, but the visits grew fewer and fewer, until it was only in the twilight sleep that we shared our moments. Today, he still visits on occasion in both dreams and while I'm dozing or awaking. I feel him snuggle briefly. When this happens, I'm filled with both love and loss.

Urisk would always be missed in the physical form, and my heart ached over the void that was now filling the space he used to inhabit. In these trying circumstances, I chose to follow the guidance of the mystery by staying put in Tucson, rather than fulfill my commitment. Maybe I wasn't as ready as I thought to face what was in store for me. Maybe there were lessons needed to be learned by Selma and her family. Maybe I simply needed to honor what was right and true in my relationship and care for this being I'd been a mother to. So much that'll never be known to the mind yet understood to the heart and soul.

66

Within a short time I'd found new employment. I began working for a new caregiving agency in Tucson that sent me to a client who'd just moved into a residential home. She had Parkinson's, and I'd be with her four overnights a week. She didn't require assistance all night, only if she awoke, so I was given permission to sleep. This felt like it would work well with my studies during the day.

Angelina and I warmed up to one another slower than many other clients. She was fairly reserved, observant, and highly intuitive, though her intuition expressed itself randomly. Since I was only with her for an hour or so before bed and a couple of times during the night, the slow build of a relationship felt appropriate.

I had the opportunity to go to bed at a decent time and was able to do my meditation before sleep and sometimes in the morning before shift change. Studies during the day were steady, and I felt like I was making great progress. The papers that I was to send into the Tree for grading were to be three to five pages long. Mine, however, could barely be condensed at eight to ten pages. Thankfully, the grading wasn't strict and formally ruled. I appreciated that the papers, though usually written on the work of scholars, also asked for the inclusion of personal experiential learning.

Having been working with the main Hebrew mantra that was given by Gabriel, I'd had enough time to feel its life and resonance. It was becoming crystal clear that the words of power, or mantras, indeed have a conscious energy force that is expressed according to the frequencies of the mantra. While reciting the mantra, I felt a sensitivity grow in order to feel its vibration in various parts of my mind or body. Just as I had learned during the yogic practices early on, the mantra and vibration of aum or om was a force that at times could be felt vibrating at the very cellular level. The Hebrew mantras were no different.

I was reminded of the Hindu goddess of wisdom, Ma Saraswati. She is depicted sitting on a swan, playing a vina. Though she carries the qualities of learning, culture, arts, and music, she also represents the power of sound and vibration. Contemplating this one night at Angelina's, after meditation, I was struck by the symbolism in all religions, which are often seen as interesting stories or ideas but are never fully realized by most for the truth that they are. Many people use om at the beginning or end of a yoga class without fully realizing the power that lies within that sound, or symbol, or connection to a deity whose qualities can be brought to life.

I was slowly learning this was a truth within the Judaic tradition, even though I had naively thought it to be limited to the Indian aspect of yoga, even though I'd been told differently. The light bulb of "aha" didn't beam bright until one night, with the resonance of the Hebrew mantra still reverberating subtly through my body. I felt the true universality of yoga.

Work with Angelina was the perfect situation, although I was beginning to feel some challenges with my sleep patterns. Four nights a week of disrupted sleep, and many times not able to return to sleep for most of the night, was taking a toll on my body. I didn't sleep much during the day because I really wanted to stay consistent with the study program I'd established for myself.

67

I had an underlying anger rumbling down under the surface by fall of 2009. I was sleep-deprived, feeling low energy, and was having difficulty focusing on my studies, and a deep unhappiness was brewing with caregiving.

My nights of no sleep had developed into an inability to stay asleep through the nights when at home. Sleep or lack of sleep is foundational to my ability to function peacefully and clearly, and without it I function not at all. As lack of sleep was the malady, I was prone to intense irritation and tight muscles (I was contracting the bubbling anger) and feeling trapped in a cycle I didn't know how to escape.

Adding to the mix, after our second and most recent high experience in July at Raw Spirit, Byron had decided he wanted to become involved in a superfood company. So, moving forward, after our return home from that weekend, he quit his job. We felt it was a great opportunity, even if it meant he might not be making much money right away.

I was also feeling restless with my direction at the Tree. I was experiencing a great deal of richness there, including the July

Interdependence Day weekend, featuring three days with Gabriel and David Wolfe. The energy and dynamic between the two of them, the diverse spectrum of knowledge and wisdom, remains unsurpassed. It was an amazing weekend that boggled the mind. But with most of the books that had been foremost on my list, I was hitting walls of resistance and doubt. I wanted to put blame for the uncertainty rising on my lack of sleep, but I knew better.

I arrived home one morning from another sleepless night at work, to Byron peacefully making his breakfast, listening to one of his favorite CDs, and I just fumed. I walked straight into the bathroom, turned on the shower, and broke down. Letting the water pour over me, I was muttering to myself, angry at him, angry about caregiving, angry, angry, angry. Once dressed and having gone into the kitchen, I couldn't even look at him. I knew it wasn't as much about him as it was about the fact that I was having difficulty taking care of myself and speaking up about how I was feeling. However, I wanted to speak tactfully, and that wasn't going to happen in this moment.

As I attempted to sleep that night, I decided that I needed to give up at least one or two of the caregiving shifts. I wasn't sure how this was going to happen, since this was our sole income at the moment, but it needed to happen. Over the next couple of weeks, Byron and I had a few talks about either this business needed to be pursued as a business or he would need to get another job. He agreed to start looking for something, at least part time, so that he could do both. And I gave up one night shift.

Each of us had a different relationship with money, yet how those relationships manifested in the world looked similar. We lived simply; saving wasn't a major priority; we were content as long as our basic needs were met, first on the list being healthy food; neither of us had grand desires for travel or for ownership of too many possessions; and only recently I had begun feeling tinges of awareness of growing older and a need to plan ahead. Although Byron had a master's degree in social work, it was never put to much use. We both chose work that allowed us our valued time, over valuing money. I personally felt the crunch when my time was impinged, like in this situation, or when I felt trapped into something that made me unhappy.

When Byron decided to quit working at the vegan restaurant, he went to work briefly for the post office, which ended up not being a good fit. Taking the leap into self-employment seemed to be a good choice for him, and I wanted to support him. One reason had to do with his scarcity and control issues around money. We thought this seemed like a great opportunity for him to learn how to let go of some of those fears. Cost of living was low in Tucson, I was working, and we had faith he'd bring in some money. The challenge of these lessons, and the superfoods, felt like a rich learning experience.

Months had passed in this way, and by December, along with the superfoods, he was also working selling advertisements for a Sedona magazine, as well as doing sales for a small organic pet food company. Though he was putting forth the effort in all these areas, the translation into income was lacking. Movement was slow, and we had very different paces at which work was being done. I wanted to support his process, his pace, his lessons. But in the meantime, I felt like I was drowning in my own struggles.

The entire month of December, I felt like I was being stirred in a boiling cauldron. Money tensions were brewing, and I was growing increasingly scattered and fragmented. There was, however, a softening occurring in my resistance to the multiple aspects of the sacred feminine tapping on my shoulder. Less resistant but still refusing to turn around and acknowledge Her presence, I noticed a buildup of energy in me that was determined to get my attention.

I had learned from experience that when the internal energy builds in such a fierce way, I need to enter into a space of journeying in whatever way called. There was a franticness building, a desire to shatter what was left that no longer belonged. I longed to step into Her fires and burn. On a December day, I danced to a powerful mystical musician, Freedom. I prayed to that divine force I resisted and feared. I did my best to ride the waves in blindness, and yet trusted I'd arrive where I needed to be. Though I called on Her assistance, I still refused to surrender completely. Through the dance, soul prayers burst forth. I cried them forth from a deep soul call: "Help me to ride Your momentum, trust Your flow. I see You circling and spiraling, dropping me through the center, and carrying me up on Your curves and waves and arches. Help me surrender!" I felt the need for darkness and depth. I closed the blinds to block out the always glowing Arizona sunlight. Soul began whispering to me, as me, "I need to die. The soul courts death in small increments. They tease at this person, the ego. Help me to die to that which is outworn, that I may be reborn." This desperation was not of my personality but of the growing desire of soul to break me free from the illusions, the blindness, the painful desire to awaken fully.

Finally in exhaustion from the dance, I fell to the floor. Sitting and weeping. Weeping and breathing. Breathing and silenced. Silenced and empty.

In the emptiness I heard soft voices. "You have embarked on the path of mysteries. Every tradition has a sister path, the path of the moon. The mother, the maiden, the crone. The sacred cycles of the feminine. It is the hidden tradition, the one of mysteries, of shadows, of the undercurrent. It is this inner path that must be taken in order to return home. The way is that which is hidden, it is the way of the She, the unseen but the known. She is the moon, the light drawing us forth with Her full Light. That light is the sun reflected in Her. In the moon they are one. The sister path is that of the internal terrain, the dance of life and death. Full Light to complete darkness and back to full Light."

Lost in words I grappled to understand, I had no faculties to recoil, so I surrendered. Stillness remained. I began to feel the right side of me peeling away. I felt the 'I' and the personality of me separating, as if a casting was being removed from the essence. With the peeling of the right side, the skin, the personality was peeled away. The left side was glowing, its pure energy, light, vibrating faster. Mind attempted to enter in but was quieted instantly. All that remained was the awareness of witness.

Something new was being born, but could it be sustained? There was a space of nine days in which that guidance and journey had time to take root. On the ninth day I was hit with a decision that felt true and laughable. In the past, I'd had difficulty accepting when friends had changed their names of their own accord. And of course, the more "woo-woo" or ethereal the chosen name, the more I was challenged. I can't say where the judgment came from. Was it a jealousy that they gave themselves permission to make such a stand? Did I feel it to be pretentious? Even though I'd longed for a spiritual name, one given to me that would resonate with my essence, was I afraid that others would judge me in the same way if I were to do such a thing?

Karma does come around in the least-expected ways. For about a year my given name was becoming so difficult to write, it was as if my hand could no longer form the letters properly. It came in a flash; the name I was to have was a name that had been in my life in a few ways already. Years back, when Fiona invited all the flower women who'd worked at the stand to receive a tattoo of their favorite flower, I chose the lotus. When a little female puppy came into my life, I chose the name Lotus. In the very brief time dancing, I took Lotus as my stage name. At no time did I know the symbolism of the lotus flower, until years later, gathering bits and pieces of information.

All of a sudden, it was as if I awoke to myself with the new name of Lotus. I felt there was a larger essence attempting to be embodied here in form. Lotus was all that this path I walked entailed. I saw a new me, an elevation of perception, yet connected to the earth. Lotus flowers grow up through darkness, the mud of the subconscious, reaching toward the enlightenment of the sun, undergoing purification along the way from the cleansing waters. There felt to be a powerful alignment and transformation in store. As the New Year of 2010 was approaching, I set the intention for a spiritual name change, through self-consciousness and all. My given oke wit h my c losest women friends in Tucson and asked

name, that aspect of me, was being allowed to die, and a new bloom was being called to radiate forth.

I spoke with my closest women friends in Tucson and asked for their assistance for a naming ceremony, which Daphne would officiate on January 1. This touched on my sensitivities of being seen in the throes of a spiritual process and also made me feel quite vulnerable. Yet I knew these places of discomfort were important for me to walk through, and who better to share in all of the messiness and brightness than my husband and those women whom I loved and loved me?

Lindley

390

68

One evening a week later, freshly into the new year with a renewed sense of myself, Byron came to pick me up from work with the plan of going directly to a gathering we'd been looking forward to. During the day I'd started feeling really tired, a little nauseous, and headachy. When the pressure subsided of having to be attentive to Angelina, on the way home I started feeling really sick. I told Byron he could drop me off, that I just wanted to go to bed. The blood flows of my menstrual cycle had been odd as of late, and I thought that might be what was going on.

Once home, I took a quick shower and was out like a light. I slept heavily and deeply. In the early morning hours I got up to go to the bathroom, collapsing at the commode, almost fainting. Byron heard me. He rushed in and helped me get up. I told him I wasn't sure what had happened, but could he please call the doctor's office and leave a message? I drank some water and climbed back into bed, feeling that I was cramping. If I was getting ready to start my blood flow, these were symptoms I'd only heard about. For the most part my cycles were minor disruptions, but nothing compared to some of my friends'.

My naturopathic doctor called and instructed me to eat a spoonful of salt and drink plenty of water. And she said I could come in that day. I was almost due for my annual, so I felt it'd be good to get it done now. I'd already called in sick. As the day went on, cramps were increasing and my thighs were feeling as if they were constricting.

During my exam, a couple of changes to my reproductive organs were discovered. My doctor did detect some abnormal small bumps, cyst-like, on the left ovary. I told her I'd been having some sensitivity on that side and often pain during intercourse. Oddly, she informed me that there was what felt like scar tissue along the inner wall of the uterus, which had never been there before. When she touched the area, it had a burning sensation, which I'd been feeling off and on at work when I felt under a lot of stress. There was difficulty getting a sample because it had seemed that although I was probably experiencing the beginnings of perimenopause, drying and hardening of the cervical tissue had prematurely occurred, making it difficult to swab the area.

She gave me some coconut oil suppositories for the cervix, saying that she would send in the sample she was able to obtain to the lab and that the next step would be to get a biopsy on the ovary. I thought for a few minutes and asked her, "What if the biopsy comes back cancerous?" She laid out some options. The one in which she would offer treatment was an aggressive vitamin and herbal cancer protocol. I suggested we just move forward with that, without the biopsy. She was hesitant for a moment but agreed to the proposal.

As a homeopath and naturopath, my doctor was also energetically aware, which was why I chose her when we first moved to Tucson. She had an understanding of Kundalini and had a strong background in the subtle anatomy system and energy work. I felt confident that we could be on the same page with regard to sensitive issues. I knew my body. I trusted that whatever was upset in my womb, I needed to help it heal with consciousness, self-love, and whatever assistance she could offer. An invasive approach was not in alignment with my deeper knowing.

The left ovary had first felt an upset when I experienced the energetic rape of the entity when still in Portland. It was also an area that the Native American grandmothers from the subtle dimensions had been helping to heal.

I was especially curious about the scar tissue, as it hadn't been there before, and I'd been noticing symptoms that sounded like what pelvic inflammatory disease would feel like. There were a number of supplements, herbs, and vitamins that formed the cancer protocol, as well as some homeopathic remedies. This was what I knew to be the path for me.

The body had been my teacher for years. When I began learning energy work in 1997, one of the first impactful lessons had been recurring swollen lymph nodes in my neck. I was given the powerful herb pokeroot to massage the neck with, to facilitate the drainage. I had to make dietary adjustments, but the most potent remedy was using my voice and expressing anger. Back in my drinking days, I expressed my anger instantly and sometimes, if you were my partner, violently. Once sober, I found it didn't come as easy. It was usually a buildup followed by an explosion. Working with the lymph node in the past and flare-up alerts taught me to pay more attention to my need to speak up. I likened this process back then to a miracle. It wasn't once or twice; it was consistent. I experienced swollen and tender lymph nodes when I negated myself in silence or disregarded my own feelings, which then drained and cleared within moments of using my voice. That was only the beginning. Part of the spiritual work I'm here for is very connected to the physical body, inquiring of its aliments and harmonizing through consciousness and energy sensitization.

I again felt as though death was strolling along in my life by my side. I felt emotional only as far as anything affected Byron. We talked about the plan when I returned home, and he was supportive and trusted my judgment. The timing wasn't lost on either of us. The reproductive organs are connected to the second chakra, which houses energies of money, security, relationship, and sexuality, and toxic emotions like rage. Most of these elements were up and heated at the moment, which felt like it was even more important to stay present with the energy and karma working itself out and to learn what I needed to in order to facilitate healing.

I began the herbal protocol immediately. The other recommendation concerned my sleep patterns. I needed to begin sleeping again and was prescribed large doses of melatonin. It was also strongly suggested I no longer work nights. I concurred.

My diet quickly changed from the salads that I loved, all the dark greens, a variety of vegetables, and minimal fruit. I didn't make the decision to change the diet; the body did, just as it had in the past. My body was repelled, virtually overnight, by greens, particularly dark raw greens. It, the body, desired yellow mung beans and rice, also known as Kitchari. Kitchari is an Ayurvedic food wonderful for healing and cleansing. I thought I should at least do brown rice, but the body was in adamant disagreement. White rice won out; the need for easy, soft, gentle food for digestion was in order. This inner guidance marked a big shift in the path I was on, taking me away from a raw food diet and things connected to that diet. But healing was under way.

It was important for me to find time to sit with the sick ovary and allow it to communicate its suffering. What didn't take long to recognize was the need to let the armor I'd worn for as long as I could remember to fall. The qualities of gentleness, forgiveness, compassion, surrender, and love were calling out for me, for my beloved Byron. I felt that the unhappy ovary was a statement of all that had gone before.

Another message I received was that it was time to choose tears over anger. Hadn't I already learned this lesson with my ear all those years ago? Clearly it wasn't done yet. I didn't see anger as bad or wrong. In this instance, though, I saw I was carrying sadness and powerlessness, masked by anger. I had the opportunity to go under the anger to heal what it was trying to protect. I understood the anger was protecting sensitive parts of my Cancerian crab from getting trampled and exposed. I talked quietly to the anger, "Thank you for your protection, the power that has served me, and the control you've given me so I can feel safe. But now I'm safe in the new softness birthing in me, safe in the care of the Universe, and safe in the arms of my husband. Your work is complete. I know I can call on you if I need you again. Thank you."

69

In the midst of these new softer, gentler calls from my depths, the money issues exploded. All the walls broke loose as Byron and I were coming home from the theater one afternoon. My anger was triggered, and I cracked, spewing all the things I'd been feeling and thinking, some valid, some not. I couldn't contain myself one more minute.

"You are so toxic right now," Byron said with a rarely raised voice. "I can't even stand to be in the same place as you. Your energy is blasting so much anger that I can't tolerate it."

"I feel toxic! I've been toxic and trying to keep it under wraps. Something has to change! You need to figure out what you're doing about work because I can't keep working these nights like this!" I screamed, picking up the phone to call Daphne.

"What do you mean? I've been looking for work, and I am working. All I'm finding is less than part time. I'm trying to figure out how to sell the superfoods, but it's not working. I'm not a salesperson." He defended himself.

"Why do you think there's only minimal-hour jobs? Why is this all you're finding? This is what you need to ask yourself!" I turned my attention to the phone. "Daphne, hi. Can you come pick me up? Now? … Okay! Thank you." Neither I nor Byron had anything more to say. I felt angry and sad. We'd never had a real fight. Our relationship had always been very grounded, clear, and easy.

"Where are you going?" he asked.

"Daphne's coming to get me. I gotta get some clarity. I feel so angry at you about this, and I feel trapped. I'll be back later. And I do love you. And I'm sorry to be so toxic," I said, afterward going outside to wait.

I felt a loss of innocence in our relationship. I felt the difficulty of commitment upon me, an initiation of a lesson I'd been longing for, how to remain committed when the going gets tough. Granted, I'd been in some tough relationships and stayed the course through addictions, infidelity, and even threats to my life. All were very dysfunctional, and my staying was based on the dysfunction. But I rarely felt trapped, because I knew when I'd had enough, I would leave. Leaving is instinctual to me. Leaving comes easy. I knew marriage would teach me how to stay based on love, commitment, and a desire to deepen.

We both were in our own fires of rigorously honest communication and self-inquiry. Neither of us was feeling supported by the other. Our lessons were bumping and banging up against one another. Much to my surprise, after this outburst, I felt a love expanding through the pain. I felt the desire to grow in our commitment, our marriage. The bigger scheme of our commitment and growth as a unit was a reality check for me, a message that I was not autonomous as I'd always been. Somehow I experienced this as a loss, experiencing it simultaneously with gratitude for that fact.

The energy that burst out in rage was transmuting into a more intimate bond and a deepening love for Byron. I was witnessing the anger that still lingered in waves, dancing with my love for him, for the road of growth we were each embarking upon.

It was clear his struggles around work and jobs had found resolve when not long after this blowup, followed by a coming back together to discuss our differences peacefully and lovingly, he found a full-time job. Bookman's, a large, popular new and used bookstore in town, previously didn't have any full-time openings when Byron last checked. This time they did. And when he began his new job, I was able to move solely to days with Angelina.

Our ground was shifting for the better, for both of us, because of the volcanic eruption. Though it's not my preferred way of functioning, it does have its own power to transform. *The blessings of darkness,* I mused.

70

Having already completed all the required classes at the Tree, I still had two remaining papers to write. They'd been outstanding for some time. I was having great difficulty getting through them. They actually went hand in hand, but I was stuck. I'd hoped to get my health stabilized and deal with the stress I was experiencing at work so I'd be able to squeeze my willpower and complete them.

There were problems with this plan. Although I didn't want to admit it, I knew I wasn't aligned with the Essene ministry. The last assigned reading was the Torah, the Old Testament, and I just couldn't get past Leviticus. I'd tried and tried. I couldn't reach the gems that I had no doubt it held. No matter how much I wanted to, I skipped around. I attempted to watch religious movies in hopes of moving forward, and I could find no alignment. The last extenuating circumstance that would inhibit my ordination even if I did complete these last two papers was that I was no longer on a raw food diet.

Here I was, two years and thousands of dollars later, living in Arizona, about to hit a brick wall. In addition, I was no longer even 10 percent raw, let alone 90 percent, which was the requirement.

Ironically, Byron was 100 percent raw. He was hooked. His body loved being raw. Veganism and raw foods was now his passion, his purpose, and his direction. We just had yet to find out what that would look like in the world.

We had moved to a new, larger apartment in February 2010. It was a two-bedroom, which meant I could offer private sessions again. I liked having more space, and the private back patio was perfect for relaxing and sunning. Byron was happy at Bookman's, and I was, well, deflated and lost. As it became clearer and clearer that I was truly not going to reach my goal at the Tree. I felt both freedom and confusion. Had we just spent the last couple of years catering to my whimsy? Was this a complete waste of time? What did it all mean?

Certainly, whimsy and spontaneity had played a part. However, to dismiss or negate intuition and the ways in which spiritual or soul's guidance spun my tale would be a mistake. There were things I embarked upon a decade ago that sometimes took just as long to recognize the reason for them. I trusted this was the same. In my more despairing moments of entertaining our adventure as tomfoolery, Byron would be quick to correct me. I began to take solace in the saying "It's not the destination; it's the journey."

Caregiving was also leading me to hone my awareness to the physical symptoms of stress. If there's one consistent lesson for human beings, it's that of control. Clinging onto what we think should be or shouldn't be, wanting what we don't have, vying to be seen or not seen in one way or another—these are just a sprinkling of the disguises worn by control. Control keeps us wrung tight and always dreading the unknown or whatever doesn't go as planned. It's grandiose and meek. It's boisterous and a whisper. It's obvious and overlooked.

My resistance and helplessness grew in the realization that letting go of becoming something, an Essene minister in this instance, touched on my stories of failure and my inability to manifest my deepest desires. There it left me, caregiving, in my mid-forties and feeling that I had nothing to show for my life, similar to how I'd felt several years ago. I was on a hamster wheel, and it was feeling very karmic. In reality, my care shifts were stressful, and there were concrete reasons for that. However, I loved Angelina, I respected and enjoyed the staff at the residential community, and I loved many of the residents.

The problem was my thinking. Only in the surrendering and emptying-out periods could I get clarity on the fact that the real problem was always in my thinking my life should be something other than it was. The three days a week I was with Angelina became a process of micromanaging the effects my thoughts had on my energy bodies. The daily practices included reciting mantras inwardly, doing breathing techniques to keep myself present, and fine-tuning the stories in my body and mind.

I felt the power of *tapas*, also referred to as the fire of transformation or discipline, clearing and purifying a deeper heart within me. I saw that my willingness to remain engaged and present in whatever suffering I was perceiving was in fact the power to purify that suffering. Because I stayed acutely connected to each discomfort, surrendered to the discomfort of it, and transmuted it, I found a new freedom.

One night after work I was telling Byron about what I was experiencing regarding the physical component to these practices.

"What I'm finding," I began, sitting down with some tea, "is that my breath isn't short and shallow like it used to be almost all the time at work. Sometimes more than others I need to remind myself to let the breath travel into the belly, and I just still myself for a few minutes. And that's all it takes."

"Are you still feeling the burning sensations in the lower belly that you were mentioning a couple of weeks ago?" he asked, checking in with me.

"Sort of. It's changed, or at least my perception of it has changed. For instance, in learning how to contain this energy that habitually wants to release by acting out in a fit, by being restrained I can feel the spot where the doc said there was scar tissue. It begins to burn. The whole lower abdomen wants to swell up. I feel it as irritated and bloated," I explained.

"Does it hurt?" Knowing the levels of work happening in that area, he felt naturally concerned.

"Not so much hurt, as in pain, but uncomfortable. It's amazing how honing our emotional energy consciously, and channeling this reactivity into clarity, does create physical responses. What I started doing over the last couple of days with the bloating feeling is to let it bloat. Angelina was napping this afternoon, and I could tell I was still trying to *control* ..." I took a moment to shake my head, again registering all the ways control manifests. "Anyway, I'd been trying to suck my stomach in, instead of allowing what needed to express, to express itself. So, when she napped I sat on the couch, rested my hands on my belly, and let it bloat out."

Once I'd shown him what I was talking about, he patted my belly and said, "Ah, this is what you'd look like pregnant." We both laughed for a minute, and then he concurred, "Wow, that's a lot of energy in there."

"I know. Right!" I exclaimed. "It just pushed out like this for about thirty minutes, and then it slowly deflated, for lack of a better word."

"But fitting," Byron added.

"The messages I got from the belly had to do with anger, of course, and protection. For some reason, it acts as a barrier protecting me from something. Maybe the stressful energy of some of the family dynamics. I'm not sure. Maybe it's energy that I'm internalizing, my own or theirs, and I'm being alerted by the bloat, the filling, the burning? More, as always, shall be revealed."

"And for how long does that scar tissue feel sensitive? That scar tissue thing is so weird. I can't understand how it just came from out of nowhere," he wondered.

"Yep. It burns for a while, but by the time the belly gave up its bloat, after I listened to it, I noticed the scar area wasn't bothering me anymore. When it dissipated, I'm not sure.

"It never ceases to amaze me how complex we humans are. There are so many levels of our being working together or in opposition simultaneously, all the time! And some of the stories I'd been carrying seem to have fallen away. Literally, I'd have to go back to look in my journal in order to access my most recent rants. It just goes to show that our stories are connected to our bodies and are connected to our thoughts, and around they go!"

71

Not long after arriving in Tucson in 2008, I'd received my first Reiki treatment from a local teacher and practitioner, Lucy. Reiki had been one of those healing techniques I perceived as woo-woo, based on nothing other than my own skepticism and adversity to anything New Agey. Something called to me, though, when I saw Lucy's card. I felt I wanted to experience Reiki for myself, and as it was a big joke to those who knew me well, it made the fact that I'd called others woo-woo nothing short of laughable.

I loved the treatment. I really enjoyed meeting Lucy. She was grounded, clear, and not, to use my judgmental term, airy-fairy. Nothing astounding happened for me from the treatment; however, I felt a profound calm and joy settle into my heart and mind that stayed with me for a couple of days. In that timing, I felt I wanted to learn Reiki. I was a little surprised, but it felt right. I signed up for her upcoming first-level attunement class and shortly after became attuned to level 2.

Now, in 2010, I was preparing to take the third level / master attunement. When I have strong resistance, it never fails to be an indicator to me of direction I'll be heading eventually. A week or so before this final training, while still doing the cancer protocol, I began noticing free-floating fear in the pelvic region, and the left ovary was growing increasingly tender.

Byron and I had been having some challenges sexually in that I was experiencing blocks of time where it was too uncomfortable for me to be sexually intimate. Fear and panic would rise to the surface, so we'd opt for holding, silence, and tenderness. These phases would come and go and sometimes last weeks. Byron was patient, loving, and supportive. For me there was an underlying knowing that had been with me for at least a decade. That knowing had to do with addressing a deeply present call to sacred sexuality. I was aware that at some point I'd have to attend to this soul guidance, which would entail more solid connection to the divine feminine. Time would tell when I couldn't avoid it any longer. We both needed to be in a place of readiness to strip to that next layer of heart and soul.

Before the Reiki training, though, something was shifting, and there were things rising up that I couldn't put words to. The discomfort in the womb grew into a low-grade pain. I knew I needed to take refuge in some time of sacred silence in order for healing guidance to occur. In our new abode, we made the second bedroom into a studio/meditation room. This is where I'd find the healing salve.

After my workweek, which ended on Wednesday, I made my bed in front of the altar space. I sent out prayers for guidance, clarity, and healing. I called in the presence of the Heavenly Father and Divine Mother, and also asked for continued opening to the sacred feminine, in whatever form she was meant to show herself for my highest learning.

The night passed uneventfully, with the exception that I was exhausted in the morning. I assumed I'd been in a very deep sleep (thanks to the high doses of melatonin I was taking) and maybe hard at work subconsciously.

Byron left for work. I settled onto the couch with some tea, lit the incense, put on some soothing R. Carlos Nakai flute music, and prepared to do some Reiki. Snuggling under the blanket, connecting to my breath, I found that tears began to flow. They came completely unexpectedly. And as they flowed, my whole womb felt on fire. In the fire, I began to see images and to experience pain that wasn't happening on this plane of existence.

I continued to stay present and to allow whatever needed to come through to do so—tears, pain, images—and I reminded myself to not resist or cling to anything that moved through. The knowing was clearer than the images or memories. What I found was rape and mutilation in the womb. Recognizing that the scar tissue had risen from this past mutilation, I was amazed. The events were multiple, over different lifetimes. I was not limited to victim status; I also carried the acts of a perpetrator. The fear ran deep. Panic moved into my breathing, and I simply allowed the body to respond as it needed. I saw the connection in a past life to one of my relationships in this lifetime. I felt a sense of resolve and closure thanks to this seeing.

The past sprung into the present over a few hours of watching and dozing. I was allowing Reiki to assist as needed. The physical pain and burning became acute and dissipated, coming and going in its ebbs and flows. Surrendering to the whole process, I also witnessed the many abortions of my creative energies and the stories of my failures, lack of follow-through, and fear of success, which carried my core fears of being seen.

Collectively, I saw in the mind's eye and felt through my body the debasing of women, the rape of our sacredness, and the misinformed debased masculine. I felt glimpses of the rape culture we live in, via language, music, and entertainment, which is more subtle but ever present. My own womb and heart ached from the darkness and ages of violence as I felt and cleared this great collective wounding.

Sleep took over at some point, and I awoke to the shadows of dusk approaching. The tea had not been drunk, and the music had long ago ended. The whole womb area felt tender. I knew Byron would soon be home from work, and I wasn't ready to talk about this yet. I felt vulnerable and protective. There were remnants of fear still floating around inside and outside. I allowed them to hover as I knew clearing was continuing to take place.

For days this healing was acute. I lay, witnessed, wept, and feared, and vulnerability made its home in me. During the Reiki training, I was still quite tender and was grateful for the additional healing provided. The womb had been activating this healing for some time, and I wasn't sure when it would end. Even as day-to-day normalcy took over, once again I was in the fire. I surrendered to Divine Mother's care every day I wasn't at work, and I felt her sweeping the womb with her love. This healing and clearing would last for six months. It came and went. Panic attacks would rise and fall, and nothing was allowed to penetrate or touch the sacred healing womb.

During this time, I felt a desire to return to dance. My body needed to move. I needed to support the process in any way I could, and it'd been too long since I'd moved in ways most natural to me. There was a Nia class right by our place. I'd attended a lovely Tucson friend's classes for a time when my schedule was aligned, and I found that now I missed them. With this studio so close and with times that fit my schedule, I made it a point to dance. Dancing allowed the energy to keep moving through. Healing and nurturance was facilitated. It connected me with community and brought levity to the depths swimming inside me.

72

"What's next, do you think?" asked Fiona. Even though she too had moved from Portland to Tucson, we didn't spend much time together, so our catch-up dates were nourishing. Her parents lived in Tubac, an artist community south of the city, and she was now residing there too. Enjoying her visit into town, we settled into the shade in the courtyard of one of the cute little coffee shops on Fourth Avenue.

"I'm not sure. I feel closure about the Tree. I mourned that for a while, not just around the stories of failure, but also because of the diet change. That felt hard, ya know. I'd really loved all I was learning about raw foods. I thought I was feeling really good until my hormones and everything else went haywire. Then when I ate that first Kitchari meal, I realized how ungrounded I'd been feeling," I mentioned, reflecting.

"You were almost 100 percent raw too, along with Byron, weren't you?" she asked.

"Mostly. I did still eat grains in the morning, but I'd switched to just soaking them and eating them pretty much raw, even though grains aren't recommended by Gabriel. But to keep my bowels regular, there are some things I need to do." I shared the intimacies we were comfortable with. "But when I ate the cooked food, boom. Back down to earth I came. I had no idea I'd been feeling so airy for such a long time."

"I haven't tried, but I don't know if I'd feel good being raw, even though I know it has so many benefits. I could see myself being pretty spacy too," she said.

"I think it really just depends on the person and timing and what the body needs. Landing back in my body in this way, feeling substantial in the body again, if that's the right word, and feeling grounded again was a big confirmation that I was needing this change." I continued, "But I also felt guilty, like I'd failed to hit this ideal mark that I wanted to achieve. So, I mourned that loss for a short time. It was brief, really, because I was feeling really good with what the body was guiding me to eat."

"How are you feeling with everything now? And how's the new name feeling?" Fiona inquired. She hadn't been able to join us for my renaming.

"I'm feeling more balanced and grounded. There are still many things shifting on subtle levels, but it's all really good. I'm finally sleeping again. I love me the melatonin! And I'm open to what the Universe has in store for me next," I said, stopping to think for a minute. "The name change has been good, awkward, interesting. I get confused sometimes introducing myself, which feels silly, but overall it's fitting. I've let go of my family using the name, though. The old me is too ingrained in their consciousness. But it's okay. I get it."

"What about the caregiving, the ongoing thorn in the side?" She laughed. She'd listened to my bemoaning the sad state of caregiving struggles since I left the flower stand.

"It's okay for now. It has to be, because it's where I'm at, and I don't see what will take its place next. I've been cultivating a new relationship with it. It's working most of the time. If nothing else, I can see clearer where I'm creating my own misery with my thoughts and allowing my reactivity to carry me away. Some days I still feel *Woe is me* and *Is this what I'm destined to do?* and I get depressed. But I'm learning a lot right now, so that counts for something!"

"Have you thought about Gurudev lately?" she asked out of the blue.

"Oh my gosh!" I exclaimed at the synchronicity of her question. "That's so funny you brought him up. I have been thinking about getting on the website. I had been missing him and was just curious. But I was wondering if it was just because I'm feeling lost at the moment and wanting something to fill the space, ya know, so I can be doing something."

"How I remember those first lessons you gave me about doing and being. That just being, and Divine Mother, changed my life, although, as of late, the doing has taken over again!" We both laughed knowingly.

"Yeah. Enough about me. What's up with you?" I inquired.

When I arrived home, I had Gurudev on my mind. Her questioning about him was so timely. I saw that there was a Yoga Nidra Facilitator's Training coming up soon. I knew I wanted to attend. I felt excitement about returning to the abbey in Colorado, where it had all started. Since my break from him, I'd learned so much, and many of the fears had subsided. All of the distrustful stories had been washed away. What was left was a love and a deep gratitude for all the blessings of my life just because of him. Though I'd been blessed to connect to the myriad of spiritual teachers and forces over all these years, he was the initial key to open the door to my heart, and that love was still present. I wanted to go to the training. I'd put it out into the Universe and see what came back.

73

The healing process was still continuing. After almost three months, I had another appointment with my doctor. The protocol had done wonders for my energy levels. I felt better than I had in years. I'd told her some of what I'd been experiencing, and she confirmed there was wonderful deep work taking place. I was uneasy with the internal exam since my protective instinct was still very strong. She understood and said she'd be very gentle and careful. Her report included the news that scar tissue had completely disappeared and the tissue on the ovary felt normal. And when the results came back from the lab, she called to say everything looked good. I was done with the protocol. She slowly began lowering the dose of melatonin, and for now, it seemed, the areas of attention were emotional and energetic.

Over the time that I'd been offering primarily compassion and love to the wounding in the womb, I noticed the presence of Magdalene surfacing once again. It seemed that in the background of awareness, perhaps in answer to my prayers, there was a falling away of resistance to the feminine. I couldn't say what was shifting for sure, but something seemed to be. There was indeed a softening happening, a lessening of judgments and criticism, both of others and myself. I was appreciating the change.

Everything fell into place for traveling to Colorado for the training with Gurudev, with many thanks to my mother-in-law, who so generously gifted me with money for the opportunity. I could see being able to begin the work I loved again. With the Reiki, yoga nidra, and some valuable techniques I'd learned at the Tree, what I could offer was expanding. It was also important to watch for the trappings of ego that needed to prove, to succeed, to be something in order to feel filled and validated. I simply wanted to be in service in the way of my highest alignment.

Upon arrival at the abbey, I felt a coming home. I had returned to the beginning of a journey, just seven years earlier, that could never have been predicted or conceived of, short of traversing these last years of direct experience. Soul had sent me on an adventure to find myself, but I couldn't say I was maintaining clarity of that goal. And here I was again, full circle, without knowing what would unfold next or who I would find myself to be at the next level.

What had been entering into my awareness was that I felt I was living a split-screen life as of late. I was experiencing two separate perceptions at once. One felt weepy, raw, and unclear with tones of loss, letting go, and a dying. On the other screen, I felt confident, enthused, and joyful with a sense of purpose returning. The two realities at once reminded me of times in the past, particularly when I'd been sick or even feeling depressed, when I recognized an underlying palpable joy was ever present. Our realities are always shifting and renewing and multi-layered. Everything will pass. Death and rebirth can exist side by side.

Awaiting the first session with Gurudev, I felt so joyful. There was a comfort and familiarity in returning to his presence. It felt natural and aligned. What he taught had been intrinsic to my nature. His teachings were so effortlessly integrated into my life, and the truth of them manifested through my practice. In just a couple of days being at the abbey and in Gurudev's presence, I felt the grace of him and the lineage lifting the confines of past beliefs and stories. New freedoms were being gifted, and I felt overflowing gratitude. There was a stripping away of a need I'd had before coming to this path. I'd always wanted a teacher to lead me, to guide me, to say, *Turn right. Go left. This is right. This is wrong.* I clung to that with him seven years ago without knowing. Then I wanted to lean on M, followed by Gabriel. It was the physical-bodied teacher I felt I needed for authenticating the guidance and teachings I received. Those of divine presence, such as Jesus and Magdalene, Babaji Krishna, and even Yogananda, who could not be seen required me to stand in my own knowing and even be subjected to ridicule for a far-out imagination. Worse yet, a core story from my childhood, and perhaps prior lifetimes, always whispered, "Who do you think you are?" It would laden me with insecurity and guilt and self-doubt.

But here I was, returning to the origins of awakening, and I felt that clinging had vanished. There was a solidity of self-sourcing that had grown, unbeknownst to me, if I held close to it. The true role of a guru is to lead one to the Source within. The goal was to rely on God's guidance, the soul's guidance, and the guidance that manifested from an inner presence. I was surprised to be sitting at my guru's feet sensing a dependency had been released. There was a peace about all of those beings who had come to assist me along this journey and who would continue to do so. The contraction of my heart that sprung from dependency on other beings, the fear-based stories about who they were, where they came from, and what their true intention was, was transforming. The past mind stuff or karmic ties that used to be divisive of my energy, or inhibit my ability to receive the blessings, were now forming a wholeness, drawing many fragmentations of myself into a devotion of divine unification.

In the expanse of this newly realized spiritual emancipation from dependency, I learned that Gurudev would be receiving private appointments through the remainder of the ten days. Humorously, I witnessed, like ants to a honey spill, the reappearance of the charging forward of dependency and need for validation that had just a moment before been dissipating. I could witness both the freedom that had been attained and the attachment, which was quick to form like Velcro, to his scheduling assistant. It took all of my will to counter the magnetic pull. I did set an appointment, and for the next few days it gave me the opportunity to play dual roles in my own private drama. It was a reminder of how quickly personality and ego, our little selves, can be forgetful of the higher truths we know.

The training itself was powerful, and the yoga nidra practice assisted all the internal processes I was experiencing. The inner peace stayed consistent, again, in the split-screen realities that lived out through me at the same time. My fears of speaking in front of others, of being seen, and of being heard seemingly vanished through the grace present. My story held no sway over me anymore. When I shared personal experiences, they flowed freely, rather than my spending time avoiding questions by focusing on others. Shame and self-judgment over being wrong or making mistakes had no ground to stand on.

When the time came to meet with Gurudev, I'd finally come to a place of surrender to whatever it was to be. Our meeting was after his morning session and lunch. He was tired and a little cranky. I witnessed my own inner recoiling in response to his mood, and feelings of guilt rose within for taking up his time. And then I let go of my stories and went with whatever it was to be. We rode to his quarters in a car driven by his assistant. During the drive he began the conversation, encouraging me to share. I felt the return of self-consciousness about sharing in front of his assistant given the private nature of my questions. But I pushed the edges of comfort and spoke anyway. Fortunately, we arrived to his quarters in a relatively short amount of time, so privacy was granted.

As I expressed a brief history of our meeting seven years ago, my abrupt awakening of Kundalini, eventually the crash, my fright, and leaving his fold, he listened and simply acknowledged what I had to say.

"I think what I'd really like to understand better concerns two things," I started, once we were in his room.

"Go on," he said patiently.

"First, after my awakening I began doing private work with others. The sessions were primarily intuitive, with a foundation of hatha postures, which then evolved into helping them through spontaneous Kundalini awakenings." As I shared, he watched me intently, nodding. "It seemed as though those I worked with already had the Kundalini awakened, or it was awakening through our work together."

"Yes," he said. "That is good. You must continue this work."

"I worry about someone getting hurt, that I'd do something wrong," I said, expressing my concern.

"You must remember it isn't you. Kundalini moves to clear and purify the entire being. What causes problems is the blockages already present. The Kundalini didn't create your experience; the blockages within you, your perceptions and fears and control, created the problems you faced. You won't hurt others. It's already what's in them that causes the trouble. It's true it can be disruptive, frightening, and sometimes dangerous, but it is what is already present being released." I felt moved, as this was so similar to what I'd been told by him during our psychic connections.

"I also sometimes feel drawn to put my hands on people. It's as if on a soul level, healing is calling out to me or my soul."

"Yes. That's fine, if it's appropriate. You will know if it is or isn't. You should continue," he said matter-of-factly. "What else did you have to ask?"

"A while ago, I had some experiences with planes of existence crossing over." I felt shy and awkward sharing this. Maybe he would tell me I really was crazy. I cleared my throat. "I had three experiences with Egyptians, like from ancient times, taking me through what seemed like initiations or something."

"Is this in meditation?" he asked.

"Well, twice has been in meditation, but I could tell I was on two different planes at once. And once was, well, while I was having dinner. They were in my living room, but they were almost invisible, although still able to be seen. It was almost as if they were translucent. Maybe in a different dimension? They called to me. I went to them, and they performed something and directed energy through my hands." I stood to show him what I could remember of the arm and hand positions.

"This is okay. You just allow what needs to happen, to happen. You are protected and watched over."

I sat quiet for a moment. I was wanting explanations, meanings, and rational information but could tell I wasn't going to get that.

"Is there anything else?" he asked abruptly.

"No. I don't think so. It's all safe? I should just keep moving forward?" I was still trying to glean more from him.

"That's right. Goodbye," he said, bowing. I returned his bow.

"Thank you so much," I said as I exited the room.

Well, he didn't think I was crazy, I didn't think. He confirmed that I should continue to do the work I'd been doing before when I was doing sessions. As an example of my neediness for validation, Gabriel and M had said the exact same things, and yet I continued to resist the permission. Would this make it different? Time had yet to tell.

On the last day of the yoga nidra training, during the morning yoga, I felt a great deal of the energy of love rising within me. The heart was exclaiming, *I love my guru! I love this path!* The love kept intensifying, and I was entering into an ecstatic state with, *I love You! I love You!* which usually I understand as *I love God!* And yet it was shifting into *I love!*

I watched the mind as it searched for the cause of the love or an object to attach love to. This dynamic had happened often. "I love!" seems to need an object of its affection, but when I leave it alone to continue to grow, like this day, there is a realization that *I am love.* Love expands into a nonpersonal quality and matures into its Divine, Universal, always present, quality Love. It resides within. Mind is in the habit of thinking the little me needs to do something with the energy, attach it to something to validate its expression. The truth is, it resides in all of us. When I let it continue to expand, allow it to fill my awareness, and allow myself to simply be in its presence, it becomes me, and I become Love. And in the container of this sacred sanctuary, infused with the spiritual energies of my guru and the gurus of the lineage, the expansion and becoming of Love happened with ease.

74

As I integrated what I had learned at the yoga nidra training, I reflected on how great it was to have had the last couple of years in the presence of the solid, intense, structured, and wisdom-filled Tree experience. There was a yangness that spoke to me, and which I found inspiration in, that Gabriel carried. The heat and fire of the desert seemed to fuel the level of integrity that I appreciated so much. In a lovely conjunction, after seven years, I felt the flow and grace of the yin energy returning, which was now being sought for further nourishment upon returning to the lap of Gurudev. I was able now, it seemed, to recognize more clearly the sacred feminine, which is at the root of all he teaches and the energies he transmits. A softening taking place in me, the edges having been filed down through the heat of Tucson, the call of my deepest feminine to heal, was helping me find balance between these two poles of life-giving forces.

Moving on from the studies and the Tree requirements, I was ready to give back. I felt excitement about bringing yoga nidra classes to Tucson. I'd already talked to the owner of the studio space where the Nia classes were held. Having private space at home also opened the doors again for offering private sessions, with the additional learning of the last couple of years. If the beginning of 2010 was any indication, it felt like it was going to be a great year.

Facilitating yoga nidra started off great, almost as soon as I returned. I had the normal jitters, but they weren't at all the debilitating type as in the past. Instead there was an infusion of genuine excitement to be stepping into a role I was here to fill. To introduce the practice to a new audience, one of the Nia instructors generously invited me to share a short yoga nidra meditation to bring class to a close. This opportunity brought both students for the class and private work.

Following through and beginning to do what I loved again felt healing. I felt like I was beginning to stand in the purpose I was here for. I loved offering sessions that could incorporate new techniques. I felt more at ease in going with what felt right in the moment, at the given time, for whomever I was working with. I continued to gain clarity and sensitivity to who was ready to awaken, my intuition was getting stronger, and I wasn't fearful anymore about what came through me. I longed for the day when I could make a living sharing this work, and for now my rates were very minimal as I strengthened this foundation. I was more open to receiving the idea that I was really helping people. I was happy to be doing what I loved, and I felt fulfilled knowing that I was being of service in a way that supported others. Students and clients were connecting to more happiness and peace. The modalities I offered assisted in clearing energy patterns, identifying stories, and sparking the awakening journey for those who were ready.

Unfortunately, there was an inner dynamic that caught the joy I could be experiencing by doing my work in a net. That dynamic was this: the more I did my work, the less patience I had for caregiving. My acceptance that caregiving had to be a piece of the puzzle grew more difficult to bear. Feelings of frustration were very wrapped up in the belief I had seeded long ago and had managed to water and cultivate, both consciously and subconsciously. The belief was that as long as I was still caregiving for a living, I hadn't succeeded.

I rode the ups and downs like a seesaw, but even the ease of the down would often land with a crash. I'd manage the acceptance for a short time, and then intolerance would take over. Failure would shout out at me. Though little by little steps were being taken toward creating a true alignment with my purpose, I was challenged by the creation of my own unhappiness with deep-seated self-defeating stories and unrealistic expectations, as well as false beliefs I'd fed myself as truth.

Working with my thought forms around my desire to be of service and stepping into my purpose in this incarnation, along with acceptance of what is, became the focus of a personal yoga nidra practice that I was integrating into daily life. The creation of intentions became a tool for me to find deeper layers of stuckness even as I experienced new freedom.

A deeper connection to the divine feminine was also taking place. I knew She was awaiting my full embrace. It was slow but steady in opening. I was willing to rely on Her to guide.

I knew Her to be the intelligence that guided my physical body when I surrendered to the divine in yoga. She was the guide informing the body of what its proper needs were: what foods or teas to ingest or not, when to retreat inward, and when it wasn't in my best interests to engage sexually. I trusted Her spoken guidance, the intuitive communication coming through in different voices of their own accord and timing, and I knew She was intrinsically connected to soul. This left me wondering, *What am I missing?*

75

Byron and I had hit a stride of ease, at least in our day-to-day routines, and we were following the ebb and flow of our intimate life based on the clearings still taking place in my womb. We had found closure as to our purpose for being in Tucson, and we were wondering what was next. We couldn't foresee staying in Tucson long term. It didn't feel like home to either of us. And we knew that going back to Portland's climate was not in the cards either.

Byron knew his passion was to write. He was able to squeeze in time to research on weekends, and he had been putting together his first book, *A Portrait of Soul: Transformational Poetry*, through a self-publishing concern. This was extremely exciting. His poetry was magical and visceral, and much of the work had simply been channeling through him since his dramatic awakening in 2006. He had notebooks upon notebooks of writings. The poems were teachings in and of themselves that could be meditated upon for raising consciousness. The expected date of completion and receiving the books was just ahead that summer. This was a beautiful creation that he manifested with such grace. I was proud of him and in awe of his process.

When we were on our honeymoon, we had fantasized that perhaps Northern California was our destination. Neither of us was interested in the dampness or clouds of San Francisco, even though we would most likely love many things about the city. On our list of musings, which were also California based, were San Luis Obispo and Ojai. We liked, but didn't love, Santa Cruz. We immensely enjoyed Mendocino, but not the weather. We both also felt that we should be in a larger city rather than a smaller town.

The only place we knew for certain we'd never live was Los Angeles. We went to a Raw Spirit Festival the year prior in Santa Barbara. Santa Barbara was stunning. I was ready to move there instantly. Everything about it spoke to me, including the moisture and the lush tropical feel, especially now that the dryness of the desert was starting to catch up with me. The drawbacks for us were the cost of living and the fact there weren't many vegan or raw option restaurants. Driving through LA on the freeway to get to Santa Barbara, we were both appalled. The traffic, to say the least, took us forever to get through. The city seemed dirty. And, of course, we chatted about all the other stereotypical negatives of LA: the smog, the expense, the elitism of the wealthy.

At one point while sitting in the LA traffic, I'd been admiring some of the architecture off to the side of the highway and up in the hills, and Byron was quick to say, "Don't even think about it. LA will never happen."

"Believe me, just because I appreciate some of the buildings, and I do love the flowers, I couldn't even imagine living here. It's too stimulating and feels out of control," I commiserated.

It was decided it was time to send our question out to the Universe and trust messages to come back as to what our next move was to be. For our remaining time in Tucson, for as long as that would be, I intended to be appreciative and receptive of what it had to offer, the relationships I'd formed, and all that it had to teach. Too often in the past, I'd spent time focusing on what was ahead or what wasn't working the way I wanted. In other words, I wasn't present to the moments of joy. In the aftermath, I'd look back and think, *Wow! That was really great. Too bad I missed it all fretting about A, B, or C.* I wanted to be more conscious this time around and be in gratitude.

The changes in my body and my cycles, and the peekaboos of perimenopause, were altering life's rhythm. Not only did I find nourishment in no longer working at night, being home, and sleeping properly again after almost two years, but also this enabled the emotional aspect of my being to balance. In this balancing there was softening occurring. I was able to feel the shoulders relax and the chest expand, little by little. This made me a kinder and more patient person in general.

Unfortunately, so much of society demands us to function at faster and faster paces, which creates stress upon stress. This erodes any semblance of inner harmony, health, and balance. It also erodes a foundation to manage stress in a healthy way.

In this inner softening, I was more inclined to listen to what I needed to do to nourish myself. Sometimes there was sadness and loss, of what I couldn't be sure. I simply allowed and released. My clarity grew that so much had been hiding under doing and ego, past programming, and judgments. I was recognizing the potency of vulnerability as I continued to surrender into those softer places within myself.

A love for myself was growing organically. There were teachings from the womb regarding the past and past lives, and they healed through my practice of surrendering to Divine Mother or just by being and emptying out in the vibrant crimson river of my blood flow. There was a new wisdom being cultivated if I allowed it and grew into the maturity to stand in it. I paid more attention to my moon-time as its own spiritual practice to be honored, to be in quietude, and to reflect, integrate, and allow wisdom to manifest.

There was a subtle knowing that my intentions were taking root. Especially in the springtime, I could feel Her presence surrounding me. I awoke a few times in the night to the mind spontaneously calling out, *Ma! Ma!* The Eastern traditions and symbolism were calling my name again. I still felt connected to Jesus and Magdalene; however, there was a sense that the feminine was calling from a new expression within, and I was growing more able to identify Her qualities in moments of both light and darkness.

76

March 2010 was the first visitation of the Blue Mother. She looked like Kali Ma, of whom I'd heard many frightful stories, of the Hindu pantheon, yet her approach was anything but fierce and wrathful. She appeared during meditation, kind, gentle, and loving. She kissed my forehead, breathed into my mouth, entered my heart. I felt Her clearing the womb area and specifically the left ovary. With this I grew nauseous, and whimpers exited my mouth. I felt the snakelike weaving of energy from left to right, left to right, weaving upward through my body, through the crown and higher. I received an inner vision in which She wore a special crown. She laid me on my back, on a lotus bed, and I entered a state of confusion for a moment, at which point She sliced me from womb to throat. I waited to be restored as in some of the journeying with the Native American grandmothers, but restoration didn't come.

Surfacing from the meditation, I felt bewildered and blessed. The aspect of Kali Ma had always been frightening to me, as to most other people not yet initiated to Her presence. She seemed to be the epitome of all that Christianity feared most in Hinduism. With the skulls and severed heads, blood dripping, wild-eyed, and vicious, what could She be other than evil?

But evil was not what approached me. All I felt was love radiating from Her blue beauty. There was a recognition of culturally programmed fear running through me, I can't deny. The pattern that had begun years ago continued to be true. I noticed my mind resisting this visitation with things like, *Why couldn't Saraswati or Lakshmi grace me? They're beautiful and feminine, and They make people happy.* The judgment was already overshadowing the blessing.

Over the next week, my dreams and meditations were the stage on which She played. Thankfully, She appeared first in Her loving aspect; otherwise, I might have been more disturbed by what followed. I dreamt of Her slicing off a hand then, in meditation, a leg and a foot. There was a dream of two very large blood-red owls. They sat at the entrance of a ceremonial snake worship I was partaking in. Though I couldn't see the snakes, I knew they too were red and the size of garter snakes. In another dream, a large snake wrapped around my leg of which I was frightened. The next night, I received a dream with smaller snakes. This time I wasn't afraid. The last dream included a wild dog with fang-like teeth, which I thought was coming after me. As it turned out, it was a protector.

I was familiar with snake symbolism as one of the prime indications of Kundalini. The Kundalini energy is actually referred to as serpent or snake energy. It's coiled at the base of the spine, which awakens when the Kundalini awakens. Snakes also signify death and rebirth, and Lord Shiva, of whom Kali Ma is a consort. Lord Shiva is also represented by the snake or Nagi, as it's called.

My first experience of this type of dream was in 2001 upon my return home from the first introduction with Gurudev and receiving Shaktipat. The most memorable dream began with me being in a dark room. The room was pitch-black, but I could feel the presence of a *very* large snake slithering around. I could sense in this darkness that the girth of the snake was the size of a thick tree trunk, and its length had to coil many times to fit into this room. In the dream, I could vaguely see Gurudev over in a corner. He was standing in a very dim light, trying to guide me calmly to him, all the while assuring me not to be afraid. As I was making my way to him, somehow a bright light switched on, and the snake bit my right hand! Both in my dream and on a subtle waking level, I could feel the pain. The arm immediately started going numb, and the numbness slowly spread through my whole body. I could feel I was trying to awaken, but it was slow going. The first sensation I was aware of was that of my right arm tingling and a soft electrical current running through my body. Once I was fully awake, the sensations began to fade or retreat—the more accurate description.

Presently, what seemed to culminate on the tail end of these experiences in March with Kali Ma was that what I referred to as my inner uglies were rising to the surface. I was faced with characteristics and traits within myself that I could barely stand to look at. Judgments and harsh opinions came flying forth without warning. Crankiness and frustration were triggered at every turn. Being in my own skin was becoming increasingly intolerable. The least desirable qualities about myself couldn't be escaped, so I was left with facing them and dismembering them.

She was going to work on me, purifying me, and bringing all of my own darkness and shadow to the surface to be released. She was cleaning house, so to speak, and I was the house. She was dismantling it from the inside out. This was the transformative process in action, all at Her fierce-love hand.

I bemoaned that I was affronted with this darkness. *Why can't I feel love? Why can't I hold on to all the warm soft fuzzies and gentle ways I was just getting accustomed to?* Instead, all of my projections of others came back home to roost, full force, to dismantle the ignorance and blindness I carried within my mind and the hardness of my heart. I was left to face the perceptions I loathed. And they weren't outside of me; they resided within.

Feeling so overwhelmed one day with the mounting clarity, and failing to recognize the clarity that I was in fact receiving as clarity, in my naivety I began to beg for just that. In my innocent perception, I thought the clarity would enable me to find the truth of compassion and love within myself immediately. The clarity hit hard and solid. It was barely palpable or tolerable. And yet I was graced with a cushion of compassion and unconditional loving energy that was not mine but was that of Kali Ma.

I saw the dislike for myself, intolerance for myself, mount. The traits I judged in others were aspects of my own ignorance. The stories poured forth like a madly rushing river. If I deemed someone as inauthentic, I was instantly hit with my own lack of authenticity. When I felt someone was selfish, bam! I was reminded of my selfishness and self-centeredness. When I would sink into self-pity regarding my lack of close friends, clarity came forward to remind me when I didn't have time for the importance of friendships and failed to be a friend. The character revealings went on and on. There was no escaping the truth that we really are or have been what we perceive in others.

The next test was to find acceptance and compassion for all I'd seen. I learned to transform some of the qualities by digging deep into the roots of their origin. Some were basic aspects of my being that I'd struggled with for years. I'd attempted to deny or demonize these parts of my being. These shadows grew looming when unchecked. For only so long can we push them deep down in the hopes that no one else will know, ignore them, or hide them from ourselves. The irony is that most people around us recognize our shadows far better than we do. This is ever so humbling.

In short, what this process taught me, first, was the fierce love of Kali, to free us from our own darkness. I also learned of Her deep compassion and love for the suffering we bring upon ourselves. Her dark mother role is to help us to find freedom. Her lesson also included experiential teachings that we don't have to be afraid of our darkness, that we can handle the pain of true seeing, and that we can heal once we cultivate the courage by going within.

The healing that blossomed forth was based on acceptance and forgiveness of myself. With this great clarity and clearing by the divine grace of Kali, and with continued work on my part, my personality became more balanced and harmonized. I was able to connect more fully to self-compassion, which enabled more freedom and joy and love and acceptance for others. But I never would have reached the deep transformational shift had I not gone into the suffering.

I had begun to accept things about myself that had been aspects of my personality ever since I was a child. In the process of integration and honoring these traits of personality and character in this lifetime, I was lying in the sun one afternoon when I heard the affirmation: "I'm an edge pusher, a shadow worker, a truth seeker, a light revealer."

Kali is transformation. Deep, lasting change and transformation isn't in the realm of pretending our way to happiness, thinking our way there, or looking for it outside. Pretending or acting as if is short-lived and doesn't vibrate with the higher qualities we are here to evolve into. We can't just wish to be compassionate, loving, or joyful; we must do the inner work of deeper knowing that this *is* who we are. Transformation removes, burns away, and purifies those aspects of ignorance, karma, and ego that cover up or veil these qualities that are already within each of us. Some qualities are just buried deeper than others. This is the inner work. It takes time and energy to raise consciousness and sustain its raising. But the truth that is revealed, that we have a great love within us, is worth the pain of clearing out the illusions.

The blessing was indeed born out of darkness, the archetype of a lotus in motion. The months of the intense in-the-face learning process eventually burned to embers. This stage of death, leading to a rebirth, had come to completion.

77

A seamlessness was forming between waking life, practice, divine connection, trusting the flow, and some sleep states. There was becoming less and less division, with my job as a caregiver remaining the exception.

By June, on my forty-sixth birthday, as I sat in reflection, I felt contented with the direction life had taken me since my vertigo breakdown or breakthrough in 2001. I was grateful for being taken off track from teaching Nia, even though I was devastated at the time. God-Goddess doesn't close one door without opening another. I was being awakened; I just didn't know that at the time. I'd come such a long way, too, from the fears of the unknown and my resistance to the feminine, and my mind had been expanded beyond what I would have believed possible at that time.

Soul had indeed been a guide and teacher, and whether or not I knew precisely what soul was didn't matter. I knew it lived within me and connected me to God. I saw that soul had kept me on track, so to speak, compelling me to delve into places that forced me into awakening, and that soul was also that which was awakening. Jack's forecast about my death was still in the back of my mind. I planned on making it to forty-seven, but I'd see what the Universe had in store.

Being a late bloomer in many ways, I was finally feeling an inkling of being a maturing woman. I recognized that the sacred feminine, the Goddess energies, was what was calling for my surrendering, and that it is what had been calling all these years. Finally, I was fully embracing Her and ready to learn from Her ways. And though I'd come to Tucson to become a priestess, I found the ways of a priestess organically unfolding with initiations being bestowed from the other side. Still, the mystery as to what it meant, how it would look, and all the steps that were laid out in front of me had yet to be explored. But I felt content. I knew I was simply in the middle of a book that had already been written, but I couldn't jump ahead to the last pages.

78

Meditation practice was bringing Gurudev back up to the surface. A longing for him was springing back to life. I was surprised to find it happening months after the yoga nidra training, rather than while I had been in his presence. I didn't feel dependence as I had years before, yet I saw on the website that initiation into the lineage was being offered. I felt a yes. I wanted to be formally initiated and receive the sacred mantra of my lineage. This ceremony would be held in Florida at the ashram rather than in Colorado. I was excited about this, as I could remember during my first or second visit to Colorado, still bright green regarding what I was stepping into, that the purchase of this land for his center was also in baby stages. I felt like it would be a lovely opportunity to be immersed in the energies of the lineage. The date was to be just after I received the final attunement as a Reiki master/teacher, which was in July, and I would be off to Florida in August. What a wonderful way to deepen through the summer.

Not long after my birthday I had a follow-up appointment with my doctor. Though the protocol had completed and I was continuing to feel great physically, with the exception of some normal off-and-on PMS'ing, traces of karmic patterns were present. Changes were continuing to be seen during her exams that indicated internal protection and trauma in my womb. I was grateful she was of similar ilk as I. She understood there was healing, karma moving out, and neither of us felt alarm or the need to intervene. We both had faith in the natural and spiritual processes at hand. She was gentle and didn't force through the fears that arose during my exam with her, and for this I was grateful.

Just before the Reiki initiation, I experienced an increase in fear and sensitivity in the womb. There was more sensation than before of the violence being carried from lifetimes past. The waves of memories that had few pictures, but carried dark and deadly energy, would assail my pelvis. I had been experiencing tinges of posttraumatic stress disorder symptoms throughout this whole process and had navigated them with all the awareness I could muster. Crying would lessen the physical pain for brief reprieves. Breath work and becoming very still helped with the energy release. Dreams of a partner I'd had in the 1990s were infiltrating my nights. We had an intense, dark love, a repetitive pattern of breaking up and coming back together, for five years. Carl was an archetypal dark man, the force in my life that catapulted me into a deepened spiritual life after surviving the underworld. He had a past. He carried danger. And he was a very wounded little boy in a grown man's body.

One day while resting on the couch, creating a space for my healing to continue, I found that my womb was revealing just how deep our connection went karmically. I began to get flashes that he had been my perpetrator in a distant life. He had been my father, and there was grave damage inflicted upon me. The snapshots raced through my mind. They horrified me, and my womb and belly cried out, allowing these imprints of another time and space to release, as I was in my cocoon of blankets on the couch in this world. It became clear why I could never access my power or my adulthood throughout our romantic relationship.

Victimization had been something I strongly rejected in this lifetime. I refused to stake claim to it in this life. Sadly, it was often difficult for me to have compassion for others who carried a strong victim mentality. I had a belief that victim energy left one disempowered and without choice. During these clearing karmic journeys, I was shown that I, me in this life, carried another aspect of self that had been severely victimized and traumatized, within the tendrils of our relationship, in another time and space. I watched from the witness vantage point as repulsion rose up in me, rather than compassion. I didn't want to go there. I didn't want to admit that I had any feelings of victimhood. But here they were. I felt vulnerable, powerless, and ashamed. There was self-hatred brewing in the core of this awareness, as well as swelling inside my femaleness.

The intensity of the growing inner reality was almost too much to bear as I attempted once again to control the situation. Finally, I could no longer keep it together. I let loose a scream and tears and felt shame and guilt from the present to the past. The emotional pain stormed forth, and simultaneously I felt a contraction of the cervix and a burning within the pelvis. The crying continued, and then came sorrow for my suffering. "I'm sorry. I'm sorry. I'm so sorry ..." repeated on and on through tears, drool, and phlegm.

Lifetimes of other aspects could be felt punishing me for being wounded, for being a victim. I saw in this lifetime that rarely I could ask for or feel deserving of help. I victimized others with impatience and judgments because they were wounded and I didn't realize the role I was taking on. This saddened me very deeply. I was sad not only for myself, but again I was feeling this shame and blame for all of us who were victims at the hands of another, based on their pain and wounds. I felt grief for the dark man who was lost in his darkness, who in this lifetime had been my lover, and who in another lifetime had been my father. I found myself coming through the other side, hours later, with a seed of compassion for both, because ultimately both were victims.

Days later I was able to see that owning that I'd been victimized, in both the present life and the past, allowed healing to continue to take place. Once again I saw how vulnerability allowed empowerment, and treating myself gently enabled me to treat others gently. Subconscious identification with or repulsion from victimhood lessened, but I could feel it still freely floating around me.

I could only assume that because this was so deep, personal, and cultural, it wasn't going to disperse overnight. It had already been taking months, but it was moving. When in the throes of these clearings, I thought it was no wonder that it took human beings so long to awaken, to reach higher states of consciousness. Each of us brings with us layers upon layers of muck. Too few of us know what we are carrying, and even fewer learn how to consciously heal these layers. Instead we unconsciously create more. I felt grateful for each step of pain and darkness that needed to move up and through me because I knew I was moving closer and closer to the light and truth and to a deeper wholeness within myself.

It was weeks later when I found myself lying in bed, half asleep, watching weird sensations moving around in the pelvis. The sensations were releasing clouds of shame as I drifted off to sleep. My last thought was, *I never could have realized all this lived within me. Help me to keep surrendering to You.*

79

It seemed obvious, but I hadn't foreseen that the trip to Florida would be colored by the womb clearings. Before I left, I began having mini panic attacks. I'd be without Byron, my grounder and protector. What if I was the only person in the shuttle to the hotel? How could the driver be trusted? I'd be alone and vulnerable. Would I be safe in the hotel at night by myself? Those were the irrational fears that I could discern with clarity. Others just whooshed by me and through me as sensations of fear and terror. The rational mind and Byron's clarity only brought temporary sanity. I purchased the tinctures I'd used before for anxiety, and with Byron's encouragement I boarded the airplane in spite of the erratic internal turmoil.

The reality is so often less dramatic than the imagination. Once I arrived in Florida, I had a moment of fear waiting for the shuttle, but it was short-lived, as there were other passengers going to the same hub of hotels. *Whew! I am safe,* I assured myself. I had a relaxing evening, feeling safe in my hotel room, and was looking forward to carpooling to the ashram in the morning with a couple I'd met at the yoga nidra training.

The entire week was fluid, healing, and peaceful. The grounds and the lake at the ashram were lush and nourishing, and within a day the humidity had anointed my skin with a suppleness I hadn't felt since leaving Portland—and then some. In the sanctuary were pictures of the lineage, and on the way up the stairs was a large image of Jesus looking with loving eyes upon all who passed.

For the first time since being connected to the lineage, I felt what I refer to as the great-grand-guru, Dadaji, blessing me from his life in ancient times. He was present a couple of evenings while I was going to bed. I smiled and felt included in the family. My dreams were filled with healing, forgiveness, and compassion for myself and for Carl, my dark love. I felt a tender love for each of us, for our pasts, for our mutual pain and wounding, and for healing in the present.

Always, listening to Gurudev talk was humorous and enlightening. He had such a marvelous way of bringing ancient teachings and universal truths down to earth and into relevance for practical daily life. The highlight for me was, of course, the day of mantra initiation. When I read his first book in 2001, I saw pictures of this ceremony. I had no understanding then, and I'd wondered if I would ever get to partake in this initiation. And here I was.

We all were asked to wear our white clothes, find the pillow with our name on it, and take a seat before Gurudev arrived. I'd already gotten a beautiful set of *mala* (prayer beads) earlier, as required. The ceremony was beautiful, and I could feel the vibration of the mantra as it was infused into the mala beads by the touch of my guru during the initiation ceremony This was one more instance in which something I'd longed for and eventually let go of needing or wanting was finding itself manifest. It was here that I received a given spiritual name by a master.

I felt blessed to feel called to enter into this lineage of spiritual fathers. Especially all these years later. I wasn't here out of need, or out of dependency, or because I had the illusion that Gurudev was the source of my salvation. I felt like he had never left my heart, and I was grateful and felt more informed after so many gifts from other beings, but I knew from my journey thus far that I belonged right where I was.

This was the path that had introduced me for the first time to Divine Mother, the feminine force of Shakti Kundalini, which changed and continued to transform my entire self. He was the path that led me home to me. For the first time in any talks by my Gurudev, at least to my recollection, he spoke of tantra, saying that this path of surrender was a tantric path. Had I been intellectually knowledgeable about yogic traditions in the beginning, I may have surmised this. But I wasn't. I was shown via experience, led to realizations of the inner realm, not by intellect but by the heart, and I always came full circle into alignment. Again this left me in a state of wonderment.

The Goddess, the divine feminine whom I consistently ran away from, is central to tantric teachings. Many may be surprised to learn, or may even reject, that Jesus and Mary Magdalene are also a tantric path when followed mystically. It was through direct communion with them that I realized this truth. And then in Florida, my guru echoed it.

Tantra has gotten an interesting reputation here in the West, lacking ancient rooting in teachings that encompass more than sexuality. There are many paths, and I won't negate that they all hold important teachings. We each have our own way of finding God-Goddess, but it's also easy to get sidetracked with false titillation. Tantra is a practice of presence in all of life, the light, dark, and grays. It makes sacred everything, recognition that the divine lives in all aspects, and utilizing every part of our life to awaken. I saw that this had been my path from childhood. I'd always lived my life in these ways instinctually.

The feminine, the Goddess, and the force of life, death, and rebirth are the cycles of life. Her expressions are loving and fierce. She is archetypical, metaphorical, and literal. She is transformational. She is soul. She isn't outside of us; She is an aspect of us. And when She is realized within us, we wed with the divine masculine, internally and externally.

Once I began putting the pieces of a lifelong puzzle together, my understanding still rudimentary, remaining perspectives of division began uniting in one complete picture. I felt that the walls constructed of illusion began crumbling. We are all a part of the same fabric, not separate pieces of fabric. It's just our perception that sees the cloth in torn swaths. When I see in separation, me against you, or when I'm comparing, or when I'm judging, I'm simply demonstrating my ignorance, showing where my blinders are still worn. And until I completely awaken, this will most likely take place. It's the nature of ego mind.

I appreciated the new framework I was gaining clarity on. I appreciated how beautifully Gurudev's path held all that came through me naturally. This was no mistake. I'd been connected long before my first recognition of his picture that day at the Bikram studio. Soul knew, and Ma Kundalini knew. I was now remembering what had been forgotten. There was hope of going deeper into identifying those areas that kept me blinded and asleep to larger truths. Glimpsing the truth was a good start, but I yearned for the day when the glimpse would become the constant. This was a prayer always going out to the lineage Divine Mother. I trusted Her to show me the way.

Grateful for everything I'd received, for the deepening of self, I left the ashram to take home what had been given to me. Gifted with the spiritualized mantra, a new name, with the lineage infused in my being, I would continue to forge on, grow in love, and find peace in the fires of burning illusions.

80

On my return from Florida, I decided it was time to let go of the caregiving and give all of my attention to what I felt was my soul's work, my sacred purpose. As always, saying goodbye to those I cared for was heart-wrenching, but the time had come. There was the practical argument of financial security, yet I felt called to trust in the deeper knowing of my purpose. And that was my choice.

Before long, Byron and I both started receiving similar intuitions about our next move. The Universe does indeed have a sense of humor, and it's best when we can laugh along with it and at ourselves. The law of irony, if there is such a thing, was once again revealing itself.

We'd both been praying for some time to be shown what was next on our horizon, where to settle next, and when the next shift would happen. In discussions regarding what was drawing us to any given area, we knew a large enough population was important for my work. We also knew that a sizable vegan/raw population was important for Byron's path, which was still a bit obscure, other than his writing, which could be done anywhere.

I was craving green grass; soft trees; flowers that weren't growing on plants with sharp points; dirt that was soft, rich, and dark; water, water, and more water; and both sunshine and rain. Northern California seemed too wet and cool. We began thinking maybe Southern California. Slowly, we found ourselves talking about the possibility of outlying areas of Los Angeles, as long as we weren't in the city. And then we found ourselves asking with scrunched faces, *Los Angeles? Really? Los Angeles? Wow. Los Angeles.*

Friends and family found this hilarious and dubious. Neither of us had ever been hippies or excessively alternative, but we had previously always lived a very laid-back, nondemanding lifestyle, and we liked it that way. We were turned off to glitz and image-driven lifestyles. Nor did we buy into the model of consumerism that LA is known for. The only exception in favor of LA was that we were into movies. The artistry of film and those who made films always fascinated me.

The programmed stories came from every direction. "It costs so much to live there." "The traffic is horrible." "You'll never be able to afford it." No one could wrap their minds around this actually taking place. We, too, were curious and amused. We had never spent time in LA and decided that if that's where we were feeling pulled, we'd better go check it out.

In February of 2011, we contacted my cousin who lived near Pasadena and asked if we could come stay with her for a weekend while we explored the city. She generously offered her spare room, and the plan was set. Byron and I were full of amazement and enjoying the irony once again on our drive to the big city of LA. He'd already made a list of raw/vegan restaurants, and we hit Café Gratitude in Hollywood as soon as we arrived.

Awe, a sense of being overwhelmed, and excitement were front and center. Shockingly, we fell in love. Literally, it was love at first sight. The creative energy, along with all other forms of energy, was abundant and palpable all weekend. We had still been toying with the possibility of outlying areas, but once we arrived, there was no doubt left in our minds that we wanted to be in the mix. Any kind of community we'd want was in LA, as was entertainment, food, the outdoors, cool neighborhoods, and things we hadn't even considered yet.

The billboards were mesmerizing. Laurel Canyon was full of amazing inspirational history; the Sunset Strip was legendary; Hollywood was sketchier than I would have imagined; and the beaches of Malibu and Venice had been 1970s fantasies. It didn't escape us that there were many ways that LA could be a slippery slope if one got too caught up.

This was another chapter waiting to unfold, to learn from, to expand into. I moved to LA in May of 2011, and Byron followed in July. The living mystery reveals itself both within and without, if we're paying attention. I felt an instant belonging in this City of Angels. For me, it felt eerily startling how familiar the city was. I knew I belonged there and felt I'd already been there. LA was home. I felt its cord connected to my heart, and in faint distant memories yet to be discovered as more unfolding and transformation had yet to be revealed.

The song that had sung through me years ago, was now an integrated part of me.

> I'm longing for You, moving toward You,
> The ache of surrender etching the way.
> Losing myself to be with You, going deeper to be You,
> The ache of surrender etching the way.

No longer did I feel it calling me into some unknown, mysterious territory. I had surrendered to the ache for divine connection, for the presence of God/Goddess in my heart that I'd been separated from. I had surrendered to its guidance, surrendered the ego for purification, felt myself lost, only to be found in the immense bosom of Spirit, which has forever been leading me along the path of my life. This path, was and is etched out before me. My part is to continuously surrender.

EPILOGUE

Life brings many phases and stages of learning, growth, integration, and time to embody the wisdom of our experiences. I've noticed the way I circle and spiral through my life. While the first part of my journey was very internal, Los Angeles, full of new excitement, drew me out of my cocoon. At least for a while.

During our six years in Los Angeles, the City of Angels, we found that it held many jewels, and indeed it tested our inner resolve with its ever-present lure into a slippery slope of materialism, ego, and desires. But the most alluring aspect is the vibrant, palpable creative force of dreams waiting to come true. The lessons were powerful. By 2014, I circled back into a more internal mode once again. It was when I again created the internal space that another jump in my own transformation introduced itself through the channeling of Light Language.

The opening to Light Language, which I realized had always been with me since my first Shaktipat initiation with Gurudev, forced me to expand my perceptions beyond anything I'd entertained before. I was compelled to explore the relevance of Ascension and its connection to the Kundalini path I'd been traversing. The mind once again began blowing gaskets, so to speak, in order to understand what this next level held for both my personal evolution and my healing work with my clients.

My sense is that as the frequency of our planet has risen greatly, moving through our own inner darkness is becoming more fluid. Even though the collective darkness appears quite grave to many, I see this as the proof that we are releasing our density quicker. My work with clients finds easier navigation through their shadows' enabling the levity of their truest expressions to shine forth more efficiently.

I've found that the early phases of awakening can be the most dramatic. After a certain point, many of us learn to navigate the big ups and downs of expanding consciousness with more ease and grace. There is a learning curve of how to truly be in the world but not be of it. To gain the power of choice over how much influence the personality self has, rather than being flung around by personality like a puppy's toy. At this juncture, I feel I'm reaping many benefits of being more easily in the present moment, consistently in tune with divine guidance, allowing Peace and Joy and Love to be my guiding light.

Byron and I now reside in the quieter, calmer, smaller city of Tulsa, Oklahoma. Why Tulsa? My returning to Tulsa thirty-five years later was a call to do my last bit of unresolved shadow work. That, of course, is yet another story.

What I can always rely on is that my life here is dedicated to transformation. I see now that it always has been, even when I was a young child. I came in ready to alchemize, transmute, and transform toward that which heals, loves, and brings peace and joy. There is not a moment when I rest in any form of status quo. I am constantly engaged in inner work. This is not because anything is wrong or broken. It's the evolutionary trajectory I came here to fulfill. The expressions and qualities of Divine Love are unending; therefore, I continue toward *that*.

The countless opportunities we each have to embrace the unlimited potential to say "Yes!" to our conscious awakening, if we so choose, always leave me in wonderment. This doesn't mean the journey is all love and light, warm and fuzzy, "just be happy." No, it's so much more. However, each time we show the willingness to come more deeply home to our own divinity and knowing the Divine is always within us, that we are one with Source, Love, and Light, the rewards far outweigh the challenging moments of dismantling of the illusions of the dream. This is important for each of us and for all humanity, and beyond.

The living mystery is still spoken of in metaphor because the intellect is still challenged to perceive through the linear framework. When we're living the mystery, though, the direct knowing is as clear as the light of day, through the deeper capacity to Love, access Joy, and trust the divine inner connectedness with all life.

May you, too, be inspired to begin or continue your personal journey of awakening from the dream and return to the altar of your heart and your own divine remembrance.

DEEP GRATITUDE AND LOVE

My deepest gratitude and love goes, first and foremost, to my parents. I believe that the parent–child relationship can be one of the most challenging given preexisting karmic ties. These relationships set me up perfectly to learn some basic lessons I needed to learn, with just the right recipe of love and presence, as well as the perfect rub against the grain to force my growth.

My parents have been the perfect souls to prepare me for my spiritual journey. I received from them the freedom of nonconformity and an alternative upbringing that prevented certain aspects of programming of consciousness from taking root in my psyche. I was a freethinker from early on, deeply reflective, and they fostered this sensitivity. I'm so grateful they raised me in an atheist home. This empowered me to explore and find a God of my understanding, to look within and know that force beyond what humankind teaches, that comes through my own heart and by living the mystery. I love you both deeply.

I also want to share my unending gratitude, love, and honor for my husband, Byron, who has been a solid, stable, safe, and grounding presence. His tenderness and love, along with his own deeply spiritual nature, has enabled us to grow and flourish together, always deepening our own spiritual calling while honoring one another's. I couldn't see traveling this path without you, babe!

To Caleb, I offer so much appreciation and love for having the keen awareness to hold powerful space for me in the first phase of this process, as we were the blind leading the blind. I'm grateful for all we healed and learned together in partnership, and for the continuing honest, clear reflection you offer in friendship.

To those friends and my little sister through Big Brothers Big Sisters of America, were not privy to pieces of this story, I thank you for your part in this journey and your presence in my life.

I also have a special place in my heart and love for my biological father and stepmother, who have known nothing of this part of my life. Though our relationship has been distanced by miles and different life paths, I've always felt your love, caring, and joy during our times together. You are loved.

To my brother and sister, though our paths weren't intertwined during these years, I feel such joy that we can share some commonality of spiritual perceptions, which make for wonderful conversations. I have so much respect for who you each are. I love you both immensely, and your support is always held in my heart.

I'd also like to thank my mother and father-in-law for their open mindedness, support and love through all of our adventures!

Last, but not at all least, I'm deeply indebted to Gurudev. You sparked my remembrance journey home to myself and changed my life forever—and it continues to transform. And to all of those beings who have guided and guide me today safely, both seen and unseen, there are no words to express the depth of love I have for you all within every fiber of my being. I bow deeply.